43 YEARS WITH THE SAME BIRD

BRIAN READE

43 YEARS WITH
THE SAME BIRD

A LIVERPUDLIAN LOVE AFFAIR

MACMILLAN

First published 2008 by Macmillan
an imprint of Pan Macmillan Ltd
Pan Macmillan, 20 New Wharf Road, London N1 9RR
Basingstoke and Oxford
Associated companies throughout the world
www.panmacmillan.com

ISBN 978-0-230-70968-3

1 3 5 7 9 8 6 4 2

A CIP catalogue record for this book is available from
the British Library.

Typeset by SetSystems Ltd, Saffron Walden, Essex
Printed in the UK by CPI Mackays, Chatham, ME5 8TD

To the 96 and the 39,

Shanks and Sheila,

Vic and Billy.

Always on my mind.

Thanks to *Liverpool Daily Post* and *Echo* librarians Colin Hunt and Les Rawlinson for digging out old articles, solicitor Ann Adlington and curator of LFC museum Stephen Done for checking the facts, David Luxton and Richard Milner for helping to bring the raw words to the published page, the fan whose flag Another Great Night Out With My Bird inspired the title, the players who fired the passion, the mates who shared it and the partners who had no option but to suffer it.

PROLOGUE

Bill Shankly's bare manhood stood three feet away from me. OK, stood is an exaggeration. We were getting on well, but not that well.

Slacks with a crease that could shave a werewolf's four-day shadow had been removed with military precision and were being placed on a dressing-room hook with his left hand. In his right was a pair of black crumpled shorts so old you could smell the Boot Room on them. In between hung a question:

'What school are you from again, son?'

'De La Salle.'

And the shorts, which had made their way to the expectant toes of his left foot, were abruptly pulled away.

'A rugby school?'

'No. Football.'

Relief. Then animation.

'Thank Christ for that. I hate rugby. I remember in the air force, turning up at a new post in Wales and asking for a football.

'This officer says to me: "We don't play football here, only rugby." So I says right, give me a rugby ball and I'll squeeze it intee a fitball.'

He burst into a raucous laugh and began to squeeze an imaginary oval ball into a round shape.

'Gi' me it, and I'll squeeze it intee a fitball.'

I join in the laughter and he knocks me on the arm and says for a third time: 'I'll squeeze it intee a fitball. Christ, it's funny what things come back to you. I'd forgotten all about that.'

Let's get this straight here. I should be at school, battling to stay awake through double economics. Instead I'm joshing away with Bill Shankly at Melwood, like a groom and his best man preparing to rip up the town on a stag night. Goolies on parade and everything. I've been in his company less than five minutes and he's already told me a story nobody has ever heard before. Granted, in the league table of Shankly anecdotes it's six points behind Stenhousemuir. But it's mine and mine alone to drop casually into conversations for eternity. As this dawns on me a shiver jolts the blood.

Fearing the joshing will stop, I tap-dance through the silence like a rhino in Air-Wear.

'And did you?'

'What?'

'Squeeze it into a football.'

He tugs on the shorts, stands bolt upright, hands, hips and eyes snapping into Cagney mode, the wrinkles on his forehead contorting into a map of the Alps.

'This De La Salle, son. Did you say it was a special school?'

There is no laugh, just a brisk turn and a march towards a big wicker hamper from which he grabs a pair of red socks, then keeps on walking. The shiver turns to sweat as an abyss slides into view below my three-inch platform heels.

Any second now he will turn and unleash a volley of insults aimed at cutting me to the size of an ant, call off the interview, and boot me out of Melwood, back to the sixth-form block and rank humiliation.

He stops, does an about-turn, and unleashes a bark: 'I'm making a pot of tea. Do you want one to set you up for all them questions you've got?'

There's a sigh of relief which I have to emit in short bursts for fear of being sucked inside out. The hands stop shaking but a stitch gnaws away at the high waistband on my Birmingham Bags and fear drifts slowly from my brain, spreading right down to feet doing epileptic taps. It's a feeling I would experience in varying degrees over the next thirty-odd years of professional life before doing an interview.

But I would never feel the pure rush of pride I felt that hot June morning, not even watching Muhammad Ali stumble from a car and limp towards the door of his Michigan ranch. Because I knew when that kettle went on, that whatever miserable hand life might deal, my self-esteem would never scrape a barrel's bottom.

I would always be able to look a boss, a foe or a put-down merchant in the eye, and tell them that Bill Shankly, the man who instilled the most achingly beautiful of obsessions into thousands of souls, once shared a unique anecdote with me.

With his cock dangling in my eye-line.

At seventeen, life could only go downhill.

P.S. Huge. Obviously.

1

MATCHSTICK MEN

20 FEBRUARY 1965 – BURNDEN PARK, BOLTON

I was perched on my dad's shoulders at the back of a sprawling, uncovered terrace, with Our Vic parked on the crash barrier in front, snarling at every banality that left my seven-year-old mouth.

Through the big hole in my red balaclava, down past the bare knees which stuck out either side of my dad's neck, I surveyed a sea of heads: flat-capped, bald, plastered with grease, flowing for what seemed like miles down to a bright green carpet, where tiny red-and-white figures moved in clusters, stopping regularly amid loud roars or deep grunts.

Smoke was everywhere. Behind the roof of a dirty corrugated stand smog belched out from mills and factories, and rising from the sea of heads was a pungent cloud of tobacco which clung to the back of my throat, while the nostrils were filled with a fug of nicotine, sulphur, Brylcreem, beer and sweat.

A decade earlier L. S. Lowry had captured this exact slab of northern working-class life on canvas in his painting *Going To The Match*, and whenever I see his bleak, emaciated figures, I am dragged back to Bolton on that cold, distant afternoon. I can feel my dad shuffling uncomfortably below, telling me to stop fidgeting and no, it wasn't half-time yet. I can hear the embarrassed, indignant eleven-year-old voice of Our Vic, telling me it wasn't Gerry Byrne who'd had that shot but Willie Stevenson.

I spent most of the time looking away from the pitch, entranced by the white brilliance of the floodlights, counting their bulbs, staring at the pigeons chasing each other across the stand roof, looking around at the mass of humanity, wondering if that tall one with the long hair and thin black tie was a Beatle. But mainly wondering if everyone was as bored as me.

I'd feigned euphoria ever since my dad, Reg, threw the tickets on the kitchen table and told Vic it was his eleventh birthday present, a sight which sent him sprinting into the back garden to run around in circles, with clenched fists, repeating the word 'yes'. I followed him out, because, well, it would have looked like I was ungrateful if I hadn't, and because when he ran out of puff I'd have a chance to ask him what the big deal was.

'It's the FA Cup fifth round, you dick.'

'Will they get the cup if they win?'

A look of pure disgust was followed with a swift kick to the shins and threat to steal my ticket and give it to his mate Kenny Quayle. Someone who wasn't a ponce. Someone who knew about football.

He had a point. In the early months of 1965 football was about as appealing as Winston Churchill's funeral. Actually, not quite as appealing. When that long, dirgeful parade of black unfolded on my nana's little telly she made me howl with laughter by yelling 'Good riddance, you feckin' whore-master,' as his coffin came into shot. I didn't have a clue what a feckin' whore-master was but the joyful manner in which she spat it out contrasted magnificently with the pious Dimbleby tones coming from the box.

Football moved me about as much as one of my little sister's dolls (less when you factored in how much damage you could do to Tiny Tears' eyes with a dart). I didn't get why Vic took the scissors to *Charles Buchan's Football Monthly* and covered his wall with pictures of men in shorts. What was cool about that? Why hadn't he butchered *Fab 208*, like me, and taped up The Beatles, The Searchers and Sandie Shaw?

For a start, you rarely saw it. *Match Of The Day* had begun that season on BBC2, but nobody had the channel, and all the radio gave you was the shipping forecast and *Sing Something Simple*.

What made Our Vic squat with pained concentration before the *Grandstand* teleprinter every Saturday? Especially when any display of emotion was met with a slap off my grandad whose horses had gone down, soon to be followed by his Littlewoods coupon, meaning that three-mile hike to the docks on Monday morning was still a reality.

Back then we spent every weekend in my nana's terraced house in Wavertree, the part of Liverpool where both my parents had grown up, and where I'd spent my first six years until Reg's job as a car parts manager moved him up to Preston. It meant that for two years he'd drive the six of us (I had two younger sisters as well) in his Austin A40 back to Liverpool every Friday night to cure my mum Sheila's chronic homesickness.

It was this geographical upheaval to a one-eyed hole called Garstang which drove me into the clutches of Liverpool FC. I was lonely and insecure and every day I was made to feel as out-of-place as a leper at a *Vogue* fashion-shoot. I was an outsider. Someone who spoke differently, thought differently and had no mates. Factors which made me assume a cockiness I was incapable of living up to. I was from a big, tough city, so I had to act like it. Which didn't endear me to the natives.

By the way, these were natives who gave interbreeding a bad name. They didn't hold a Miss Garstang contest, they just gave a cup to any girl who had less than two heads. The biggest humiliation of all was that I was being humiliated by the cast of *Deliverance*.

And it was ritual. At break times the other boys in my class would pick a football team consisting of the number of lads who were around, minus one. I was always the minus one. Because most of them would have struggled to win a place in a one-legged girls' under-4s team, their footballing pleasure was derived from seeing the dejection on my face as they ran off with their arms around each other for their kickabout.

To compensate for the lack of opportunities to show I could play, I took an interest in Liverpool. Our Vic's team were the champions of England, going for the European Cup. Preston North End? It was a superiority that spoke for itself. And most Monday mornings I'd rub it in, which usually ended in a fight, being sent to the head nun's office, told I was a disruptive Liverpool council house yob who was a bad influence on the rest of the school, and caned by the most inappropriately named woman on earth, Sister Immaculata. A hatchet-faced Grim Reaperette, whose vow of chastity was made slightly redundant by the fact that God had yet to create a male desperate enough to give her one.

Vic kept his distance, believing I deserved what I was getting due to being a loud-mouthed gobshite. He was facing his own problems but handling them much better. Although he was fanatical about football, it was more or less all theory. He'd worn National Health specs since he was five and possessed the physique of an anorexic crane-fly. It may have worked for Phil Thompson, but not him.

So even if he had the will, he didn't have the means to fight my fights for me. Like the one on a Monday lunchtime in January 1965 when, after being left out of the class side again, I picked up their ball, shouted 'I'm Ian St John' and booted it over the wall, into the path of an oncoming car, which burst it instantly. I became the substitute football. And Vic looked on shaking his head as I was once again led away to be tortured by God's Hatchet.

So that's why Kenny Quayle wasn't having that Bolton ticket. It was mine. And I had to be there to discover with my own eyes what it was all about. To assemble the raw material which would allow me to gloat over those Garstang hillbillies who couldn't play football, and who never went to a game. I'd learn so much watching this match, grow so much harder, they'd have to pick me out of respect.

What a shame it was boring me rigid.

At least it confirmed I'd been right in December when my

uncle Tommy offered me a choice for my Christmas treat: go with him and Vic to the Blackburn game at Anfield, or with my auntie Eileen to Lewis's grotto. Santa's knee won hands-down.

Obviously there was a possibility that the man in red may have been a child molester, but at least he was giving me a toy gun. What were the eleven barely discernible red men on that Bolton pitch giving me other than a freezing nose and a dead bum? Nothing. I wished I'd brought my gun. I could have had a pop at the pigeons or even the referee and got it abandoned.

'How long to go, Dad?' I whined.

'A few minutes. Now sit still. You're breaking my bloody neck.'

Vic could contain his rage no longer.

'Why did you bring him? He's not interested.'

'I am.'

'You're not even watching.'

'I am. And I know as much about them as you.'

'Ha.'

To prove my point beyond all reasonable doubt, I started to repeat the names of Shankly's first great side. The one he called the same team as last season: 'Lawrence, Lawler, Byrne, Milne, Yeats, Stevenson, Callaghan, Hunt, St John, Smith and Thompson . . . Lawrence, Lawler, Byrne, Milne, Yeats, Ste—'

'Dad, tell him to shut up.'

'Why, 'cos I know as much as you?'

'No, 'cos you've got the wrong team. Gordon Milne's not playing. It's Alf Arrowsmith you stupid little . . . GOOOOOAAA-AAALLLLLLL!'

There was a surge that sucked me and Reg a dozen yards down the terrace and past our Vic, who was forced up against the crash barrier, both hands in the air screeching 'Yes!' at the top of his high-pitched voice.

Reg swayed like barley in a hurricane, shifting his balance from right foot to left in an attempt to keep me on his shoulders. It was the first thrill of the afternoon. A Big Dipper ride that blew away the boredom of the preceding 85 minutes.

Men clapped and patted each other on the back. Fists were clenched and rattles clattered. 'Good old Cally, eh lad,' said a man with one yellow tooth left in his head, referring to Ian Callaghan, who had scrambled the ball over the line with five minutes of tedium left.

'Yeah,' I said, disappointed the Big Dipper ride was over.

Vic had joined in with the singing: 'Liv-er-pool (clap-clap-clap) . . . Liv-er-pool, (clap-clap-clap).'

The little red-and-white dots carried on moving around in clusters, as hunched men in the stand to the left pulled down their caps, slunk out of their seats and off into the dark fug, back to their Lowry wives in their Lowry homes, with little comfort to take to their Lowry mills on Monday.

'How long left?' I asked Reg. But by now words weren't leaving his mouth, just sighs and groans.

'I'll have to put you down,' he said, slowly lowering me from his shoulders, his face grimacing with pain. 'I've done me back in.'

He motioned Our Vic to leave, but he stubbornly refused, pointing out on his Timex that there were only a couple of minutes left, and he was staying until the end. Reg relented, transferring his weight to a hand that was propped up by the crash barrier, while his other one held on tightly to mine.

And there I stood for the next five minutes, in a black world of my own, staring at the back of a man's overcoat which smelt of pipes and dogs, catching hairs in my mouth, gutted that Ian St John hadn't scored with a diving header I could recreate. Reconstructing an Ian Callaghan scramble doesn't carry quite the same kudos.

Then the whistle went, and a roar erupted from everyone around me. Except my dad, who was using the raucous outburst to disguise his own 'aaghs'.

He'd slipped a disc and hobbled back to the car like a war veteran with shrapnel for kneecaps. Me and Vic helped lower him into the driver's seat where he proceeded to wail every time he changed gear and swear he'd never put me on his shoulders again to watch a football match. I feigned concern, but my mind was many miles away, in a school playground, trying to work out how a goal that looked like it went in off Ian Callaghan's arse could ever be made to look sexy.

2

SAINTLY CONVERSION

1 MAY 1965 – BISHOPGATE STREET, WAVERTREE

The way I figured it, even if St John had scored a beauty, the Garstang hillbillies would be none the wiser. What seven-year-old inbred would be glued to the teleprinter when he could be watching his mum arm-wrestle a pig in the back yard?

So, contrary to newspaper reports, Liverpool weren't in the last eight of the FA Cup thanks to a Cally scramble but a St John diving header, which I rehearsed throughout Sunday like a Method actor priming himself for an Oscar-winning performance.

By the time I reached the playground on Monday morning I was Brando on heat and every one of those woollybacks was going to get burnt. I'd even thought of an ingenious way of getting around the team-picking farce which always left me eating my bogies next to girls with skipping ropes. I brought my own ball in.

Before the whistle alerted everyone to trudge off to lessons, the school witnessed its first-ever live act by a performing seal. I threw the ball against the classroom wall and dived at the rebound, nodding it into an imaginary goal. If it came back too high I'd try a scissors kick. Too low, a volley.

A crowd formed to witness the bizarre spectacle of a manic seven-year-old with blood trailing from gashed knees and palms, to hear the thud of spine and cranium on concrete, and the chanting whenever an imaginary goal was scored: 'Dan-dan, dan-dan-dan, dan-dan-dan-dan, Saint John.'

Eventually they were packed off to class and I was told that unless I stopped the seal show I'd be straight round to Sister Immaculata for more wood therapy.

After this scream of defiance, the school was split into three distinct camps: those who pitied me, those who feared me and (by far the biggest group) those who hated me. But at least they were united in one respect – all now avoided eye contact. I was referred to as The Liverpool Loony and shunned.

If you've never been subjected to a lengthy Sent To Coventry order, you won't be familiar with the feeling of liberation. Suddenly there's no pretending. From being an outsider trying reluctantly to force yourself into the inside, and failing miserably, you become an empowered individual who doesn't care if he's in or out.

They didn't want me to be there and I'd rather have been in Sonny Liston's gym as a stand-in punch-bag. But the mutual loathing was becoming as irrelevant as Sister Immaculata's chastity vow. By now Sheila's get-us-out-of here ultimatums to Reg had reached the threat of a hunger strike (with him doing the starving) and I knew it was only a matter of time before this prison sentence would be over. So the sheep became irrelevant.

All I had to do was show that I was consumed with an object far more desirable, and figures infinitely more interesting than those who chose to shun me. That object had to be Liverpool FC. I may have drawn little pleasure from the trip to Bolton, but look at the respect I'd won on the back of it. Liverpool FC had inspired me to take a stand against the sheep. It had even earned me a nickname which I loved. Being called a loony by a shower of mentally subnormals surely singled me out as Einstein material.

Besides, football was growing on me. I was drawn to the teleprinter, sneaked the back page of Reg's *Sunday Express*, even delved into Vic's *Football Monthly* when he wasn't looking, and listened to every minute of the second-half radio commentary on the FA Cup semi-final, floating on air when we whupped Chelsea 2–0 to reach Wembley. That was the day I lost my cherry. The day I dropped all resistance and let it take me. If only I'd known how I'd feel the following January, watching my first FA Cup tie at Anfield, seeing the same Chelsea side knock us out in the third round, I mightn't have rushed in with such wild abandon.

The ecstasy felt from the first big win leaves the memory far quicker than the agony of the first big defeat. If I try hard enough I can still feel the hot tears streaming down my cheeks as I left Anfield and the urge to rip the flesh off Reg's face for saying 'There's always next year.'

Here was the harrowing pain football could inflict, as others celebrated wildly over the same set of circumstances that were leaving you on the floor. That feeling of total isolation, despite knowing there were countless thousands of your brethren equally bereft. The sense that this was a tragedy unique to you, which would never be overcome so long as there were record books around to remind you of the mental wound.

But in March 1965 as Liverpool closed in on winning the FA Cup for the first time in history, Mother Football had yet to wound me. It was the first flush of love, and like a religious convert I threw myself into the cause with a rare fanaticism. Wacky Mop Tops were ripped from the wall to be replaced with any badly cut photo (even from a Spot-The-Ball coupon) that bore the visage of The Saint. No matter how small a pinprick he appeared in the background.

Vic took this sudden conversion with a mixture of bemusement and resentment. On the one hand he was glad to have someone else to impress with his knowledge, especially someone as desperate to be armed with factual ammunition as me. But he wasn't too keen on his personal space being invaded by a little brother. Especially a gobshite prone to spouting his ignorance both loudly and in public. A gobshite who, as he constantly pointed out, only months ago chose the grotto over the match.

At school he chose to ignore my public screams for attention, which now consisted of imagined radio commentaries on goals from Saturday's games, combined with reconstructions of those scored by Ian St John.

He'd be walking around the playground, forgetting my existence, only to see out the corner of his eye a small duffle-coated blob, diving to head an imaginary ball, with no one paying attention. If they had bothered to put names to mental illnesses back then (the only head problem a kid was allowed to suffer in the mid-sixties was nits) I would probably have been assessed as a Tourette's Syndrome sufferer whose tic was a diving header, and whose involuntary swear-word was 'St John'.

At the end of April, in the week leading up to the FA Cup final my knees were bleeding so badly, and I was hyperventilating so frequently, that Sheila kept me off school on the Friday. I can't remember if I'd drenched too many socks in blood or I was running a temperature close to a fever. Either way it was to be the only time I ever protested about being kept off school.

I ached to be there, telling everyone that tomorrow Liverpool would do what Preston had failed to do the year before and win the Cup. But Sheila kept me at home, and like the ungrateful little prick I was, I hated her for it.

It had been her idea to send my dad down to Jack Sharp's sports shop in Whitechapel to buy the full Liverpool kit of red shirt, white shorts (with red line down either side) and red-and-white socks as a Cup final present. She'd been the one who sewed the oval piece of cloth bearing the Liver Bird on to the shirt. And she was the one who realized when they got it back to Garstang that it lacked the finishing touch. A number 9 on the back to signify my undying love for Ian St John.

So she set about solving the problem by taking a needle and white cotton and stitching the outline of 9 on the shirt, imagining this final gesture would make my joy complete.

The plan had been to lay it on the bottom of my bed so that when I awoke on FA Cup final day I would be overcome with joy and gratitude. But that Friday morning was going badly for Sheila.

As well as running round after my five-year-old sister Karen and trying to get my one-year-old sister Cathie off to sleep, she had me climbing up her anaglypta walls, unable to wait the thirty-odd hours for a Cup final.

Which was when she decided to give me the kit. A gesture she thought would make me as placid and humble as Buddha. Not quite. Upon setting eyes on the front of it I struggled so hard for breath she thought I was having a seizure. The joy was life-threatening. But on seeing her cack-handed attempt to place a number 9 on the back of it, my eyes expanded like a deep-sea diver hitting the bends, and I struggled so hard to keep down the swear-words I threw it to the deck, called her a 'stupid bitch' and ran out of the house and down the street.

She followed, screaming at me to come back, but I just kept running, yelling back that I was leaving home for good. For hours I hid under the sink in a kitchen of a house that was being built on a new estate, moping over how near yet how far I'd come to owning my own Ian St John kit.

In the end the stitched abortion didn't matter. After I'd returned home to face the music, Vic smugly pointed out that the traditional red-and-white kit was now defunct. They'd tested an all-red one out against Anderlecht in the European Cup. Shankly loved it because he thought it made them look fearsome, and Liverpool would be wearing it in the Cup final. So now the entire kit was a joke and I'd be better off sitting in Bishopgate Street tomorrow dressed as Andy Pandy.

You have to realize that back then teams only changed their kits every couple of decades, dictated by fashion. If they hadn't, they'd still be wearing what they wore in the 1870s – knicker-bockers, laced-up shirts and Wee Willie Winkie hats. (Think David Beckham's Next Look.) Unlike today when it's four kits every three years, parents were never forced to wilt under pressure from a brat pleading that he would look a total divvy and povvo, if seen out in last year's strip.

So Reg was rightly enraged and wasn't having any of this new kit lark. He'd forked out 7s 6d and I was wearing it. We reached a compromise – if the offending number was removed I'd wear it. Which is what happened.

So there I sat in front of my nana's telly dressed head-to-foot in a kit which now belonged to the dark days of the 1950s, like one of Jesus's apostles about to be visited with a flame.

If you've ever got close to experiencing the best dream you've ever had fused with the best sex you've ever imagined, you may feel the way I did that afternoon. I'm yet to have the lightning-striking, tambourine-clashing moment that comes about when you turn into a born-again Christian. But thanks to a moment 21 minutes into extra time, with the score at 1–1, I now know how the tambourine sounds.

Ian Callaghan went past Paul Reaney, floated a hopeful ball into the box which Gary Sprake failed to get near, and there, steaming in with his socks down, was Ian St John, who met it with the most glorious diving header. His body arced into a crescent, the ball rippled the net, and time stood still.

The first thing I had ever wanted so badly in my life it made me bleed, had happened before my eyes, and I was being lifted in the air by an uncle and shaken, as the room filled with whoops and cheers. But I was paralysed, overcome with the sheer magnitude of what was passing before my eyes.

God was doing this. God was looking after me. Telling every kid and teacher up in Garstang that I was a Chosen One. That I had walked among them and they had spurned me, even though I spoke about the deeds of a Saint.

I could smell the flames of hell licking around their trembling hillbilly legs. I had visions of them all falling to their knees and begging forgiveness, telling Him they would treat me like a messiah when I returned to school on Monday. So lost did I become in this fantasy of hope and retribution that I didn't hear the final whistle. I just joined the rush out into Bishopgate Street and a scene I'd only ever seen on New Year's Eve. Hugging, kissing, dancing, swaying. Everyone drunk, but without a whiff of pale ale on their breath.

It had taken Liverpool seventy-three years and 207 ties to finally win the FA Cup. It had taken me seventy days and three ties after I made my bow at Bolton to see them lift it. Clearly they'd waited for me. It was another sign from above that me and Liverpool were destined for each other.

Celebrations went on long into the night. Uncles and aunties descended on my nana's with their kids and left them there as they all went over to Bent's back parlour for a night of revelry. Crates were dragged back by the men and the women made sarnies. Reg got on the piano and the party began.

The old songs about 'Red Roses for Blue Ladies' and 'Slow Boats to China' were interspersed with 'Ee-aye-addios' and 'We'll Be Running Round Wembley With The Cup'. Even the Evertonians joined in. Well, some of them. Swaying men pressed tanners into kids' hands and kissed them on the head. My uncle Mickey, a fanatical Red, sat me down on the stairs and told me what this meant. How it was the start of something big under Shankly. We were playing Inter Milan that week in the semi-final of the European Cup at Anfield, and when we battered them (as we did) we'd go on to be the first British team ever to lift that trophy (which we didn't).

He talked about this being Liverpool's time. That the football team was a symbol of a reborn city, made famous across the world by The Beatles (at Number One again that week with 'Ticket To Ride'). One of our MPs, Harold Wilson, was Prime Minister, our comedians and writers (remember *Z Cars*?) dominated popular culture, while our poets were shaking up all those arty-farties in London.

An hour after midnight my grandad's mate Billy Jones staggered through the door (now he did smell of pale ale) bearing exaggerated tales of what had really happened at Wembley. How it looked and felt in the flesh. How everyone down there said our songs and flags had been a revelation. How there had really been 120,000 in the ground because 20,000 Scousers had bunked in. How even Lizzie herself had laughed when they all started singing, 'Ee, aye, addio, the Queen's wearing red.' How he'd been near the front and Ian St John had winked at him on the lap of honour. Honest to God.

And then he made a shushing sound, threw back his arms and started belting out these words to the tune of 'When Johnny Comes Marching Home':

> Here's to Lawrence, Byrne, St John – haroo haroo,
> Milne and Yeats and Stevenson – haroo, haroo
> Hunt and Thompson, what a man,
> Lawler, Smith and Callaghan,
> And we all got blind drunk when Liverpool won the Cup.
>
> It's Wembley on the first of May – haroo, haroo,
> It's Leeds United Labour Day – haroo, haroo,
> We were there for Shankly's side,
> And brought the Cup to Merseyside,
> And we all got blind drunk when Liverpool won the Cup.

I was stunned into a muteness which Billy Jones couldn't fail to see. He put his bottle down and crouched so he was at my eye-level.

'Here y'are son,' he said, pulling the match programme and ticket stub from his mac. 'That's for you. Proof of the greatest day in Liverpool's history. Keep 'em safe.'

Unable to speak, lost in a trance, I took them upstairs to bed, stuffed them under my now dated Liverpool shirt, and smiled at the ceiling as the reassuring laughter, clanks of the piano and tuneless singing from the drunken voices boomed up through the floorboards.

I was as happy as a feckin' whore-master.

3

PUPPY LOVE

27 FEBRUARY 1970 – KELLITT ROAD, WAVERTREE

It was one of those bitter February nights when the rawness of the wind and the blackness of the sky eats away at your soul and makes you realize why men join the Foreign Legion.

On the badly lit terraced streets frowning strangers with hunched shoulders scurried past, eager to get home for light and warmth. A journey I should have been taking too, as I traipsed off the 60 bus in Wellington Road weighed down with my school-bag. But for the past six months my heart had dragged me on a lengthy diversion.

We were living in Huyton now, on the outskirts of Liverpool, having moved back from the land of sheep in early 1966, after Sheila reached into the knife drawer and threatened to do a Lorena Bobbitt on Reg. I was in my first year at De La Salle in Croxteth, and a regular in the school team, although the St John impressions had long ago ceased.

There was a new man in my life, a blond bombshell called Alun Evans. And here I was again, outside the Wavertree terraced house where he shared digs with two other players, going through the same ritual I'd gone through at least forty times in a vain attempt to share his oxygen. I knock on the big red back-door gate and brace myself for the standard procedure. An Alsatian barks, my arse goes, I think about legging it, bollock myself for being a sad stalker, hear the bolt taken off on the back kitchen door, then the gate, and a middle-aged woman in a pinny and curlers gives me the Jehovah's Witness brush-off and slams the wooden mass in my face.

But the unexpected happened that night. This time, when the bolt came off the gate, standing before me was a sideburned vision from the back row of the team pictures. Peter Wall. Not a god by any stretch of the imagination, but undoubtedly a demigod whom I'd watched come through the reserves, play solidly at full-back and earn the right to be described on the back of football cards as a 'promising fringe player'. No doubt about it, he was a capture.

'Erm, can I have your autograph please, Mr Wall?'

(The formality had come from an incident two years earlier in British Home Stores when out of the blue Reg said, 'There's Billy Liddell over there, why don't you get his autograph,' before giving me his pen and ripping a piece of paper from his wallet. I legged it down the aisle, stopped the legend in his tracks and breathlessly panted, 'Can I have your autograph please, Billy?' Only for him to boom, 'Mr Liddell to you, sonny.' He signed the scrap of paper after I'd addressed him with his required title but I could never hear stories again about the winger who was so revered they called him Liddellpool without thinking, 'What a miserable old sod.')

'Yeah. No problem,' said Peter, signing away with a knowing grin. He had me sussed. I was still in my school uniform and it was six o'clock. I hadn't put off my tea on this horrible night to ask for the signature of a promising fringe player. He handed me back the pen and paper, waiting for the inevitable request.

'Erm, is Alun Evans in?'

'Yeah.'

'Could you ask him for an autograph for us?'

'Sure,' he said laughing, no doubt thinking the snub would annoy the even bigger star who lived in the house, Emlyn Hughes.

The wait for my trophy took on Newcastle proportions as scores of uncertainties kicked in. I was about to meet Alun Evans face-to-face. How would he look at me? Would he think I was just another little tosser wasting his time, or realize I was such a huge fan I'd stood up for him in the playground when he'd been ridiculed as a pretty boy who wasn't fit to lace Roger Hunt's boots?

I'd loved Alun Evans from the first time I set eyes on his blond mop in his debut against Leicester in September 1968. As with every other home game back then I went with Our Vic, wooden stool tucked under my arm, entering an Anfield Road turnstile as soon as it opened at half-past one. Once inside, I'd buy a programme, find a crash barrier a third of the way up towards the Kemlyn Road, place the stool down, hear the opening bars of the song that always kicked off the Tannoy service, 'Let's Go' and spend the next hour-and-a-half alternating eyes from programme to pitch.

As with most kids who didn't go to the Boys Pen, a zoo-like monkey cage at the top left-hand corner of the Kop, I felt like a bit of a fraud. A bottler who'd copped out of military service after hearing dark tales about snatched bus fares and yockers all over the back of your head.

The uncomfortable truth was, à la Prince Edward and the Marines, me and Vic weren't hard enough. The kids who took their Kop apprenticeship in the Boys Pen learnt it the tough way; the kids who chose to fork out an extra shilling for the Annie Road earned a smoother passage. That said, as the sixties became the seventies, and hooliganism was rife, spending an afternoon in the Annie Road was hardly likely to leave you with a passage that was smooth. On a good day your bum was tighter than Ken Dodd; on a bad day, it was looser than Linda Lovelace.

The away fans used to congregate at the back of the Annie Road and as kick-off time (in both senses) approached, with the hardcore of skinheads and piss-heads falling in from the pubs and streets to sound the war cry, the fun would begin.

The police, in their naivety, didn't bother to segregate the away fans from the home crowd, a mistake the local boot-boys saw as manna from heaven. During a game against Stoke (who always brought a handy crew with them) I received such a nasty butt on the head that I flew off the stool.

The chants of 'Zigger-zagger, zigger-zagger, oi, oi, oi' (Stoke's version of 'Come and have a go if you think you're hard enough') had been ringing out for a while, when the foot soldiers of the

Annie Road Army decided to prove they were indeed hard enough by ambushing them from both sides. The Stoke mob spun like an exploding Catherine wheel on to the terrace below, a blur of boots and fists and scarves tied on wrists. One lad was legging it so fast from the pursuing brown leather that he tripped, the momentum carrying him through the air and his head smacked into mine, taking me from the stool to the concrete beneath.

Vic picked me up. He was panicking because I'd blacked out. One of those where you stop hearing anything for a few seconds and incidents and people kaleidoscope through your head, before a loud buzzing takes over, your eyes open to see two sets of four faces staring down at you, followed by a surge of pain that feels like your head's been slipped into a vice. And then a numbness.

'Is my stool OK?' I asked groggily. But the fellas around me wouldn't let me get back on it in case I fainted. They sat me on the crash barrier and formed a wall around me. I felt like royalty. But as we hated royalty in our house, I couldn't have been less comfortable if I was sitting on a spiked ball. When Roger Hunt put us one up after 15 minutes, I pronounced myself fit to return to the stool. We battered them 3–1.

I'd been touched by Vic's show of compassion after the butt, but I sensed it was more for what he would have got off Reg had I ended up in Alder Hey hospital. The truth was that he didn't want me to be there with him, especially with the stool he regularly threatened to burn. But he had no option because Reg had said that if he didn't take me then he didn't go.

I'll be honest, there weren't too many other kids carrying stools to the match. I must have looked like a midget with a huge rattle, or even worse what I actually was. A geeky trainspotter so consumed with my lifetime passion, I didn't care how odd I looked to outsiders. Vic knew though. Which was why he made me walk to the 75 bus stop in Huyton village like a Taliban wife, ten yards behind him. At Anfield he'd make me walk ten yards in front, tailing me from a distance like a private dick.

But he was to blame for the embarrassing wooden prop.

Without the stool, unless I stood right at the very front of the Annie Road (which Vic refused to as it was full of primary school kids like me) or sat on a barrier (a no-no as Vic wouldn't offer the necessary back protection from the swaying crowd) I was knackered. The one-and-a-half-hour wait inside the ground made utterly futile by some big fat fella who'd fallen out of The Arkles at five-to-three planting himself in front of me, blocking all views of the pitch, and blowing a huge Sayers meat-and-potato pie fart in my face.

That piece of wood was a liberating lifeline. When I stood on it and soared to 5ft 11in, I was the master of all I surveyed. And that Saturday afternoon when Alun Evans made his debut, oh what glory there was to survey. We'd won the toss and were attacking the Annie Road End in ferocious waves. After four minutes we were 2–0 up. After ten minutes Evans brought the ball down on his chest, swivelled past his marker and buried it. Two minutes later Cally scored a fourth, so 4–0 up after 12 minutes. Against our bogey team to boot.

It felt like the dawning of a new era, especially when we went to Wolves the following Saturday and thrashed them 6–0, with Evans scoring twice. That clinched it. He'd won my heart and I had to do the decent thing. I had to finish with The Saint.

Actually, like most splits, we'd been growing apart for a while. Tony Hateley had been bought to partner Hunt up front, and St John was switched from number 9 to number 10. From being a 20 goals-a-season man to half-a-dozen.

He was still a vital team player, but a kid needs more than that from a hero. He needs a goalscorer. He needs to see his man producing a little bit of magic that flummoxes a defence, before bursting the net and running to the crowd to soak in the mass adulation.

When you're ten your hero has to be the one who does the things that you want to do. The one who is fleshing out your dreams. There has to be real envy. And sadly I didn't envy The Saint's engine and ability to deliver a cute, defence-splitting

pass or his unselfishness at laying on the goalscoring chances for
Hunt and Hateley.

But then neither of those two strikers did it for me idol-wise.
I couldn't suddenly flirt with Roger after dating his mate for
three years, and Hateley was too much of a big ugly lump, too
easily injured and so lethal in the air the team was tempted
to switch from their trademark pass-and-move system and play
it straight to his head. Shankly agreed, moving him on quickly
(despite scoring 16 League goals in his first season). Shanks, like
me, decided heroes had to have a bit more class about them.

Back at Kellitt Road I heard footsteps on the kitchen step and
a presence slowly making for the gate. My sphincter was so tightly
clenched it could have supported a troupe of hanging acrobats.
This was the moment then. Our first date. And then my guts hit
the deck.

'I'm sorry mate, but Alun's a bit tied up, will I do?' squeaked
Emlyn Hughes, wearing a trademark face-splitting smile. I didn't
have the heart to tell him he wouldn't.

'Er, yeah Emlyn, thanks,' I replied, handing over the pen and
piece of paper which had been squashed into a sweaty ball as I
awaited the man who'd left me in the lurch. The shock of the
snub hit me so hard I'd dropped all that 'Mister' bollocks and
unleashed a subconscious revolt against Billy Liddell and the
entire football-playing class.

'On your way home from school, are ya?' he said, handing me
his stylish signature (opened with a beautiful swirling, almost
Elizabethan 'E').

'Yeah, I've had football training.'

'Play for your school?'

'Yeah.'

'Who's that then?'

'De La Salle.'

'Where d'ya play?'

'Midfield.'

'Like me, eh? Keep behind fo'wards do ya?'

'Yeah.'

I'll tell you how my brain was working here. At first I was answering him on autopilot, the shock of Alun Evans' betrayal still dominating my thoughts. As Hughes spoke I could see that behind his lips he was still chewing. Probably steak. That's what Shankly made them have every night. Which meant he was halfway through his tea. Which meant so was Alun Evans. Which meant (according to my warped juvenile mind) when Peter Wall told him there was a lad outside after his autograph, he's gone: 'I'm having my tea.' Emlyn's gone: 'You can't disappoint the boy if he knows we're in here.' Evans has shrugged, shovelled a few more chips on his fork, gone back to the *Echo*, and Emlyn's pushed back his chair, head shaking, and come out.

You albino-headed bastard, Evans, I thought. You lovely man, Emlyn, I added.

'Are you any good then, son?'

'Not bad. Never get dropped, like. But nah, there's better players in our team. That's why I'm in midfield not attack.'

He laughed out loud. At me. And I wasn't even being funny.

'Eh, don't worry about what position they play you in, son. Alf Ramsey plays me at left-back.'

'I know. I saw you the other night against Belgium. You were sound.'

'Well, I'll make a deal, eh? You keep playing your heart out behind the fo'wards and I'll do the same at full-back. I'll have a word with Alf, and in a few years we might both be in the same England team, eh?'

'Yeah.'

'Right, off you pop, I've gotta finish me tea.'

'Thanks, Emlyn.'

The red gate slammed into my face, which was a similar hue. Was it due to embarrassment at having such an intimate conversation with a man who Shankly declared would one day captain England (which he did, 23 times)? Was it because he'd said he'd have a word with Alf Ramsey? Was it because I'd made him laugh (little did I know at that point that Hughes could unleash a fit of sycophantic convulsions by merely catching a whiff of a Junior Royal)? Or was it the first flush of love?

The answer became clear the second I arrived home and made for the garage to perform a rechristening ceremony. I took my dad's black marker pen from his toolbox, went to my hamster's wooden cage, scrawled furiously over the word ALUN, and wrote next to it, with loving care, the name EMLYN.

Hell hath no fury like a twelve-year-old football fanatic scorned.

4

THE IDES OF MAY

9 MAY 1971 – ST GEORGE'S HALL, LIVERPOOL

Between the ages of eleven and sixteen I had only one conversation with Reg. It happened every Saturday lunchtime during the football season when I came through the back kitchen door after playing for the school, threw down my bag, grabbed soup off him and rushed past to watch Football Preview on *Grandstand*.

'Did you win, son?'

'Yeah, seven–nil.'

'Who were you playing? The blind school?'

'No.'

OK, it wasn't seven-nil every week. Occasionally it was a bit tighter, but we always seemed to be handing out batterings. Unless we were playing St Kevin's, who had twelve-year-old kids with facial hair and Mister Universe muscles. When you lined up against them on their wind-blown Kirkby wilderness it felt like you'd landed on the Planet of the Apes.

De La Salle's pitches have always teemed with talent, producing the likes of Wayne Rooney, Franny Jeffers and Paul Jewell, and in the seventies there was no better school in Liverpool. I played centre-midfield, chipped in with ten goals a season, and quite fancied myself as a half-decent player, until one Saturday morning in the third year when we went to St Francis Xavier's, I came up against Sammy Lee and he put what small talent I had into sobering perspective.

He was fifteen months younger than me, half my height, twice my girth, and when I set eyes on him I sniggered to Pop O'Brien alongside me that this shower must be getting desperate if they've drafted in a ginger Jimmy Clitheroe from the year below. Never have words been rammed down my throat with so little effort.

Sammy rarely moved out of the centre-circle, preferring to stand there, pick up everything loose and direct it with precision into the path of an attacker. Trying to win a ball when he was within three yards of you was like trying to pick up a cuddly toy with an electric claw in an amusement arcade after ten pints of cider. He held up a mirror that day, showing me the gulf in class between those who think they're good at football and those who know they are. He made me realize any dreams I cherished about playing for Liverpool should remain between my head and my pillow.

Years later, when Sammy became a regular for Liverpool and England, and some fans dismissed him as a talentless hod-carrier, he taught me another priceless lesson: never trust the opinion of the ranter sitting next to you at the match because there's a good chance he's never played football at any level, and he's merely spouting the last thing he's heard from the loudest bore in the pub.

Those Saturday conversations with Reg never progressed past the blind-school reference because as soon as Football Preview had finished discussing Liverpool's game, I was out of the house. Either joining in the twenty-a-side free-for-all in the park in the middle of our Huyton estate, or heading off to Anfield. Fortunately for Vic I no longer had to troop along behind him like a flood victim carrying what's left of the household furniture. Neither he, nor the stool, accompanied me to the match any more. Instead I tagged along with other lads from our estate like Nicky Williams, John Fleming and Icky Littler. Vic had graduated to the Kop but I still wasn't ready to flee the Annie Road womb.

The biggest myth about Liverpudlians of my age is that we were shameless glory-seekers, medal-chasing Muttleys, who spurned the chance to follow Everton for a trophy-machine with a fan base whose accents hinted of too long spent near combine-harvesters. That LFC were Man United-on-Mersey and its fans a shower of shallow, gold-digging prostitutes.

If only. During the first six seasons I was an Anfield ever-present (1967 to 1973) we won precisely nothing. Like 95 per cent of teams we were potless also-rans, praying for a decent Cup run to disguise an inability to win the League.

Everton, on the other hand, were a purring Cadillac with their midfield of Kendall, Ball and Harvey leaving most neutrals drooling. When they won the 1970 title the School Of Science, as they termed themselves, looked likely to dominate the new decade and beyond. It was why my school class, like virtually every class on Merseyside, was split fifty-fifty between blue and red. No Kopite was on a superiority kick. No Blue Nose had a boulder on his shoulder.

Silverless years they may have been, but they were golden days nonetheless. Away from home we weren't much better than Burnley, at home we were better than Real Madrid.

The players, galvanized by Shankly's tongue and the 'This Is Anfield' sign he had placed in the tunnel, steamrollered opponents into submission, and the Kop was the greatest collective mass of passion, wit and song in any walk of British life.

I stood 100 yards away but still felt a surge of pride at ten-to-three every week when the teams were read out, in anticipation of what was to come. The chewing gum would move faster, the pit of the stomach would begin to churn, slowly at first, then accelerating towards that sudden adrenalin rush in the split second after Liverpool's substitute was named and Gerry Marsden uttered 'When you walk . . .' – the signal for that massive red-and-white shutter at the opposite end of the pitch to rise, blocking everything else on the horizon.

As 'You'll Never Walk Alone' got into its stride I'd look at the men in the Kemlyn Road and Main Stand, turning towards our Mecca, watching grace being sung before the meal.

I'd peel round to the away fans, hoping to see them struck dumb by a vision which, like the greatest of players, was worth the admission money alone. And they were. Time and time again. Some taking pictures, others lifting their kids on to their shoulders to glimpse the Eighth Wonder of the Footballing World.

The thing about real football fans is that they know when they're in the presence of greatness. They respect it, mentally tick off the experience and log it for future tales. That's how I felt when Man United hammered us 4–1 in 1969, with George Best and Bobby Charlton at the height of their brilliance. They may have been inflicting untold pain, but something told me I'd remember seeing Best torturing Peter Wall, turning him inside out at will, until the day I died. That I would be eternally grateful to have watched a genius in the flesh.

Earlier that year I'd watched the Kop applaud Leeds, our bitterest rivals, from the pitch, chanting 'champions' in their honour after they'd drawn 0–0 to leave us runners-up. I'd gone home gutted. All that changed the next morning when I read Don Revie in the papers saying the Kop's generosity 'brought tears to my eyes'. He sent a telegram addressed to 'The Kop, Anfield'. It said, 'Thanks for your very warm-hearted gesture: We nominate you as the Sportsmen of the Century. You and your great team and wonder manager deserve one another.'

Of course the Kop (being, like its idol Shankly, as vain as it was vicious) lapped up such praise. Kopites were the best around and they knew it. The first terrace in football history to be awarded iconic status. At every home game they starred in their own movie as the players vied for best supporting actor. There were few banners then as Europe had yet to be conquered, no team shirts with names and numbers on the back (money had yet to conquer us all) but what an inventive and extensive repertoire was emitted by that wall of sound.

It wasn't only the away fans who looked on in awe, or the opposing goalkeepers astonished at being so warmly applauded back on to the pitch after half-time. Film and sound crews turned up to record a social phenomenon. Pink Floyd put them on a best-selling record, Kop albums were recorded and foreign documentary-makers flocked to L4. *Panorama* sent a plum-gobbed Oxbridge type to stand before it and have the piss taken out of him, and in between songs he remarked, 'This famous mound, named after a Boer War battle in which a local regiment suffered many casualties, is today as rich and mystifying a popular culture as on any South Seas Island.' His editor had cut out the cruelty but it was there in equal measure with the wit.

Folk-singer Stan Kelly tells of the time he sat before the Kop to make a sound-recording for one of his albums. 'When we got back to the studio and played the tape the first thing we could hear under the song was this voice saying: "Hey mate, get yer head down will yer, I can't see the fuckin' match." '

But what an enduring football legend it is. This choir, and they were a choir, had taken a 1964 pop variation of a Rogers and Hammerstein standard and turned it into an anthem which became the world's football hymn. A hymn which didn't just endure but grew in stature year after year, to the point where the Germans played it to console teams knocked out of the semi-finals of the 2006 World Cup. A fitting tribute to a rare marvel.

I plunged into it, alone, on 21 November 1970. Derby day. And my second day as a teenager. The previous Monday I'd got off school early and queued for five numbing hours to get a ticket. I must have stood out a mile as I walked down a dark Walton Breck Road at 7 p.m., a twelve-year-old in a school uniform from a different part of town.

And I couldn't have wished to have been mugged by two nicer lads.

'Give us your derby ticket, la'.'

'I haven't got one.'

'Well you won't mind us looking in your pockets then will ya?'

'Ah, eh,' I pleaded, lower-lip trembling like the hands of a last-bus alcy. 'I've been queueing up for five hours. Don't take it.'

His mate felt slightly sorry, and went to intervene. But it was too late. The freshly minted ticket had been grabbed from the inside pocket of my blazer. The gold dust was in the prospector's hand.

'Sorry, la'. You're just unlucky you bumped into us. See ya.'

They walked off laughing, my voice too weak and shocked to make a final clemency plea. I felt raped. Seconds earlier I'd been so proud to get my mitts on a derby ticket. I'd been walking alone picturing the build-up to the game, telling everyone who asked, 'Oh yeah, I've got a ticket. Bunked off school and queued for five hours.'

I was still shaking when I got home to receive a bollocking off my mum for being so late. A bollocking that stopped when I unburdened my tale of grief: 'Don't worry son. We won't let them win,' she said. 'I'll get you another ticket. A better one.'

And she did. She worked on the counter of Green Shield Stamps in Hanover Street, and when word got round, all stops were pulled out. Two days after the mugging a ticket had been found, given up by one of the women's husbands. I may have sagged off from a Christian Brothers school for the afternoon but I'd learned a lesson the men in frocks could never teach me. For every heartless shit out there, there's a Good Samaritan. And this one had given me a derby ticket for the Kop, and entrance to one of the most memorable games I would ever see.

Everton were champions and playing like it. The Horse (Joe Royle) and the Rat (Alan Whittle) had put them 2–0 up with 20 minutes to go. Misery stared me in the face as well as a surrounding knot of Evertonians on the outer edges of the Kop (I was told to keep away from the middle sections as they were feudal plots handed down by fathers).

When Heighway jinked inside and let one rip towards the near post, leaving Gordon West stranded, a human wave lifted me and nearly unhinged my neck from my spine. When Heighway crossed six minutes later and Toshack soared above Brian Labone to plant the equalizer in the top corner I flew a full 30 feet down the terrace and was thrown back like whiplash. When Chris Lawler connected with a Toshack knock-down to volley the winner I went under like a dog in a lake tied to an old bed. I was sucked up, heaved back, tossed into the air and ended up lodged between two men who looked as though they were trying to make love.

For the next few minutes my feet didn't touch the floor, and when they did I was minus one patent-leather Chelsea boot and my bus fare.

I walked the five miles back home to Huyton, down Walton Breck Road where I had been left so desolate days before, a grin splitting my face and the concrete splitting my sole. I wanted to bump into those muggers and let them see how happy I was. No I didn't. I wanted to hear that the big one had used my ticket to get into the Annie Road, said to an Evertonian psychopath when the winner went in: 'Sorry, la'. You were just unlucky you bumped into us,' and woken up to a hospital breakfast.

It was a win that kept me warm inside for weeks. A memory that could block out all the embarrassments, frustrations and uncertainties that dominate the crash through puberty.

The downside of obsession is the hollowness you feel when things aren't going well. You have nothing or no one to help you take your mind off the pain. The upside is that when things go well you are as close as you can be to nirvana. Joy and fulfilment burst your heart.

I struggled to fathom how outsiders could not appreciate the beauty of this infatuation. Or even that it *was* an infatuation, which by definition means a total love for a specific object of desire to the exclusion of all else. An object you think about constantly, which becomes the lens through which you view life. I've since learned how to rein it in. These days if I'm asked to write a piece about the happiest moment of my life, or how I'd spend the perfect day, I veer away from Liverpool FC, even though it is right there, smack in the middle of the answer.

When I was thirteen, I couldn't see the need and didn't have any meaningful experiences outside of my obsession to offer an alternative. A situation which used to anger teachers, none more so than the one who took us for English – an acute Small Man Syndrome sufferer, with a whining voice straight out of Midlands polytechnic training college, who tried to assert himself through shouting, dishing out the strap or making us write out the preface to some 1930s grammar book. I was forced to write that preface so many times I could virtually recite it. My recurring crime being whenever I was asked to do a creative essay I would always bring it round to football. I remember one particularly violent verbal assault after he'd asked to write about how we'd spend a perfect Christmas Day.

It was so obvious I banged it out in ten minutes flat. Get up at 3 a.m., read my footie annuals, put on my new footie boots and go out and play until dark; come in and play my new footie game, then get an early kip because Boxing Day kick-offs were usually a few hours early.

He exploded, dragging me to the front of the class and screaming about how pathetic my life was as it 'revolved around a football pitch'. I toyed with saying at least it doesn't revolve around spanking boys with leather.

I got revenge when he tried to cast me in a drama production of *The Lord Of The Flies* (because I was 'a gobby show-off'). I had no problem with it until he told us initial rehearsals would take place on Formby beach, over the next three Saturdays. He turned to me smugly and asked if I had problems with that, to which I replied, 'Well, yeah. On two of the next three Saturdays Liverpool are at home, and that's where I'll be.'

He got up so close his coffee-tinged halitosis was threatening to singe my nasal hairs. But I knew, and he knew, that he couldn't make me do this. It was Saturday. It was voluntary. And if I chose to spend it at Anfield rather than romp around sandhills chasing an imaginary pig with that greasy prick shouting at me for not being dramatic enough, that was the final word.

Logic should dictate that I had other interests but I hadn't. There was no other toy or hobby, no other comic or magazine than *Goal*, *Scorcher* and *Roar*, football programmes, *The Football*

League Review, *The Kop* magazine and *Charles Buchan's Football Monthly*. There was no other non-football-related TV show apart from *Top Of The Pops*.

It's an uneasy truth hammered home whenever I see those dreadful 'I Love 1971' (or whatever) telly shows, which line up unknown talking heads to spout on about Space Hoppers and Spangles and divulge their love for a specific year of their adolescence. How can they know so much about *The Magic Roundabout* or care so deeply about *Alias Smith And Jones*? What were they doing on Chopper bikes when there were footballs? Where were all these fond memories of childhood bliss coming from? Surely when they think of 1971 all that comes back is the memory of that gut-churning ten-day car crash at the end of the season when Leeds knocked us out of the Fairs Cup semi-final and Arsenal beat us in the FA Cup final?

How can you dish out chirpy anecdotes about your love for a *Magpie* presenter when the only abiding memory of that year was that long streak of Cockney piss, Charlie George, lying on the Wembley turf with arms outstretched, blinking into the sun as, behind him, Ray Clemence is on his knees gripping the post with the net still rustling.

That 2–1 Cup final defeat was a horrible blow to take, especially after we'd beaten Everton in the semi-final with a glorious goal from Alun Evans. Especially after Stevie Heighway had put us 1–0 up in extra time and Arsenal seemed unable to break our defence. Especially when Alun Evans was substituted and we gifted them an equalizer. Especially when that Charlie George goal gave them The Double, and their fans celebrated with that turgid dirge 'Good Old Arsenal', newly composed for the Cup final in a TV competition, so they wouldn't be embarrassed by the Kop.

I was too emotionally drained to cry. As the final whistle went, before my mum could get in her usual 'it just wasn't meant to be', I fled the house, and got it out of my system by joining in a game in the park, flying at every Evertonian who'd had a lovely afternoon in front of the telly. I was taking defeats better now. Mainly because I'd had plenty of practice.

I was growing up. My sentimental sixties childhood had passed. This was the seventies now and I was a teenager with half-a-dozen years' experience of miserable blows. It was time to coolly work out the *why*, rather than mawkishly dwelling on the *if*.

Shankly had got round to breaking up the mid-sixties side (two years too late) after a humiliating sixth round FA Cup defeat at Watford, a year earlier. Out went the likes of Tommy Lawrence, Geoff Strong, Ron Yeats and Ian St John. In came Ray Clemence, Alec Lindsay, Larry Lloyd, Steve Heighway and John Toshack.

It would take time and a few more players before they were back challenging for the League. I knew this. So too did half of Merseyside who made it known the next day when 500,000 turned out to welcome the beaten finalists home. I stood in Lime Street, watching in awe as Shankly took to the steps of that Neoclassical masterpiece St George's Hall, and spread his arms out under those huge columns, looking like Caesar on a triumphant return to Rome.

Silence cut dead the ear-splitting din as Shankly took the mic. 'Yesterday we lost the Cup. But you, the people, have won everything. I've always drummed it into my players that they are playing for you, the greatest fans on earth. If they didn't believe it, they will now.'

His speech was punctured with wild applause which was stopped by the raising of his hand. Like Chairman Mao he appeared as a little red dot to those of us at the back of the crowd, but had us all transfixed.

He promised us this team was going places. He vowed that he would take them back to Wembley and win it for us. And we believed him.

When it was over I walked to the Pier Head to get the bus back to Huyton, utterly convinced that the Cup final defeat had been our darkest hour before the dawn. That Shankly's new side was destined for greatness. That they would win the FA Cup next season and that I would be there, finally at Wembley, in the middle of it all, and my life would be complete. But then if Shankly had told us all we were twelve-foot tall, had four arms and were about to invade Mars we'd have believed that too. And invaded.

5

THE PROMISED LAND

I know you're going to think I'm a dirty little slag, but I hadn't
gone looking for it. Honest.

I hadn't spent that summer staring at my Emlyn Hughes posters
thinking, there's definitely the beginnings of crow's feet round
those grinning eyes. I'm going to bail out now before the face-lift.

I'd been with Emlyn for almost eighteen months and, to be
frank, had few complaints. I hadn't stopped voting for him in
the *Football League Review*'s Handsomest Player of the Month
competitions, although I did have a slight heart-twinge when my
old flame Alun Evans won it once, and felt a surge of pride (not
to mention bemusement) when Ian Callaghan nicked it.

I also had a very interesting conversation with my mum, as I
was heading out of the front door to the post box, where she
revealed the fears she was harbouring over my sexuality.

'What's that letter?'

'A vote for Emlyn Hughes.'

'What kind of vote?'

'For Handsomest Player of the Month.'

Quizzical frown. Pursed lips. Crossed arms. Desperate search
for tact.

'Why do you want to vote for that?'

''Cos I want him to win.'

'Yeah, but "handsomest" player? Why?'

''Cos I don't want Georgie Best or Rodney Marsh or Jim
McCalliog or anyone else to win.'

'Don't you think it's a bit . . . you know?'

'What?'

'*Queer.*'

The word fell on to the carpet like a bouncing bomb, bobbling along until it went past me out of the door. My eyes followed it. I was stunned. My own mother labelling me a poof because I was voting for my hero in a poll in a magazine stapled in the middle of every football programme published by every First Division side. Which meant every football fan had a say. Which meant I was only doing my duty. This was a chance for us to win a title at a time when we couldn't win a goldfish on an 'Every Throw a Winner' stand at the Liverpool Show.

I just shook my head in disgust. Storming to and from the letter box though, the head began to boil at the cheek and hypocrisy of the woman. When I walked back in through the kitchen door I didn't mince my words. Although she probably thought I was mincing.

'You sat there in front of the telly last week watching *Miss World*, going on about how lovely Miss Sweden looked, what gorgeous eyes Miss India had, what a fabulous figure Miss Australia had, and we didn't say a thing. No "Is she a big lezzer or what?" sniggers. Nothing.

'You don't hear me going, "Ooh look at the thighs on Mick McManus" when I'm watching the wrestling, do you? But when I show a little bit of loyalty to a Liverpool player I'm a queer. Think about it.'

And after I'd stamped up to my room and she'd stopped laughing, she must have thought about it because she apologized. And gave me extra chips with my corned beef rissoles. And she never accused me of being queer again. Well, until she saw me dressed in her maxicoat for the 1974 FA Cup final.

I felt vindicated. More than that, I felt good about myself, even though I was making a fundamental mistake promoting the handsomeness of our players. It wasn't my fault though. I couldn't possibly have known at the time that the last thing you wanted your team to be was easy on the gay or female eye. Good-looking teams never win anything unless the players are called Roberto or Giuseppe. Look at Liverpool's Spice Boys who turned Wembley into a catwalk in 1996 to model cream Armani suits. Jamie Redknapp, David James, John Scales, Stan Collymore. They may well have been Calvin Klein model material, who had women swooning in their Paco Rabanne tail-winds, but as a team they stank.

Now look at those great Liverpool sides of the 1980s filled with the likes of Ian Rush, Steve Nicol, John Wark, Peter Beardsley. Uglier than all of the seven deadly sins, as the *Manchester Evening News* often used to point out, but they rarely ended a season without seeing their less-than-gorgeous looks reflect back at them from polished silver. (As the *Manchester Evening News* often used to avoid pointing out.)

I was to learn that a player whose mush scares ten shades of shit out of the opponents tends to be a winner. But I didn't know that back then. If I had, Tommy Smith would have covered my wall for twelve years.

But it was still Emlyn Hughes, even if the hamster had long ascended to the great miniature wheel in the sky. Crazy Horse may not have scored too many goals, but those he did were stonking, 30-yard, half-volleyed, net-ripping Goal of the Month beauts. He was an England regular, a war-horse, an inspiration. We were happy.

Obviously if I'd known of his love for the Royal Family, his legendary tightness and his eventual adoration of Margaret Thatcher, his posters would have met the same charred fate that Salman Rushdie's books did outside mosques. But I didn't know that and as the 1971–72 season started we were very much an item.

Until 12 minutes into the opening game against Notts Forest when a midget with a feather-cut who looked like he'd spent too long in the gym smashed the ball into the Kop net, leapt like a salmon, and landed in Tommy Smith's arms. Arms I wanted to be mine.

Forget all the lovers who'd caught me on the rebound from Ian St John – Kevin Keegan was the love of my life. Amid the thunderous roars of approval from Anfield regulars who sensed they were witnessing the birth of a new legend, I heard wedding bells. Brian Keegan had a ring to it.

The problem was there were very few pictures of him. The only one I'd seen was of him sitting glumly on a bin outside Anfield (dressed like Dave Hill from Slade) in the week leading up to the FA Cup final. Shankly had just paid Scunthorpe £35,000 for him, and the caption that went with the picture said something about us landing a kid for the future while the men got on with the present task of winning the Cup.

Yet there he was, three months later, wearing the number 7 shirt, causing all sorts of chaos with his darting runs, flicks and chest-downs, looking like he'd been in the side for years. This was completely unheard of. Back then lads from lower division clubs – Ray Clemence and Larry Lloyd, for example – did three years' hard labour in the reserves, learning their trade before getting close to warming the first-team bench. Not Keegan.

I asked him twenty years later if he knew how he ended up in the side that day, and he said he basically selected himself.

'I was having a good pre-season and the boss came up to me at the end of the final practice match and said, "What team do you think I should pick you for on Saturday? The reserves or the first-team?"

'Straight away I told him I hadn't come here to play for the reserves but the first team and I was ready for it.

'He said, "good." And the next thing I knew I was on the team-sheet. He was being very clever, testing me out. It was all about my response. If I'd have hesitated, had to think about it, or come out with stuff about there being some great players here who I looked up to, he'd have dumped me in the reserves.

'He might have thought I was ready but he needed to hear it from me first to be sure.'

It was one of Shankly's most inspired decisions. Not just the spotting of this pearl among the dross, but giving him the chance to shine so soon. Keegan galvanized Liverpool. He awakened a team that had been slumbering for five years. You often hear football pundits talking blithely about final pieces of jigsaws and missing links but most of the time it's just empty rhetoric. Not in Keegan's case.

He was the ignition key that started up the red tank which would eventually roll across Europe and flatten the continent. The general who would deliver Shankly's Napoleonic dream of 'conquering the bloody world'.

And I loved him because he never let you down. Game after game, season after season, he would spill the last bead of sweat in his body for the Liverpool cause. On some days I would look at his bulging chest in that tight, short-sleeved shirt and its redness would appear more vivid than any other shirt on the pitch. As though his blood was dying it a deeper shade.

We eventually fell out of love when he let it be known in early 1977 that he would be going abroad at the season's end. No fan could understand it. It had never happened before. The deal back then was that the clubs squeezed the life out of players, discarding them like old dishcloths when time caught up with their knees, and the fans wished them well as they went off to run a pub or sell insurance. But *we* were never dumped.

When Keegan announced he wanted a 'fresh challenge' we took it personally, and turned on him. At first we thought he was joking; when we realized he wasn't, we questioned his sanity. When we discovered he was in full possession of his marbles we concluded he was an ungrateful little money-grabbing git and wished him a lengthy stay in a German hospital.

My how we laughed when, in his final game, we became European champions. How in his absence we signed an even bigger legend in Kenny Dalglish. And in the following season's

European Super Cup how we annihilated his new side Hamburg 6–0.

It felt good but it was quite shameful. Football fans like to lecture modern players about the notion of loyalty but they can never occupy the moral high ground. The vast majority are 100 per cent loyal to their club, but 0 per cent loyal to the players. Break a leg and you're a forgotten man cursed for weakening the side. Hit a bad run of form and you're barracked for not earning your wages. Decide you'd like to pursue your career somewhere else and you're a callous mercenary.

Ultimately Liverpudlians only stay loyal to the Liver Bird, not the man who wears it. And we're not alone. In truth Keegan did nothing wrong. He gave six magnificent seasons to Liverpool before trying to make a wider impact on the world. By becoming twice European Footballer of the Year at Hamburg, it's fair to say he did. When the hurt died down and we learnt of the restrictive wages at Anfield back then, and the money foreign clubs were willing to offer, most fans forgave him. Especially when Graeme Souness and Ian Rush took the same route not long after, with little dissent.

But forget the hurtful break-up. Between 1971 and 1977, Keegan was our very own Superman and I embraced him with more passion than I had any other footballer. I came late to Ian St John and Emlyn Hughes had been around Anfield for four years before I gave him the eye.

Yet here I was at Keegan's birth and with him every step of the way until his retirement party in Rome. And because my first six years as an Anfield regular had been so barren, when the trophies started arriving it felt like I was mainlining on ecstasy, and he was at the core of it.

I guess a Liverpool fan who has followed the club since the mid-sixties could pick any of twenty seasons as their favourite. Few my age will see further than 1972–73.

Going into it, despite the signs being there that we were capable of winning the title, I was less optimistic than I'd ever been. That summer I'd tried to wean myself off my fanaticism. It was screwing me up.

The climax of the previous campaign had left me dead on the floor. Mentally I stayed out cold for weeks. We'd almost done it, you see. No, for a few seconds we had won it and the big wait was over, only to be snatched away in the cruellest fashion.

We'd had an incredible run-in. After losing away at Leicester (where else) a week after New Year's Day, we went unbeaten for fifteen games, winning all but one of them. In the penultimate game we lost 1–0 at Derby, after which Brian Clough took his team to Majorca confident they had done enough, even though a Liverpool win at Highbury would make us champions.

Reg tuned the stereogram in the living room in to the game while Sheila watched the telly. Such a distraction was clearly unacceptable so me and Vic listened to it on his small transistor in our bedroom. The second half produced a tension I had never experienced. We threw everything at Arsenal but couldn't score. I threw everything around the room, as the threats from an equally nerve-wracked Vic grew ever darker. With ten minutes to go a promising Liverpool move broke down near their penalty box, and I snapped, picking the radio up and hurling it at the wall.

Vic was on me like a panther, smacking me on the head, knocking me to the floor, booting me in the back and called me every expletive under the sun. It didn't hurt, but what happened next did. He plugged his earpiece in, lay on the bed and flooded the rest of the room with silence.

My pleas, screams and bangs went unanswered, but were picked up loud and clear by my mum who was trying to put my sisters to bed. Reg dragged me downstairs, telling me to cool it. My head was in turmoil. It had been a good two minutes since we lost contact. They could have scored. We could be champions now and this old fart was telling me to shut up.

Turning away from another clip on the ear, the solution glared at me from on top of the gas cupboard. His car keys. As soon as his back was turned I nabbed them, was out the front door, into his beige Austin Maxi and frantically turning the radio dial to regain contact. And there it was. A clipped BBC voice saying, '. . . and the ball goes out for a Liverpool throw, down to our right, 20 yards from the corner flag, with six minutes left on the clock.'

I'd barely had time to check if there was a chewy in his glove compartment when the voice quickened with the words 'It's played into Toshack in the penalty area . . . 1–0 . . . the title's heading for Anfield' screamed from the dashboard. The background roars confirmed that the commentator's eyes weren't lying.

I raced from the car, yelping with joy. I jumped into the garden screaming 'Champions' as loud as my lungs would allow. The front door opened to reveal Reg standing there with a gob tripping him. Anticipating a smack for stealing his keys, and waking every baby in the road, I yelled: 'Toshack. We've done it.'

His mouth delivered the blow, and it was far more painful than anything his hand could muster. 'It's disallowed. Still 0–0.' I fell to my knees, picked myself up and slumped back into the car. Sure enough it was still 0–0 with minutes left. Sure enough that little, fat baldy shit of a referee Roger Kirkpatrick had disallowed it on the grounds that Toshack was offside. I could see from my dad's car in Huyton that he wasn't. Kirkpatrick – I still struggle to say that name without spitting – had landed himself at the centre of another controversy. Funny that, isn't it? You can pick any footballing era you want and there's always one referee making the controversial decisions.

This time the bastard in the black had decided the destination of the League title. It was Derby. For the second year running, a trophy that seemed to be heading to Anfield had been snatched away from us late in the last game of the season against Arsenal.

I couldn't look at the back pages for weeks, and as the new season approached and my head started to dance in expectation of the thrills that lay ahead, I tried to stifle any optimism. My system couldn't take being shocked so grotesquely for a third year running. This time I would view every run of wins with a detached scepticism. Until we opened up with a couple of 2–0 wins over the Manchester sides, and I was mentally scrawling 'League Champions 1972–73' on the team poster above my bed.

This time they didn't let us down. The boys were developing into men. They'd taken strength and knowledge from the depths of despair, knew when to hold, when to play and when to turn the screw in the toughest of scraps. The fluidity, energy and class in Shankly's latest side meant that, apart from Frank Lane and Trevor Storton who played a couple of games, only fourteen players were used.

We had a second team to recite without thinking: Clemence, Lawler, Lindsay, Smith, Lloyd, Hughes, Keegan, Cormack, Heighway, Toshack, Callaghan. They were the best side in the country and crucially they had the mentality to prove it.

A glorious 2–0 win over Leeds in the penultimate game saw us virtually there. All we had to do was draw at home with Leicester and the wait was over. That's right, Leicester. Surely not?

For some bizarre reason Vic suggested we went together. Without any of my little 'side-kicks' as he put it. I felt honoured. It was as though he'd recognized a joint agony between us these past six years, a hard and bloody war we had fought as brothers, and he wanted us to share the spoils of victory together. But really it was because his mate had got a Saturday job in Tate & Lyle's.

It was just like the old days (minus the stool) as we queued outside the Annie Road at 1.30. But this time we needed to be queuing because the gates were shut an hour before kick-off.

From 2 p.m. onwards, not an inch of concrete lay empty in Anfield's standing areas, but the atmosphere was far from carnival. Most fans had waited six years to see the League trophy shine at Anfield – some of us had waited all of our lives. We were sick with fear and anticipation.

There was a feeling we'd celebrated prematurely after the Leeds game and we were about to get our comeuppance. After all, hadn't history taught us that's what Leicester were for?

I didn't want to see the match. I wanted the ref to blow his whistle after two seconds. I couldn't take the thrills and spills, the oohs and aaahs, the possibility that we'd have 'one of those days' while plucky opponents with nothing to lose rose to the occasion, writing themselves into the history books. I just wanted it to be finally over. To push 'You'll Never Walk Alone' past a lump in my throat as big as a gobstopper while below me beaming, sweat-drenched players, weighed down with scarfs tossed that trophy in the air.

And guess what: our fears were fully justified. Maybe the nervousness of the crowd got through to the players, maybe Leicester remembered their destiny in life was to be Liverpool's bogey team, maybe there is something in the finest of humans that makes them question themselves just as they are about to be bathed in glory. Who knows. But we were dire, and never looked like scoring.

Just for a laugh, Fate took us to that precipice on the lip of Hell for a third season running, by letting Leicester score and the hearts of 56,000 people plummet to the soles of their shoes. Then Fate disallowed it. Maybe to even up last year's heartache.

After that I knew it would stay at 0–0. What followed was an explosion of relief. The pent-up tension of that frustrating 90 minutes had been a microcosm of the last six years. The release was a collective scream from every pore of the club. Whenever I imagine what VE Day must have felt like, this is where I am.

We hugged, we kissed (not me and Vic, obviously), we pogoed, we joined in with any of the six different songs that were going on at any given moment. We sighed, we inhaled, we looked up to the blue skies and said our thanks. We clapped the players, and when they lifted that quaint old trophy, Anfield (the district, not the ground) shook as the word 'Champions' was bellowed out. A statement of love, respect, relief and venomous defiance to anyone who ever doubted us.

Then a single word was chased around the ground like a Mexican Wave. The entire audience, including the Leicester fans behind us, picked up its cue from the person next to them. 'Shankly, Shankly, Shankly . . .' The emperor entered his colosseum, arms held aloft, and took off his jacket to reveal a red shirt and red tie. Scarfs fell at his feet like victory wreaths and he picked up each and every one. Lads with Bay City Roller hair and outfits danced around him. He looked part Pied Piper, part Moses, leading us to the Promised Land again.

He lapped the ground slowly, a scarf tied round his neck like a docker, his cropped head glistening in the glaring sun, drinking in all the years of hard work and disappointment. He looked at us the way the risen Christ looked at his disciples, eyes blazing with an intensity that said: Tell me you never questioned me. Tell me you harboured no doubts. Tell me all the pain and emptiness was worthwhile.

Tell me I've just put flesh on your dearest dream.

6

A MAMMOTH DESCENDS

12 JULY 1974 – CARR LANE EAST, CROXTETH

'You're going to be late.'

I roll over, scratch, attempt to yell, 'I'm coming,' then shiver and pull the blanket up to my chin.

'There's a letter here for you.'

Yawn, roll over, breathe, watch the cloud rise in the cold air, scratch.

'Who from?'

'The House of Commons.'

There's the kind of upright bolt that happens on America's extraordinary rendition flights when electric currents are sent through suspects' testicles. I fly downstairs in my undies, grab the letter off the table, sit down on the couch, place it on my knee and stare.

It's a lovely big white envelope, with an indented seal like the back of a threepenny bit. The words 'HOUSE OF COMMONS' are printed on the bottom left-hand corner and at the top is a crown with the words 'OFFICIAL PAID'. It's franked 'House of Commons, SW1, 9.30 p.m. 10 Jan 1974' and it's addressed to 'B. Reade Esq.'.

B. Reade Esq. Jesus, no one's ever called me an Esq. before.

This will be it then. Confirmation that B. Reade, Esq. has written his name indelibly into the Liverpool FC history book. I carefully open the envelope and out falls the most serious-looking letter I've ever seen. It's from the office of the Rt Hon. Harold Wilson, OBE, FRS, MP, and in biro it says 'confidential'. I must have clinched it then. Here goes:

Dear Mr Reade,

Mr Wilson has asked me to thank you for your letter of 3rd of
January.

He appreciated your writing to him about Mr Shankly, but he
has asked me to explain to you that the honours list is no longer
something on which Mr Wilson has any powers to intervene in any
way since it is entirely a question for 10 Downing Street.

Mr Wilson has however asked me to say he will certainly bring
to their attention the strong views you have expressed about Mr
Shankly and he will ask that Mr Shankly's name goes forward for
consideration in the usual way.

Yours sincerely

Mrs Marcia Williams, CBE

Personal and Political Secretary

OK, so I'd overlooked the fact he was no longer Prime Minister
when I wrote to Harold Wilson slagging off a system which kept
Shankly off the Honours List. But he was Labour leader, my MP,
and surely had the ears of the besuited Humphreys who handed
out these things.

At least he'd promised to bring it to their attention, and noted
that my views were strong, which was clearly politician-speak for
'Marcia, get this deranged, non-voting constituent who's obsessed
with some wrinklie in a tracksuit off my bleedin' back.'

Strong was an understatement. I had been apoplectic when I'd
read the New Year's Honours List the previous week to find that
Shankly had been snubbed, while Bobby Charlton had had his
1969 OBE upgraded to a CBE. For what? Finally dragging his old
legs off the pitch and into management at Preston where he was
a failure.

It added further fuel to a long-held view in Liverpool that
Manchester United, gawd bless 'em, had been given Queen
Mother status ever since the Munich Air Disaster. Matt Busby was
given a CBE for surviving it that year, which was upgraded to a
knighthood when they won the European Cup. And now Bobby

'cry those peepers out and drag that last strand of hair back across the scalp' Charlton had got a Palace double whammy too.

As for Shankly, oh he'd done nothing really. Just rebuilt a huge club which was sliding towards dereliction into one of the greatest in Europe. Won them promotion to the First Division, two League titles and an FA Cup in the sixties, then created a new side which last year regained the League and won the UEFA Cup in the same season. (In the month after the Leicester game they demolished Borussia Moenchengladbach 3–0 at Anfield, fell two behind in the first-half over there, but held on to win the club's first European trophy.)

So in 1973 Shanks had become the first coach of an English club to lift a domestic and European double, but when it came to recognizing his achievements, he was ignored. Before you start thinking this is classic Scouse paranoia, ask yourself why it took the next United manager to win the European Cup (in 1999) a matter of days for the government to leak that his new name was Sir Alex Ferguson. Whereas three-times winner Bob Paisley made do with the token CBE.

By the time of that last snub I was applauding the fact that Paisley had been overlooked. Who wanted to have anything to do with a corrupt system which allowed politicians to put forward sportsmen and soap stars for headline-grabbing minor trinkets, which camouflaged the pay-back going on behind the scenes? Who wants anything to do with a system which props up an antiquated monarchy by letting their subjects see them as benefi-cent father-figures, at one with the public mood of the day?

But back in 1974 it was different. It meant something. It was recognition at the expense of our rivals. The snub was a kick in the balls to the fans, and a slur on Shankly's reputation.

So yes, Mr Wilson, strong views were expressed. Words I expected to be acted upon. And they were. The following month Ted Heath asked the nation to choose between him and the miners. It wasn't too difficult. He was out, Harold was back where he belonged, and in what I guessed was his second task after giving the unions the keys to the Treasury so he could call and win another election six months later, he sorted out The Shankly Question. By the end of the year, Shanks had an OBE.

It may have had something to do with hundreds of other Liverpudlians venting their anger over the contempt shown to the great man, but I still like to think it was my letter, and as Harold said 'the strong views expressed', which made Whitehall see sense. Either way I was fiercely proud of the reply from Harold and the hope it held out. And I wanted Shankly to know us fans cared even if the government didn't. So I forwarded it to him.

Let's be honest here. I was a snivelling little creep searching for teacher's pet status, who wanted Shankly to know what a martyr I'd been on his behalf. So I went down to the Picton Library, dug out his address from the electoral register, and sent a copy of Wilson's letter to 30 Bellefield Road, West Derby L12 1LS. It was shameful, cringeworthy and undoubtedly sent in the hope I would gain a place, if not alongside him in the Boot Room, at least at his table for the odd Sunday dinner.

But, oh, what I received back. Just something I've known for the past thirty-odd years I would take to my grave. Banged out by Shankly himself, on an old typewriter, on headed LFC notepaper (with the odd grammatical error) it is the most moving piece of paper I will ever receive. The one luxury I would pack along with my Desert Island Discs, a treasure I wouldn't flog at Sotheby's for all the money in Chelsea.

Dear Brian,
   Received your letter, also the one you received from Mr Harold Wilson, thanks very much indeed.
   It is very good of you to write on my behalf. I appreciate it. However Brian I am not really disappointed about not being recognised. The people who dish out honours are not my people, my people go to Anfield. If I can make you all happy, then that is my greatest ambition.
   Very sincerely,
      Bill Shankly

Forget the writings of Marx and Engels, here was socialism laid
bare. 'The people who dish out honours are not my people, my
people go to Anfield. If I can make you all happy, then that is my
greatest ambition.' Of all the Shankly quotes, this is my favourite.
Not because it was addressed to my impressionable sixteen-year-
old self, but because it sums up the essence of the man. 'Some
people think football's a matter of life and death . . . I can assure
them it is more important than that,' was an off-the-cuff gag.

The intent behind it comes from the genuine Shankly belief
that you cannot underestimate the emotional power of the game.
But he doesn't mean to elevate the seriousness of football over
the birth or death of a single human being.

Yet the declaration that he has no time for the Establishment, and that his sole desire is to spread happiness among the
working-class people who turn up in old stadiums to watch
the working-man's game, hits at the nub of his philosophy, and
begins to explain why almost three decades after his death he is
so deeply loved by everyone connected with Liverpool FC.

When Shankly arrived at Anfield in December 1959 it was a
club going nowhere, run by a board that was happy to hang
around in the upper half of the Second Division, where, on
average gates of 35,000, and little need to spend big, no financial
risk was required. And managed by managers who were happy
not to rock the boat.

Shankly initiated a seismic shift. He demanded money to buy
the best young players in Britain. He rebuilt the crumbling shack
and relaid the barren turf at the Melwood training ground. He
introduced modern training methods and treatment rooms. He gave
the club a new professionalism, a new meaning, and instilled a
self-confidence, optimism and ambition which saw it fly.

Nowhere was this feelgood factor felt as intensely as on the
terraces. By the mid-sixties, when Shankly started to deliver the
trophies and restore the pride, the fans' love for the man was
bordering on adoration. Players, directors and journalists who had
been on the wrong side of his temper may have had unkind words

to say about him, but rarely, if ever, the fans. How could they, when everything he did was solely for their benefit?

In the lean years we loyally stood by him, refusing to doubt that he would turn things around. In the early seventies when the trophies came flooding back, we ditched mere adoration and worshipped him like a pagan god.

Individual stories abound which testified to the sincerity of his feeling towards the lowliest of the club's followers. A feeling summed up by an act witnessed by Kopites and players on the day they drew with Leicester in 1973 to clinch the title.

As Shanks did his lap of honour a boy threw a scarf at his feet. A policeman kicked it away only for Scottish wrath to descend: 'Don't do that,' said Shankly picking up the scarf and putting it on. 'That scarf's the boy's life.'

British football had known other great managers before Shankly: Herbert Chapman, Matt Busby, Jock Stein and Don Revie, but none had his magnetism. Here was a little, bald, old man whom few of his new admirers could recall as a player (unless you were around playing fields in West Derby of a Sunday when he would join in kickabouts with the kids) yet he possessed the charisma of a 30-goal-a-year, Casanova-lookalike striker.

Such a bond with the crowd had never been seen before. He started something unique in football: the manager as idol. A tradition Liverpool fans respect to this day under Rafa Benitez. Walk around the streets where Liverpool fans are gathered before any Cup final and you'll see a framed photo of the Spaniard, carried like a religious effigy with fans bowing before it. Look at the huge Liver Bird flag that spreads across the Kop shortly before every kick-off and you'll see, down either side of it, not drawings of the greatest strikers over the years, but the managers.

Listen to the songs sung about Benitez, as they were about Gérard Houllier, and you will hear a crowd reaching out to its leader, demanding a communion between the dug-out and the stands. It's a cry to be loved, a request for the man who holds the club's destiny in his hands to recognize his flock. To reciprocate the trust and tighten the umbilical cord. And it dates directly back to Shankly.

Imagine how that must have felt for Houllier and Benitez. Chubby, middle-aged foreigners who'd won nothing in mediocre playing careers, walking into this level of worship. At no other club on earth does the manager receive that kind of support or attention. Because no other club had Bill Shankly.

The day this bond was laid clear before the world was the day Shankly delivered on his promise, made on the St George's Hall steps after the defeat by Arsenal in the 1971 Cup final, that he would be returning to that very spot, some day soon, with these players and the FA Cup.

In 1974 he did just that after murdering Newcastle 3–0. It was the day Liverpool finally put on a show in an FA Cup final. The day the TV cameras caught Shankly orchestrating a glorious eleven-pass move, like a Proms conductor, which finished with Tommy Smith crossing for Kevin Keegan to score his second of the afternoon. The day the cameras caught two grown men lying prostrate on the floor kissing the great man's feet as the travelling Kop sang his name to the tune of 'Amazing Grace'.

In the multitude of wild dreams I'd had about Wembley I'd never expected that my first trip to the place would get anywhere near matching the fantasy. As me and Vic travelled through the night on a Home James coach, we'd never been so fired up. Before leaving the house an ITV panel of 'experts' had concluded that it would be Newcastle's day, because our defence would be incapable of living with Malcolm Macdonald.

A few years later it made me realize why Bob Paisley used to relish his side's chances being damned so publicly. How, whenever a chancer spouted off in the papers about what they were going to do to Liverpool he'd cut out the article and pin it to the dressing-room wall. If the players felt half as wound up as me and Vic felt after listening to the ITV panel, vengeance was assured. As it transpired, a massacre ensued.

Neither of us slept on the journey south. Instead we actually talked to each other, about football, which was a tipping point in our relationship. The moment in time when Vic ceased to look at me as a weight around his shoulders and accepted me as an equal. He was twenty by then.

He'd gone to Warwick University at first, hated it, and left by Christmas. He was now at Leeds and hating that too, and was about to be given the boot once his lecturers got their hands on his first-year test papers. His distance from home brought me respect. He was rarely at Anfield, whereas I was there every game. He was watching from afar, whereas I was at the heart of it all.

Suddenly he was asking my opinion on players and tactics and team selection. Me, the irrelevant gobshite, who nine years earlier (at our first ever FA Cup tie) he'd wanted to stab in each eye and leave dying on the Bolton terrace as punishment for the embarrassment I'd caused him.

Not that I was any less of an embarrassment on the Newcastle trip. The red, full-length maxicoat, complete with lady's belt that I'd pinched from my mum's wardrobe, saw to that. He threw the wobbler to beat all wobblers when I pulled it out of a bag after Reg had dropped us off at Picton Clock.

'What are you doing with that?' he asked as I put it on over my denim jacket in the queue for the coach.

'Wearing my colours,' I replied.

'No you're not, you're wearing a middle-aged woman's coat. You look like a fuckin' trannie.'

He walked off muttering about not sitting next to me and how my mum was going to kill me. But when he realized half the bus was dressed in an equally ludicrous over-the-top way – think badge-encrusted boiler suits and top hat and tails – and thus he had a fifty-fifty chance of sitting next to a member of Billy Smart's Circus, he relented.

Vic was right about Sheila killing me when I got home though. And it wasn't the first time she'd gone ballistic over that Cup final. Take the ticket she got me. Well, the ticket Bill Shankly thought she'd got me. I still wince when I think about it.

I didn't have the correct number on the end of my ticket stub to qualify for a place at Wembley, and I didn't know anyone powerful enough to have spare tickets lining the inside of his suit, so what was I to do? I decided to be extremely liberal with the word 'know'. I convinced myself that technically I did know somebody in high places. In fact in the highest of places. Well, we'd exchanged fond letters a few months earlier, and we were so chummy I'd written to the now Prime Minister on his behalf.

Oh yes. Without an ounce of shame I wrote a begging letter to Bill Shankly's home, reminding him who I was, and asking for a ticket. Days later a standard reply from club secretary Peter Robinson thudded on to the doormat explaining that wasn't how life worked.

I was in a state of mild shock as I struggled to explain the snub. I'd convinced myself I'd be the only fan writing to his house, that he would read my emotional plea and answer my prayer as soon as he reached the office. I decided to kid myself again that hundreds of fans had done the same and he'd just handed them over to his secretary in a bin-bag, without opening them, and got on with his job.

I had to be cleverer, so I tried a different tack. I don't know where the idea came from but all I know is I was desperate to the point of despicable. At sixteen I was a decent forger who had escaped many a school lesson through impersonating my mum's rather basic handwriting. If suspicious adults who knew me fell for it, then why not an unsuspecting one who doesn't?

I can't remember every maudlin arrow I fired at Shankly's heartstrings, but it ran along the following lines:

Dear Mr Shankly,
    I am Brian Reade's mother. The boy who wrote to Harold Wilson on your behalf, and who last week asked if you had any spare tickets for the FA Cup final. I fully understand that you are unable to help out everyone who asks. But I just had to write to let you know that he is so devastated he is walking around the house in mourning. Not

because you let him down, but because he won't be able to take his place at Wembley and see you, the man he looks up to more than any other, deliver his promise made outside St George's Hall three years ago, and send out a team to bring the Cup back to Liverpool. As I said, I just thought I'd let you know. And if you can do anything for him, I've enclosed a stamped addressed envelope.

    Yours sincerely,

    Sheila Reade

I know you're wincing reading that. So imagine how I feel, the fraud who wrote it. What a phoney.

Anyway, for the next three days I was up at seven to intercept any letters addressed to Sheila Reade, written in my scrawl. On the fourth day, having convinced myself Shankly had seen through the wheeze (or had other things to occupy his mind, like winning an FA Cup), I arrived home from school to find Sheila sitting on the couch, wafting an envelope under her chin.

Coolly, she pulled out an FA Cup final ticket, with a slip saying 'Regards, Bill Shankly', and threw it on the coffee table. She tried to question me, but she wasn't getting anywhere. Delirious tremors had set in.

She wanted answers, saying that as the ticket was addressed to her, she would be waltzing down to Wembley with it, unless I coughed as to what was going on. But I just stared at it, remembering the last time a Cup final ticket had ended up in my possession. The night they won the Cup in 1965 and Billy Jones had pulled the sacred relic out of his mac and told me to cherish it for life.

I palmed her off with some lie about the club only giving out tickets to over-eighteens, so I had to pretend she was asking on my behalf, which she eventually fell for. What she couldn't understand was the long, morbid face that was tripping me.

How could I explain that I was overcome with the magnitude not just of Shankly's generosity but of my deceit? I was going to an FA Cup final under false pretences. I'd conned Shankly, lied to him for personal gain. Instead of being overjoyed at the prospect of going to Wembley for the first time, I was filled with a sense of foreboding.

My guilt-obsessed Catholic head was convinced Fate would punish me for this heinous act. That the Cup final would be a disaster for Liverpool, and all because of my duplicity. That the bond of trust between Shankly and me had been broken irrevocably and things would never be the same again.

The weird feeling stayed there right up to kick-off. The belief that I was about to walk head-first into a disaster intensified the more smoothly the day progressed. I'd walked around London for the first time, strolled down Wembley Way dressed head-to-toe in red, the banter and the build-up had been more intoxicating than I'd ever imagined, and me and Vic had bonded like Bostik. Surely God was about to smack me in the face at any moment?

But when that third goal, Brazilian in its beauty, went in, and Liverpool's masterly slaughter of Newcastle was complete, I began to realize what a superstitious, God-fearing lightweight I'd been to believe Shankly would bring no more joy into my life.

Until one Friday afternoon, two months later, when a woolly mammoth fell from the sky and crushed me through the concrete. When I clambered out of the crater, I sprinted into a newspaper shop down the road from our school hoping to refute the rumours that were infesting every corner of the playground.

Via the *Echo's* front page, God caught me with a left jab, an upper-cut and a haymaker. Before landing the head, and swinging his boot as I hit the deck:

SOCCER BOMBSHELL – SHANKLY RETIRES

7

EVERY SINGLE BRICK

It was one of those blistering summer mornings when you can fry an egg on a well-polished shoe, but that wasn't the reason my sweat pump had jammed on maximum. As I sat on the wooden steps outside Melwood's changing rooms, it could have been colder than an Eskimo's nuts, and my shirt would still have been glued to my body. I was nervous.

This was the moment. Any second now a car would pull up, the driver would climb out, bark at me for wasting his time, and warn that my questions had better be good.

Chris Hill, a classmate and fellow Kopite, had badgered me into letting him come along. So I said he could be my photographer. Oh, the power. This six-foot rake with a Led Zeppelin haircut had a rebellious sense of humour, and his nihilistic tendencies were surfacing: 'Photographers don't wear school friggin' ties. They're artists,' he said.

'Yeah, but it's a sign of respect, isn't it? Shows we're serious, like,' I replied.

'No, it doesn't. It makes us look like we're third-years doing some poxy Duke of Edinburgh medal,' said Chris, whipping off the tie and sticking it in his blazer pocket.

He had a point, I thought, pulling mine off and letting the air get to the ocean of sweat that was lapping around my shoulders.

Shanks had to realize we were deadly serious sixth-formers. Me with my tape recorder and Chris with his camera. More than that we were Press, working for a school magazine with the highly unpretentious title of *Le Journal*. (That had been Bernie Horton's idea after our history teacher, John Phillips, said we needed a name that was different. Bernie had started picking up his big brother's Jean-Paul Sartre books and the rest of us couldn't be arsed thinking of another title. So *Le Journal* it was. Tragically.)

Obviously I didn't tell Shankly the name when I wrote once again to his home, telling him I was the sports editor (a lie) who wanted a chat about his views on football (another lie). All I wanted to know was why he'd done it. To hear it from his mouth as I looked so deep into his eyes I reached his soul. I wanted the truth. After all, good, decent men don't just walk out on people without a credible explanation. And while Shankly's claim to decency was beyond dispute, his explanation was anything but.

Even the letter he wrote back to me showed the psychological mayhem he was going through.

> Dear Brian,
> Received your letter re: having a chat regarding your newspaper at De La Salle, thanks very much for same.
> I am at Melwood most mornings between 10 a.m. and 12 noon. If you can come down we can have a chat.
> Yours sincerely
> W. Shankly

Virtually a year after he'd walked into the Anfield boardroom to announce his retirement, feeling (as he put it) like he was walking to the electric chair, he still saw Liverpool's training ground as his office. He still made it down here most mornings to pick up his life. To cut away from the irrelevance of outside influences, and concentrate on the only thing that had ever mattered to him. Being close to footballs, football pitches and football people.

But on the loose phrase 'most mornings' hung a heavy sadness and a tragic reality. It wasn't most mornings, it was any morning when the first-team players were absent. And this being pre-season, when only the groundsmen and the odd apprentice were in, Shankly had the keys to his old empire. An empire that was deserted.

Although he'd retired the previous July, he'd carried on turning up, changed into kit, strolled out to the Melwood fields and readied himself to suck in the odour of footballing men at work. He couldn't see anything wrong with that. After all, hadn't he laid every blade of this ground? Hadn't he nurtured every sinew of every player? What harm was he doing, now the reins had been passed on to his loyal deputy Bob Paisley, by keeping himself mentally and physically active at the spot he loved better than any other on earth?

The club saw it differently. Halfway through the season, chairman John Smith was forced into doing what a few months earlier would have led to his mansion gates being stormed and his head carried away on a stick. He barred Shankly from Melwood. He politely told him to stop turning up every morning on the grounds that Bob Paisley was finding it hard enough trying to step into his shoes, without having him around young men who, throughout their Anfield careers, had called one of them 'Boss' and the other 'Bob'.

There was a growing perception that Paisley was too soft, lacking the nous, guts and charisma required to be a great leader like Shankly. Had Liverpool made a poor decision and the exciting young side of the early seventies been entrusted to the wrong hands?

Things weren't going too well on the pitch. A bright start to the 1974–75 season turned into a disastrous November, with no wins in the League and exits from the European Cup Winners' Cup and League Cup. Reasons were sought and Shankly's enduring presence was one of them.

It may have seemed harsh, and with every passing year it seemed harsher, that Liverpool should be the stake that pierced Shankly's heart. But what choice did they have? Wasn't it Shankly's own core belief that Liverpool FC existed purely to keep the fans happy, and anything which threatened that state of bliss should be eliminated? Didn't his presence threaten it? Wasn't the mere sight of an icon who had held each and every player under his spell, undermining Paisley? How could the modest, unassuming Geordie, who for fifteen years had ploughed away tirelessly as a loyal lieutenant, begin to imprint his own style and authority on impressionable young men with Shankly looking over his shoulder?

We're talking about a personality and a charisma of unprecedented size in football history. How do you accommodate that? Look what had happened at Manchester United when Matt Busby 'moved upstairs'. His successors in the dug-out felt stifled by the living reminder in the directors' box of great days now passed. And with all respect to Busby (he was a decent wing-half for Liverpool in the 1930s), when it came to sheer weight of presence, he was no Shankly.

'Who's car is this d'ya reckon?' said Chris as a Ford Capri sat at the training ground entrance, its driver lost in conversation with the gateman.

I knew, but couldn't find the dexterity of tongue to reply. He pulled up in front of us, leapt out, and as we jumped to attention a canny grin cackled across his face.

'You'll be the reporter, then?'

'Erm, yeah, Mr Shankly. And erm, this is my photographer.'

'They've given you a photographer too? Jesus you're almost at the top already. Come inside.'

He bounced up the steps and led us into the glorified hut as though he were a monarch throwing open his palace.

'Sit down in here, boys,' he said as we entered the changing room where every god I had ever worshipped had sat. I felt the ghostly forms of St John and Evans, and the living, pulsating presence of Hughes and Keegan. Shankly could see how awe had descended on me and Chris and he was pleased.

'Magnificent, isn't it?' he purred with pride, picking up shirt and shorts from a big wicker hamper. 'This is where we prepare for greatness.'

And with that he hung up his windcheater jacket, took off his three-button casual shirt and slacks, went for the underpants, and asked us to remind him what school we were from, before making that cup of tea.

He started talking. About breathtaking triumphs and heart-busting players. It was like having your own Audience With God. Best night at Anfield? Inter Milan in '64, when we 'tore the best side in Europe apart, only to go over there and be robbed by a travesty of justice'.

Best player? Of all time? Tom Finney by a mile. Best player he'd had? Out poured the love and admiration for Kevin Keegan, Emlyn Hughes and Peter Thompson – 'the most talented winger of his generation who could dribble past an entire team, then do it again just for the hell of it. And often did.'

Ray Clemence, he reckoned was the finest British keeper of all time: 'If I'd signed him ten years earlier I'd never have lost a game throughout the 1960s.' He'd had many, many great players, he said, randomly name-checking Tommy Smith, Ronnie Yeats and Steve Heighway, but if he were pushed to name one who stood out above them all it would be Gerry Byrne.

'The best professional of the lot. Hard and skilful every game, but above all honest,' he said. 'And that is the greatest quality of all.'

I listened open-jawed, nodding in agreement, laughing when his eyes gave you the cue to do so. Listening back to the tape I can hear myself trying to butt in with observations but I'm patted away contemptuously by this rasping Scottish voice.

Even funnier, I can hear the one, solitary intervention from Chris Hill. Apropos of nothing, it just comes out, in a deep gruff blurt:

'What d'ya think of Toshack?'

There is a silence as Shankly remembers another presence in the room, gauges Chris and says: 'Aye, good player Toshack. Very tall. Like you.' Chris blushes at the blessing from on high. It was what he'd wanted to hear. As did all of our mates back at De La

Salle when Chris's stunning contribution to the interview was endlessly replayed.

Seeing as we'd moved into check-out-your-hero mode, I threw my hand in: 'What about Ian St John?' There was a brief laugh, as Shankly carefully chose his words.

'St John? My first great buy. Him and Ronnie Yeats started it all. Clever, canny, bags of skill, made things happen. Liked a scrap too. Jesus did he like a scrap. I sometimes wanted to tie his fists behind his back. Great player though. Gave you everything on the pitch. Mind you, a lazy bugger at training. He hated it. Always trying to pull one on us. But what a player.'

There was a distant look in his eye as he dredged up the memories. Was he thinking about The Saint's goal that won the Cup in '65 or was he thinking about their acrimonious break-up that should never have happened? Was it pride or regret, fulfilment or unfulfilment lacing his words?

The spark in his eyes had dulled. An air of sadness hung over him as he surveyed the changing room. It had been his home for years, where his sons still lived. But he inhabited this house no more. Now he was a weekend dad, who'd seen his kids taken away, and despite his love for them being as strong as ever, he was denied all but the most fleeting of contact.

'You see Melwood,' he said when I asked him what the club was like when he arrived in 1959. 'It was a wasteland. I built it with these hands. Every blade of grass. Every single brick.'

It was as though he were talking about a love he had rashly abandoned. As though he'd jilted a woman for all the right reasons, then realized when she'd left that it was the irreplaceable passion of his life and he would never have her back. His soulmate gone for ever.

I could tell he was beating himself up, searching for something to fill the great void in his existence, and failing woefully. He had no other interests. The two daughters he felt he had let down by devoting his life to football had grown up. He hated holidays and golf, didn't have the patience for books, cinema or theatre and all he'd watch on the TV, apart from the occasional old film, was football. He couldn't even get bladdered to blot out the sadness because he didn't drink. Football was his drug. And he had sentenced himself to a life of cold turkey.

Eventually I summoned up the bottle to ask him why he'd done it. I hoped for the answer he'd given no one, but got the one he'd given everyone.

'I felt the time was right. We'd won the League, the UEFA Cup and then the FA Cup, so I knew I'd given Liverpool a second great team that could reach the heights again. It felt time to go.'

'So why didn't you reach the heights with them?'

'I felt tired. It comes to us all. I wasn't getting any younger and the break had to come at some time. I couldn't go on for ever. And I felt I owed it to my family, after forty years in the game, to step back.'

'You could have handled it,' I said, expecting him to laugh at my audacity, ruffle my hair and call me a cheeky scamp. But his craggy features only became more intense, as though this was the fear and regret that kept him awake every night.

'Maybe I could, son. Maybe I could. But you have to understand what this job is like. My work followed me everywhere. At every moment. You never have a spare second to think of anything outside it. It grinds you down. I needed a break.'

'So why didn't you take one and come back?'

'Oh no,' he laughs unconvincingly. 'That's not the right thing to do. Unfair. The right decision for me and the club was to make a clean break. To give someone else a chance. And Bobby Paisley is doing a fine job.'

'Do you regret it?'

Another laugh. Forced I'm sure.

'No, son. You can't afford to have regrets in life. It gets you nowhere.'

'Would you ever come out of retirement to manage Liverpool again?'

An even bigger laugh. This time not so forced. 'No, no. As I say Bob's doing a fine job. Why would they want me back? Besides I'm having a great time. Never felt better. I've plenty to keep me happy with my family. And the phone never stops ringing with people asking me for advice, offering me jobs. I give the advice but I won't take the jobs. I'm enjoying retirement too much.' Sure, I thought. That's why you're down here every day, getting changed into your old kit, aching to have your men back under your command, priming them for immortality. Or even Stoke away.

The blatant emptiness, and the act he was putting on to disguise it, was tragic to behold.

On that hot summer day in 1975, like virtually everyone outside of his family, I didn't know the inner turmoil Shankly was going through. How the knowledge he had gone too soon, plus the cold shoulder he was being shown by the club, was eating away at him. How a belief that the Liverpool hierarchy was deliberately ostracizing him would eventually kill him.

Critics say Liverpool should have done better by Shankly and maybe they should. But look at the shameless way Bobby Moore was neglected when he retired from football and you'll realize it was a completely different game back then.

The men at the top don't treat loyal servants better today because they want to, but because they have to due to the high-profile industry it has become. Put simply, they can't get away so easily with treating their employees like old carthorses. An intense media spotlight, watertight contracts, agents and heightened fan power has seen to that. Back then, none of that existed.

I didn't find out why Shankly walked away, but then neither did many better men than me. The reason being, I don't think Shankly knew. I guess it was a combination of things – he was feeling tired and old and needed a break from the pressure.

Maybe after that classic demolition of Newcastle, and the plaudits that followed, the student of boxing thought back to the greats who had punched on for too long and persuaded himself that the only way to go was at the top.

The seven years Liverpool had spent in the wilderness and the breaking up of that first great side had left mental scars. Maybe he decided he couldn't risk facing that painful wilderness again. But I think it had more to do with the principle Shankly held closest to his heart. Loyalty.

When he joined Liverpool in 1959, the backroom staff of Paisley, Joe Fagan and Reuben Bennett expected to be shown the door. But Shankly believed in giving men a chance. He told them their jobs would be safe so long as they stayed loyal and worked 100 per cent for him.

Shankly had demanded and received loyalty throughout his life. Possibly he thought it was time to pay back some of the same to his long-suffering wife Nessie. That by letting her have some of the hours in days which had all been given to football, he was doing the right thing. I'd love to think he was sharing himself around and staying true to his unflinching belief in socialism.

'If I became a bin-man tomorrow,' he said to me when I asked him about his politics, 'I'd be the greatest bin-man who ever lived. I'd have Liverpool the cleanest city on earth. I'd take over the whole cleaning operation and make it work. I'd have everyone working with me, succeeding and sharing out the success. I'd make sure they were paid a decent wage with the best bonuses, and that we all worked hard to achieve our goals. Some people might say, ah but they're only bin-men, why do we need to reward them so well for a job anyone can do, but I'd ask them why they believe they are more important than a bin-man. I'd ask them how proud they'd feel if this dirty city became the cleanest in the world? And who would have made them proud? The bin-men.'

I've been a socialist all my life. My Irish nana was a Dublin Republican who told tales (many fanciful) of the 1916 Easter Rising, how the martyrs were shot and how the Black and Tans raped her land. She passed on her loathing of monarchy, empire, Conservatism and injustice to my mum, and down it came to me.

It wasn't hard. My dad, despite being the son of a docker and a cleaner had passed the 11-plus, gone to grammar school and gained nine O-levels. He was a talented artist and wanted to be an architect, but had to leave school and work as an apprentice warehouseman to bring in a wage that would help feed three younger brothers.

I'd seen my mum's dad forced to walk to the docks to stand in pens and hope to be picked out for a day's labour, only to be sent down the road because he was a Catholic whose religion wasn't shared by the ruling Masonic mafia. Being RC in Liverpool during the 1940s, '50s and '60s necessitated voting Labour, because the Conservative and Unionist party who ran local government, docks and industry were there to reward their Protestant supporters.

Oh, what joy it was in the sixties and seventies when our very own Harold Wilson won four victories that took Labour into power. Wavertree Labour Club on election night was like standing on the Kop. A hysterical camaraderie filled the air, and us kids were afforded a glimpse of it by sneaking in through the doors and watching from under tables.

Shankly's philosophy struck a raw chord with myself and many other Liverpudlians. His socialism was not built around petty party politicking. It came from inside. It was of his essence. With Shankly it defined how he treated other people, as his equal and with respect. How he built his football teams as communal forces by drawing the fans into his vision.

No other football manager at that time had dared to talk about politics, least of all bang the drum about socialism. Probably because they feared being kicked on to the dole by the fine, upstanding Tory businessmen in the boardroom, who kept their grounds like abbatoirs, their players like slaves, and themselves in the lap of luxury.

God, I loved him for that. I loved the way he seemed to encapsulate everything I held close to my heart and aspired to be. A Liverpudlian, a football man and a socialist. And captured it with such wit and fire.

Unless you accept the flaws in your hero, they are no hero at all, but simply a myth. I never want what Shankly was, what he gave, to be discarded as mere sentimental guff. A cliché about football being more important than dying.

So let's list the faults that made him human. He was a vain man, evidenced by what looked suspiciously like a lousy syrup sitting on his scalp during his last TV interview. He could be cold and dictatorial. The stuff about him treating injured players like lepers is true. He cut them out of his life until they were of use to him again. During Ian St John's final days at Anfield, when he was frozen out of first-team plans, he referred to Shankly as 'that bastard'.

Conversely he made mistakes due to being too soft on players who had served him well in the mid-sixties. That side should have been broken up much earlier, but Shankly refused to discard men he'd begun to regard as sons, and Liverpool suffered as a consequence. He was an attention-seeker who would threaten to resign virtually every summer, and more than once meant it. He was a natural comedian, but he was a shameless plagiarist, stealing lines from quieter souls and passing them off as his own. He distrusted most things foreign, refusing to adjust his watch to local time when he travelled abroad, because he saw it all as a conspiracy against the British. He had an overpowering belief that his way was the only way. He was pig-headed, he was so driven by his ambition he neglected his family dreadfully. He expected journalists who worked on his patch to be as blind as the fans, and he would savage them if they were critical of his work. He could be a bully towards young players, keeping them in line with a cruel tongue and an aggressive manner.

But for all of that, Shankly was special, unique and inspirational. Miner-turned-MP Dennis Skinner, veteran trade union leader and Spanish Civil War fighter Jack Jones, D-Day veterans, the sacked Liverpool dockers, Barbara Castle and Muhammad Ali are a few who have moved me almost beyond words. But none can touch the effect Shankly had. No one's philosophy and selflessness has stayed with me through life more than his.

I can still see him, as Chris Hill took a photograph of us, standing there with ramrod back, flat stomach, teeth and skin glinting in the sun, a cross between Kirk Douglas and Jimmy Cagney.

I can hear him say, 'Right boys, I've work to do,' then offering his iron grip, thanking us for our interest and asking if I'd send him a copy of my piece, which I never did through embarrassment.

I can see him turn, walk on to the grass, and break into a jog, floating off into the distance, past those famous sweat-boards he introduced to improve the players' touch and control, across the pitches he helped re-lay when he arrived at a training ground so dilapidated there was no running water. Pitches that laid the foundations for the most successful club in the history of British football.

I watch him disappearing, getting smaller and smaller, in this deserted training ground, wondering what's going through his head. Is he reliving past glories, enjoying having the run of his old kingdom, or lamenting his disastrous decision to abdicate?

We watched in silence that long-gone summer's day as his shadow grew smaller and smaller, until it was just a dot in the green distance. Then, as now, I see him show us his old, lined hands, and hear his voice, rasping with pride and love (but laced with a deep sadness) saying, 'I laid every single blade, every single brick.'

Every single blade. Every single brick.

And I know as sure as day turns to night that I'll never meet a finer human being than him as long as I have breath in my body.

8

THE FALL OF ROME

25 MAY 1977 – PUTNEY HILL

It wasn't exactly a Who Can Piss the Highest competition, more a Who Can Piss the Most. Into the potted plants outside George Best's flat. Before his door opened.

A painful afternoon had passed, with much sorrow inflicted, and much beer drunk in an attempt to drown it. A nightmare had unfolded at Wembley. No other word would suffice. It is bad enough losing an FA Cup final, especially when it's by a spawny goal. It's even worse if that spawny goal stops your team doing its first-ever League and Cup Double.

But to be deprived of the Double by a spawny Man United goal which had been deflected off a mishit shot from Lou Macari who, when he moved from Celtic, knocked us back in favour of Old Trafford. That is surely a level of torture not even the holder of the Most Evil Japanese Prisoner of War Camp Commandant 1943–45 title could conjure up.

This time I didn't have a ticket, but I had refrained from sending a begging letter to Bob Paisley. I was a big lad now. A student at Warwick University no less. That specific seat of learning was chosen not because of its emerging standing in academic circles nor because it had a tailor-made course for me. Our Vic had graced its student union for five minutes four years earlier. When I asked his opinion of it, he replied, 'Midlands shit-hole', and that hadn't swayed me either.

No. I chose Warwick because of its prospectus cover. While other places had shots of famous spires or august red-brick buildings, Warwick's carried a picture of its most famous graduate: Steve Heighway, Liver Bird on chest, in full balletic flow, skinning a full-back. No contest.

Proof that Heighway's portrait had distracted me from the crucial task of picking a three-year degree course which I had any chance of completing came on day one. The sight of English lecturers handing out reading lists longer than any novel I'd read, and high-minded students (i.e. pretentious pricks) discussing the pros and cons of Goethe and Chekhov, paralysed me with fear.

How many months, make that hours, would it take them all to realize the only literature I kept in my bedroom were Charles Buchan annuals and 1,200 football programmes. (One for each of the ninety-two clubs, by the way. A feat I'd accomplished as a sixteen-year-old in one historic week, when Plymouth, Bournemouth, Torquay and Hartlepool all responded positively to the heart-rending letter from this 'fan in exile'. How noble of them to do their bit for this life-long supporter who, after a tragic accident, was now a paraplegic being looked after by relatives in Liverpool, and anything they could send, such as a recent programme, would cheer him up and aid recovery. Thanks chaps.)

The economics department accepted me on day two, but it soon became clear my non-acquaintance with numbers made me even more afraid of failure than my non-acquaintance with literature. The course required students to be up to A-level maths by the end of the year, as well as keeping up to scratch on neo-endogenous growth theory. Our divorce was inevitable.

As Easter came into sight, with fractionally more than nil lectures and seminars attended, it was clear I was about to get the boot. So I lied to the English department that my parents had forced me to do economics against my will, even though my heart lay with literature, and the corduroy-clad mugs mopped my furrowed brow, offered Kleenex for my fake tears and told me to pick up my plume again in October.

I didn't even lose my grant. So a state-sponsored six months of wine, women and song had ensued, leaving me free to take advantage of Coventry's greatest natural asset, namely the ease with which you could leave the place and reach more interesting cities. Its position bang in the centre of England meant virtually every Liverpool away game outside of the North-East was accessible, especially in the Midlands which then boasted seven First Division clubs.

It's quite possible this fact had dawned on scores of football-loving Scousers, because Warwick was flooded with us. Within a week we'd put together a team, imaginatively called The Scousers, decked out in Liverpool's all-red home kit, which walked the university's Sunday League tournament for the next four years.

It may be hard to accept today, when the Merseyside derby is a hate-filled war game, but back in the seventies Blues and Reds could co-exist in spiteless harmony. It may have been down to a mutual respect, a self-preservational bonding, or the fact that many families were genuinely split down the middle. Most likely it was that Liverpool had yet to leave Everton behind.

A form of equality still existed and Blue Noses weren't bitterly resentful of a Liverpool whose dominance at home and abroad had made Everton, in the eyes of the wider world, the city's poor relations.

The nasty edge between the two sets of fans just wasn't there in the mid-seventies. It meant that when Liverpudlians were in the majority in the Warwick Scousers, and John Kempster managed to get hold of an entire set of Liverpool home kits, Evertonians donned the colour of their foes from across Stanley Park. The absence of hatred also meant we occasionally went to their away game in the Midlands and they came to ours.

There was something liberating, almost intoxicating about away games back then, in so far as you never knew what to expect, or who to expect it from. Like the Arndale Centres and the concrete subways you were chased through minutes after stepping off the train, it was ugly, but it possessed a certain anarchic charm. A bit like *Tiswas*.

Wolves always guaranteed an underground tear-up, the added

thrill being that, because there were so many entrances to the miles of subway, you were running blind, never knowing what lay in front or to the sides. Keeping one step ahead of the roars and the boots didn't half build up a thirst for that first pint though.

I'd gone down to Wolves as a schoolkid on the final game of the 1975–76 season hoping to see Bob Paisley pick up his first League title. Me, Mike Sinnott and Terry Pettitt bunked out of De La Salle for the afternoon and got a lift down from Mike's uncle. So it seemed had 30,000 others. Meaning that when we arrived at Molyneux the ground had been shut for an hour. A gate had been flattened allowing thousands more in – you see them all in mad flares, high-heeled boots and perms leaping up from their makeshift seats on the grass in front of the advertising hoardings, invading the pitch after every Liverpool goal – but the police regained control.

Like a displaced tribe the red hordes marched to the top of a nearby hill which afforded a view of roughly one-third of the Molyneux pitch, and there they camped. (They'd clearly all been to Goodison and didn't mind putting up with that scale of obstructed view.)

By the time we arrived you couldn't even pitch up at the base of the hill, so we drove to a pub and pulled out a transistor radio in time to hear Steve Kindon put Wolves one up. If it remained that way Wolves would stay in the First Division and the mighty QPR (yes QPR) would be champions.

With 15 minutes to go it was still 1–0, and West Midlands and West London prepared to orgy. Then Keegan, Toshack and Ray Kennedy did their stuff and normal service was resumed. It was our turn to party, although a half-empty Wolverhampton old man's alehouse with a collection of faces that would have struggled to make it as extras in the *Star Wars* bar on grounds of being too ugly, wasn't the place.

So we headed back to Liverpool and The She nightclub where the regulars were slightly more attractive. OK, a few were. Slightly.

A couple more lagers and the surge of optimism induced by winning the title injected me with such confidence I plucked up the courage to ask an older woman for a dance. She asked if I'd been working. I told her I'd sagged school and gone down to Wolves to see Liverpool. She started to walk away. I shouted after her, 'But we won the League,' and she turned around and gave me a 'wanker' sign. I think that meant, 'How sad would I be to waste my time with a pissed-up, spotty schoolboy when there's real men around who'll take me for a chicken chow mein in Wong's followed by a lift home and a grope in his Capri.'

Like I gave one. I've never expected, or even wanted, women to be interested in football, but when something happens which is bringing unbounded joy into my soul, I at least expect the pretence of empathy. Every woman I've ever been out with, or married, has seen that. None have been true football fans (if they were their passion for the game undoubtedly waned during our relationship) but they all realized that when a victory made me deliriously happy, it was something to be tolerated, even indulged. Mainly because they knew the flip-side. The darkness that sets in and the antisocial thoughts a hurtful defeat can inspire. Which brings us back to George Best's flat.

Our Vic was married now, working as deputy editor of the comic *Whizzer And Chips*, and living in a London flat with his wife Chris. Sheila and Reg had moved to London too, after Reg's job went the way of many others in Liverpool during the seventies. With little else on offer, he took on running the parts side of a small export firm in Brixton. They were living with my two sisters in a flat in Putney, the venue where me, Terry Pettitt and Mike Sinnott were forced to watch the FA Cup final after Vic's promise of four tickets being sent down from his Scottish father-in-law turned out to be a joke.

Mike and Terry had been my two best mates at De La Salle, would each eventually put in abysmal best man performances at my two weddings, and stay drinking partners for life, despite their Anfield attendance records plummeting close to zero.

Terry is a razor-sharp nark from the Dingle, whose fighting skills have saved my gobshite mouth from taking dozens of hidings these past forty years. Back in the mid-seventies, due to his dark colouring, flowing black locks, slim build, bushy moustache and silky footballing skills, he was known around Liverpool as Ruben Ayala, the Argentinian striker. Sadly during the eighties, all of those attributes disappeared apart from the colouring and the moustache, and his nickname changed to Poirot. Mike, from Norris Green, is built like a whippet, has the dress sense of a Texan, and a habit, whenever he's taken a drink, of turning into a cross between Frank Sinatra and Sammy Davis Jnr, and tap-dancing up the nearest staircase singing 'I've Got You Under My Skin'. Badly.

So there we were, me, Vic, Terry and Mike, tanked up after hours spent in a boozer lamenting the fact we didn't have a ticket, then worked up after watching Lou Macari's mishit shot deflect off Jimmy Greenhoff for the spawny winner. What happened when we left the flat to drown our sorrows was thus inevitable.

Vic had pointed out, as we walked past it before the game, that George Best lived in the block of flats around the corner, so why not pay him a visit and see what he made of the result? See if he admitted how jammy his old side had been and if he fancied coming out for a pint.

Going up in the lift, we started to ask each other what we'd do if he answered the door. Go easy on him if he's OK, seemed to be the general consensus. But he wasn't in and consequently we weren't easy on him, as his plant pots testified. Brimming as they now were with gallons of recycled lager. Well, he'd been asking for it, hadn't he?

Twenty years later I struck up a working relationship with Best, to the extent that I had the honour of taking him on an all-day bender, in the name of research, to test the effects of alco-pops. During the session he mentioned his Putney flat which brought back the memory of that drunken Saturday and almost gave me an internal convulsion. For the hell of it, I asked if it ever got vandalized by people who knew he was living there. 'Not that I can remember,' was his puzzled reply before adding, 'Why?'

I couldn't resist. 'Oh, a couple of lads I knew reckoned they went up to give you a knock once and when you weren't in they pissed all over the plants.'

He just shrugged and said, 'I wouldn't know if anyone had pissed in them because they were carrying enough of my own piss most nights as I struggled to get my key in the door.'

Best was tremendous company. A shy, intelligent man with a natural defence mechanism honed from years of being shafted by back-slappers, that made him wary of strangers. But once he realized you weren't after a piece of him or trying to garner some shagging story to brag about, he opened up and told some great tales. That said, he wasn't one to be crossed, as I discovered when we fell out spectacularly over a piece I wrote, in July 2000, after he had almost died of alcoholism.

Best's doctors had told him his liver was in such a bad state that one more drink could kill him, but that hadn't stopped his wife Alex knocking it back in front of him. So I had a good rant about her in my *Daily Mirror* column, and this was his reply:

Dear Mr Reade,

I was just settling down to a nice meal last evening with my wife on our fifth wedding anniversary. But something was niggling me.

When I realised what it was I suggested to Alex that I call you to ensure it was okay for her to have a drink when I was getting stuck into my lobster. Unable to obtain your phone number I carried on regardless and managed to get through the meal without slumping my head into my spotted dick.

I did attempt to persuade the four gentlemen dining at the next table if they would refrain from drinking whilst I was eating. They told me to 'fuck off', which I thought was fair comment.

Undeterred, the following day I paid a visit to my local supermarket to persuade them not to sell booze from the shelf when I was shopping. I don't hold out much hope of a favourable reply.

If that fails I aim to contact all TV companies and ask them to
cancel all ads selling booze during my viewing hours.

I have been pushed into this drastic action after reading your
award-winning article. Alex and I were deeply moved by your
obvious concern. Thank you.

Yours sincerely,

George Best.

P.S. I also noticed your use of the word 'dipso' in regard to myself.
I checked the dictionary (that's the one with some words with more
than two syllables) but I failed to find the word. I also couldn't find
the word 'cunt'. I suppose that pretty much evens us out.

George Best. A true genius in every respect. If only we'd signed
him. How he'd have loved playing in the team that swept towards
our first European Cup. How, more than once, the Kop would
have given him a bone in his kecks the way he said crowds could
on the big European nights.

None more so than 16 March 1977, the second leg of the
European Cup quarter-final against St Etienne. The rawest, most
emotional night since Inter Milan in '64, and the most glorious
one Anfield would experience until Chelsea in 2005. Ten of us
hired a minivan, dragged along an 88-pint barrel of lager we'd
nicked from the yard behind the Athletic Union bar in the middle
of the night, and headed up from Coventry.

The M6 was chocker with Citroens and Peugeots, green flags
streaming from the windows, packed with Gitanes smokers (some
wearing berets, honest) singing 'Allez les verts', whenever they
noticed the red scarves on the van that had pulled up alongside
them.

You couldn't get near the ground an hour and a half before
kick-off. Which is why we all leapt out of the van in Walton Breck
Road leaving Migsy the driver (a Blue Nose, so that was acceptable) to find a parking space, and made it into the Kop minutes
before the gates closed.

I'd never known it so full or so loud. I'd never heard such a buzz of expectation or sense of destiny. We knew we were up against it. We'd seen it in the first leg over in France when we were lucky to escape with only a 1–0 defeat. And we'd seen St Etienne narrowly beaten by Bayern Munich up at Hampden in last year's European Cup final.

They were a quick, dangerous attacking side who could cut you to pieces on the break. Were they to do that only once, we'd need to score three. Against a side who were yet to concede a goal in that year's competition. Two minutes in, with the Frenchmen crapping themselves amid the noise (as Chelsea's would be twenty-eight years later) Heighway played a short corner to Keegan at the Annie Road End and he overhit a cross looking for Toshack's head. The goalie flapped, and in it went. A fluke, but it was one-all and we relaxed in anticipation of a pleasant rout. Which never came. Shortly after half-time Bathenay beat the offside trap, sprinted on to a long ball and sent it dipping over Clemence from 25 yards. It was a dagger to the heart. But the Kop upped its game and with half-an-hour to go, Paisley did the same by ordering the players to cut out the neat passing and go for the jugular.

Callaghan put a cross in, Toshack flicked it on, and Ray Kennedy ghosted in from deep and sliced a low shot past the keeper. Then, with 15 minutes to go, and the French swaying on the ropes, the gods decided to sprinkle some legend-dust on us. Toshack was replaced by David Fairclough, the red-haired Scouser with the uncanny habit of scoring whenever he was unleashed from the bench. Six minutes before the end Kennedy chipped a peach down the left which caught the French off-balance. And Fairclough pounced on it. Instinctively the Kop sensed something was on. Twenty-six thousand mouths gave one of those involuntary gasps that are so intense the air shakes. Hadn't we seen Davey do this time and time again, against Leeds, against Everton, in that very same position from the half-way line? Pick the ball up slowly, cagily, then wind up those spindly legs for a run which seemed erratic, but was full of purpose. Davey knew what he had to do, and how he was going to do it.

He waltzed round one, two, then three green shirts, ice running through his veins despite the heat of the Anfield furnace. Curkovic, the keeper, advanced from his line and spread himself big, knowing that if his body got in the way St Etienne were in touching distance of victory. But before his right glove had reached the turf Fairclough had shot low and hard. It went under him and daisy-cut its way into the Kop net.

What happened next was the nearest I've seen or felt to pandemonium. All those thousands of Kopites were sucked towards the goal by a giant Hoover of emotion. Bodies clasped hard on other bodies, faces were twisted with delight. One journalist looking on from the comfort of the press box described the scene as a mass human trampoline. And that is how it felt. Fairclough's celebratory leap almost took him to the corner flag where he lay under a mountain of team-mates. On and off the pitch we just wanted to jump on each other, and keep jumping.

The French slumped to their knees. They were done for. Any heart and energy they had left was drained from them when the Kop went into an ear-bursting rendition of Our Hymn. We were in no doubt that we had just been a part of history. That a moment had happened before our eyes that would have immortality bestowed on it.

Afterwards nobody wanted to go home. We found the van, took it into town, hit a dingy, all-night drinking club at the back of Slater Street and tried to empty the stock, as Mike ran the length of the bar, screaching Sinatra. The French had found it too, and in between large brandies and renditions of 'Fly Me To The Moon' they agreed that, even though the game had broken their hearts, they'd felt privileged to have been there. They told us how special it felt reaching a European Cup final the year before, how they'd been desperate to be in another one and expunge the awful pain of that defeat. And they wished us well.

Especially if it were a German side we faced in Rome. And they don't get more German than Borussia Moenchengladbach.

It's the biggest regret in my life that I wasn't in Rome. Thirty years on I still run the reasons that stopped me going past myself, and they all sound utterly inadequate. Since 1965 my radar had been solid when it came to knowing the games that would turn out to be much more than a date on the fixture list. Games I had to be at. But to my shame I missed out on the glory that was Rome first time around.

I'd left Warwick before Easter and had been working by day in Reg's warehouse and at night behind the bar in The Nashville pub, where groups who were about to change the face of music were learning their trade. The Clash, The Jam, The Sex Pistols, Elvis Costello, Blondie, The Stranglers – they were all there, being watched by a handful of weirdos with pink hair and face-piercings whose idea of a good night was pogoing and yockering at the stage. Just how I thought the Boys Pen would be when I was perched on my stool in the Annie Road End.

I'd made my mind up that I'd work for four months solid, and travel around America for the summer. So I needed every penny I could get. In between grafting my balls off, California dreaming and The Clash, I took my mind off the ball. It would have been different if Our Vic, Mike or Terry had mentioned the possibilty of a Rome trip, but they were all in debt and miles from Liverpool with little hope of finding a ticket (Mike had gone to Warwick with me and was pretending to study history while Terry had gone to a college in Northampton where he was majoring in drunken sex).

It's still a disgraceful lapse in loyalty. A terrible error of judgement, which saw me consumed with self-loathing the second the BBC crossed to the Olympic Stadium on 25 May to show 30,000 Liverpudlians, each seemingly holding a red-and-white chequered flag, dominating the vista, emptying their lungs of song into the warm Roman night.

Me and Vic sat in the Bricklayers Arms in Putney, muttering

over and over, 'Why aren't we there?', vainly trying to pin the blame on each other. We were surrounded by the usual bunch you get watching a Liverpool game in a London pub. The Scouse expats still in their dust-stained building clobber, on the way to being legless; Cockney Reds always dressed in the latest, pristinely washed and ironed replica shirt; fans of London clubs and Man United who want to see us pummelled, and bored locals at the bar exaggerating yawns and asking for the jukebox to be put on.

There was a combination of anxiety and fear (especially after the FA Cup final defeat four days earlier), despair and self-loathing at being sat in a nondescript room with a shower of no-marks when I should have been in Rome. Terry McDermott's beautifully fashioned goal just before the half-hour saw the snakebites slide down our throats in rapid fashion.

By half-time we were rocking, pushing past the locals en route to the toilet with a swagger that said in three-quarters of an hour that big-eared beauty would be shining above our heads. Six minutes into the second half and we were hiding our faces behind beer mats. A Jimmy Case cock-up, a Simonsen equalizer, a spurt of pressure from the Germans and thoughts of last Saturday's cruelty flooded back.

The next 15 minutes are a blank. I went outside for air, came back in, threw another snakebite down with half an eye on the telly, then went back out again. The nerves were eating me up. I couldn't sit, watch or speak. I just needed to be at one with the moon, knowing the noise from the pub would keep me updated on the score. And then, as I picked up another pint, we won a corner.

As I saw Heighway shape to take it, I had one of those rare, instinctive experiences that happens to all fans. I knew they would score. I didn't know the who or the how, but I knew in the future I would see hundreds of replays of Heighway arching that back, looking up like a golfer about to hit a chip to the green, then delivering a perfect stroke.

Upon leaving his boot the TV pictures went into slow-motion. Tommy Smith came thundering into the box, rose, met it like a train, and nearly took the net off. That was it. That was the moment that tied together history, knotted a neat bow on top and handed it over.

How could we lose now? It was fated that one of Shankly's originals, who had first donned the all-red kit against Anderlecht, who'd thrown his arms around St John when he hit the third against Inter Milan, should be the man who killed off the Germans. It was also fated that the last act from the mighty Kevin Keegan, in his last game for us, should be a thrusting run into the heart of the Moenchengladbach defence which resulted in a penalty that put it all beyond doubt. I could make out Emlyn Hughes's grin splitting his face as he held the enormous trophy high, but the rest is a blur. Too much emotion, too many mixed feelings of pride and regret, at being on the outside when I should have been in the middle.

We left the pub and gusts of fresh air from the Thames cleared the head slightly and drew us towards the river where we sat on a bench, saying nothing, lost in our thoughts. It wasn't the Tiber or the Mersey but it would do. We began to talk about what it meant to be the champions of Europe. In fact, champions of the whole of Europe. We argued over whether this was the greatest night in the club's history, but there was no argument really, just me trying to play it down because of the unforgivable decision not to go.

We started singing 'You'll Never Walk Alone', swaying on the bench, our throats tight with emotion. We stood up and started to walk back up Putney High Street, arm in arm, defiant, going through the whole repertoire, hoping a Chelsea or United fan would try to take the piss out of us so we could sing 'Champions of Europe' back in their face.

On we walked up Putney Hill, swaying and singing, finally after all those years, brothers-in-arms. I didn't realize it at the time, but it wasn't just Tommy Smith and Kevin Keegan who were fated that night. I was too. There was a reason why I didn't go to Rome with my mates or on my own. It was the best of nights, it was the worst of nights. But either way, it was meant to be.

9

CABBAGES AND KINGS

10 AUGUST 1983 – ANFIELD CREMATORIUM

I'd been staring at the bound pages of the Wokingham District Council's Planning Committee for ten minutes but my brain was incapable of digesting a word. I could hear speeches being made and interruptions taking place, but not a syllable was registering. I could see men in suits and women in polkadot blouses and pearls standing up, sitting down, waving papers and pointing, but had no desire to interpret a single gesture.

As a junior reporter on the *Reading Evening Post* I'd been handed the graveyard job of spending an evening in the company of blue-rinsed Tory councillors to discover if their plans to turn another school field into a supermarket (it was all the rage in the eighties) would make locals get sufficiently up-in-arms. See how easily the clichés come back?

But on that July night in 1981 they could have passed an application to flatten the town centre and build a nuclear weapons plant with an option to bomb Russia when it was up and running, and I'd have missed it. My head was somewhere else. Liverpool, or rather Parley, was burning – not Toxteth or Liverpool 8 as the media reported it, but the once-grand spread of Georgian houses around Upper Parliament Street, a stone's throw from Wavertree – and there I was, listening to people from a different solar system.

What was I doing here? I knew the how, but not the why. In my final year at Warwick, with no idea how I wanted to earn a living when the grant cheques ran out, I decided to have a shot at journalism. There was no burning desire from within to change the world, just a realization that I would rather set my genitals alight outside Coventry Cathedral than do what most of my mates were doing – applying for managership schemes at Sainsbury's or Jaguar.

So I cut out anonymous clippings from the Warwick University newspaper, stuck them in a folder alongside the odd music review and match report I'd done, and passed it off as proof that printer's ink ran through my blood. I bullshitted my way through a couple of interviews, won a place on a Thomson traineeship, was sent on a five-month training course in Cardiff, and ended up as a reporter in Reading.

But it was at times like this, when the Toxteth Riots were kicking off and I was forced to report on the irrelevant whines of these hideous Margo Leadbetter clones, that I felt as out of place as a haddock up a tree.

Before I'd left the house the BBC were showing footage of old buildings I'd known since I was a little kid raging with fire, and streets I'd walked down filled with coppers in science fiction gear firing CS gas at locals who responded with fire-bombs. It was surreal and incomprehensible.

I couldn't think straight. Until a row broke out between the Conservative leadership and the few Liberal members who were opposing plans for a conservatory being built in someone's garden. The Tories gave emotional speeches about why this person should have the freedom to build themselves a little light cubby-hole, somewhere to relax with their *Daily Telegraph* and their prejudices, but the NIMBYing Liberals weren't having it. Talk about people with glass windows having nothing better to do than throw stones.

I shook my head in disgust. Not so much at them as myself. What was I doing in leylandii-land (just outside la-la land) when my city was on fire and I called myself a news reporter? When the nation's second-densest concentration of Georgian buildings outside of London was being razed by a community who'd been pushed over the edge by politicians like these who didn't care what their economic policies were doing to the fabric of the nation.

I stood up, threw the minutes down and deliberately walked a circuitous route to the exit door muttering as loud as possible without making it an outburst: 'Fuck this.'

It was double-takes all round. 'Pardon?' said one. 'What did he say?' asked another, followed by 'How dare he?' and 'What paper's he from?' I just slammed the door and walked to the car, barking obscenities. I knew when it got back to the news editor it would be another nail in my coffin, but quite frankly I was hoping the company undertakers already had one measured up. I'd had enough of this parochial reporting lark. My heart wasn't in it and it showed.

I'd walk to work of a morning dreading the banalities that lay in store. Would it be a Reading family of chain-smoking slobs showing me a damp patch on their council house wall which they claimed was a health hazard? A WI meeting in Maidenhead for snooty old cows with nothing better to do before they die than make jam and hate youth? Maybe a trip to Newbury magistrates to see the latest batch of inbreds up on cider-related assaults, or an attempt at trying to interview the Greenham Common Peace Women who would employ twenty different looks to tell me to get my dick off their dick-less territory.

I tried to convince myself how lucky I was. I was twenty-three years old and in a job thousands of young people would have killed for. I was still playing Sunday League football, there were plenty of loose women around and I was sharing a house with two old schoolmates (one of them Mike) who'd come down from Liverpool to find work. Yet my life felt as superficial and pointless as, well, Berkshire.

It was a mid-twenties crisis that even spread to Liverpool FC. For once, not even their heroics could eliminate life's drudgery.

The club had never been more successful, they were far and away the best in England and champions of Europe for a third time in five years, but I wasn't getting the same kick out of it as I used to.

When I did go to games it was nearly always League Cup finals, Boxing Day matches which were half-asleep affairs seen through bleary eyes, or ones that saw them stroll to another League title at Anfield. Lord Mayor's processions, the lot.

Disgustingly, I was bored with success. It's inconceivable and most probably indefensible to those fans who have never been allowed to treat a minimum of two trophies a season as normality. But it happens. When you binge on success it makes you arrogant and greedy and allows you to take excellence for granted. You can't see it happening at the time, you can't explain it, and you can't do anything about it. But that saying about only knowing what you've got when it's gone, is never more true than when applied to football greatness.

Take the 1981 European Cup final. Part of the reason the Liverpool obsession was cooling was that I had no one to share it with. No one to feed it with on long, self-indulgent away-days. Vic was mortgaged to the hilt in London, Mike was managing a Reading sports store and thus spent every Saturday chasing shop-lifters, and Terry was still studying drunken sex in Northampton. Even if I'd fancied forfeiting my only lie-in of the week and driven to away games I'd have had to do so on my own. The odds were stacked against it.

But there was no way I was missing out on the 1981 final against Real Madrid in Paris. I didn't have a ticket or a fellow Red to travel with, and was about to head off on my own when two Evertonian members of the Warwick Scousers side, Billy and Cainey, decided to tag along.

Billy was drier than a gecko's tongue, specialized in climbing through windows and nocturnal arson attacks, and was doing teacher training back home in Kirkby. He'd been with me to many Liverpool triumphs during our time at Warwick and I'd filled in many a Saturday afternoon watching Gordon Lee's Everton fail humorously at grounds across the Midlands. Afternoons which always seemed to start at Yates's Wine Lodge near Birmingham New Street Station and end with Billy climbing the roof of that city's cathedral, and, on more than one occasion, being invited to spend the night on a concrete bed in Steelhouse Lane police station.

Cainey, from Norris Green's Boot Estate, had been in the year below me at De La Salle, and was a talented footballer who went on to play in South Africa, Hong Kong and New Zealand where he ended up as national coach. But back then he was bored, unemployed and in need of a laugh. So a sickie was thrown at the newsdesk, and Paris it was (a sickie which turned into a verbal warning after an office stooge claimed he'd seen me conga-ing around the Eiffel Tower). Still it was worth it to spend five days spent fleecing bars along the Champs-Elysées, sleeping three in a bed in a flea-bitten Pigalle dive, and, for one of us at least, discovering that the perfumed lady you'd just given fifty francs to had the required tackle between his legs to become a hooker for Toulouse.

I hit lucky on the ticket front when a mate of Terry McDermott's sold me a spare for face value. Cainey hit lucky by following Billy into a multi-storey car park adjoining the Parc des Princes, copying his Spiderman act and leaping on to the stadium roof before shimmying down a drainpipe and in through a window.

It was a terrible game (don't swallow the myth about Real Madrid being a non-stop line of pure attacking beauty from Puskas to Zidane – this side was so dull and clueless they couldn't find the pulse never mind make it throb) settled by a typical Alan Kennedy goal: head down, run like Barney Rubble when he's making Fred Flintstone's car move, get yourself in range of the goal, batter it and see what happens. But it was enough to make us rule Europe again. The feeling when Phil Thompson rocked up and down with that beautiful big cup above his head still left you feeling incredibly privileged. 'You'll Never Walk Alone' was still belted out with the same raw pride.

But then, heading back into the centre of Paris, we hit a lull. Waiting at the Metro station I joined in the moans with a few other Liverpudlians about how uninventive we'd been and how David Johnson was no great shakes as a partner for Kenny. Which was when Billy exploded at me. 'You've just beaten Real Madrid to win the European Cup for a third time and listen to you. If that had been Everton I'd be so off my head now you'd have to stop me from jumping under a train. You don't know you're born.'

Of course we didn't. We were spoilt little shits who'd been blessed with incredible good fortune. The succession from Shankly to Paisley had, after the first barren season, exceeded everyone's wildest expectations. Against all predictions Paisley had developed a more patient, sophisticated and skilful side than Shankly, which enabled him to conquer, then rule, the continent.

But was that through luck or design? Had God decided to become a Kopite or were we now seeing the fruit of all those trophyless years in the late sixties when Shankly was laying the foundations of greatness, perfecting the good habits, garnering the experience, logging the knowledge that would allow them to see off the best in Europe? Experience that would breed a mindset which instinctively knew when to play it slowly, silence the crowd and keep possession, and when to go for the jugular.

It was Paisley's team now, and those three European Cup victories along with a UEFA Cup, six League titles and three League Cups, which mark him out as the most successful manager in the history of English football, cannot, and should not, be disputed. But, and Paisley was the first to admit it, Shankly made it all possible. Without his fifteen years in charge, without his ceaseless dedication to creating the conditions that would allow a succession of sides to dominate the continent, those European Cups would never have happened.

He'd even followed the Shankly blueprint of building a side with a Scottish spine. For Lawrence, Yeats and St John read Alan Hansen, Graeme Souness and Kenny Dalglish. Paisley watched Hansen as an unfocused, happy-go-lucky defender at Partick This-tle and saw a star. He signed the twenty-one-year-old for £100,000 in April 1977, and within months he was making his debut. Within a year he was picking up a European Cup winner's medal against Bruges at Wembley. Although his talent was criminally under-used by Scotland – just as St John's had been – Hansen went on to become arguably the most intelligent and skilful defender ever to play for Liverpool.

Another piece of Paisley genius was the snapping up of Graeme Souness for £350,000 from Middlesbrough in January 1978. I remember going to his debut at West Brom, and beaming at his every effortless contribution. With his first couple of touches you knew we'd signed someone who could stroke the ball around like an opening batsman. With his first couple of tackles you knew we also had someone who could hit an opponent like a world champion cruiserweight. Whatever I was to later think of Souness as a manager, as a player I had nothing but love and respect for him. He was quite simply an awesome warrior.

Before Steven Gerrard came along he was undoubtedly the most complete midfield player to wear the red shirt. Gerrard's growing stature now disputes that, but he's yet to completely refute it. Souness matured rapidly in one of the most skilful and hardest midfields English football has seen. Only a brave man or a fool would have tried to pick a fight, or complete a drinking session, with Souness, Jimmy Case, Ray Kennedy and Terry Mc-Dermott. By the end of his first season Souness was delivering the subtle, defence-splitting pass that would allow Dalglish to chip the Bruges keeper and send us all home from Wembley with a second European Cup.

Dalglish. Oh Dalglish. It's still difficult to pronounce that word without my face lighting up and melting into a mask of defiant elation. For a dozen years just saying his name to a rival fan was throwing down a gauntlet. Match that if you can. But they couldn't.

Here, I believed at the time, was my last great hero. The biggest of them all, even though I was twenty when he took over the mantle. He still remains the greatest player I ever saw in a Liverpool shirt, a point I was making to Des Lynam in Brussels during Euro 2000, before the old smoothie cut in with his theory on Kenny's greatness.

'You know what his secret was? You know what set him apart, why nobody could get near him? It was his arse,' he yelled across a bemused Chinese restaurant. 'He had a huge arse. Huge. Used to stick it out when he was shielding the ball and no one could take it off him. All the great players had huge arses. Look at Maradona's.'

Des had a point, but like Maradona, there was slightly more to Kenny than his arse. What his brain could see, and what his feet could deliver, have only been matched by a couple of dozen players in the history of football. He thought like a chess player, passed like a clairvoyant and fought like a lion. Had he played for one of the top countries in the world he'd have gone down in that second tier of all-time greats below Pele, Maradona and Cruyff.

To my mind Dalglish was the equal of Zinedine Zidane and Michel Platini. And he showed it again and again throughout a career of stunning consistency and dedication. His signing for £440,000 from Celtic, a month after Kevin Keegan left, was another Paisley masterstroke. He was the roof on the building. As a player and a manager he was the definition of everything Liverpool FC aspired to be, and for many years were. Peerless but dignified.

After Kenny I ceased to fall head-over-heels in love with players, not because the production line jammed, but because he shattered the myth of the hero. As a journalist I came into contact with him in a working capacity and he did me a huge favour. He showed me unknowingly, that if you want to worship earthly idols you should never get too close to them. Footballers aren't gods, just talented lads with as many flaws and nasty edges as the rest of humanity. If you want to carry on a childish love affair with football you need to get away from the men inside it. Get too close and the reality will shatter your cosy illusions irreparably. But back then, when I was still in the passionate throes of uncynical youth, I worshipped him above all else.

Everyone of a certain age can remember where they were the day John Lennon was shot, on 9 December 1980. So can I. In a Cardiff bedsit, during my time as a trainee reporter, gutted after picking up a paper whose back-page splash bore news that Dalglish was injured and would be out until after Christmas. And we were away to Man United on Boxing Day. I was floored. So floored I took my driving test that morning with a mind so far off the road, when the test sheet was handed to me it possessed more Xs than a sixty-strong syndicate's Littlewoods coupon.

I walked ashen-faced into the room where I was doing my journalist training to be greeted with sympathetic glances. 'I suppose as a Liverpudlian you'll be upset at the news,' asked one woman.

'I'm distraught,' I replied. 'But doctors say he should be all right by the New Year.'

'No, he's definitely dead,' said another, staring at me strangely.

It wasn't my fault they'd got their priorities wrong. Of course I was immensely saddened by Lennon's assassination, but that day Dalglish's gammy leg was more of a worry. It had, after all, brought me more pleasure than Lennon's voice. If it had been up to me Scousers would all be jetting off from Kenny Dalglish Airport.

I enjoyed my five months in Cardiff. Up until the last night, when, en route to a nightclub after a farewell party, I was overheard singing 'Poor Scouser Tommy' by a couple of rugby boys who decided to remove my two front teeth with their shoes. It dawned on me before the 2006 FA Cup final with West Ham at the Millennium Stadium, that I was singing the same song on the same spot, through two yellow crowns, that I'd sung that night over twenty-five years ago. And I realized that human beings don't really change throughout life or even sing a different tune, we just grow uglier.

If journalism training proved to be a good crack the actual role of reporter in Reading bored me more than a Latin mass. In fact I became so uninterested, I set up a singing telegram firm called Looney Tunes with Mike (Sinatragram) and our two housemates, Mugger (gorillagram) and Ces (bell-boy). We weren't so much into it for the performing or the extra income, more the chance to be the boss of girls we could make dress up in basques and suspenders who would inevitably beg us for an advance on their wages.

The first time the van pulled up outside the *Reading Evening Post* after my day shift and I dressed up as Frank Spencer in the newsroom, news editor Bert May boomed, 'When I hired you I thought I was getting a reporter, but I got a fucking clown didn't I?' I had to agree.

Things picked up slightly when I did a three-month spell as a sub-editor, mainly because it was next to the sports desk and I could spend most of the day talking about football. But any hopes I'd nurtured of staying a deskbound headline writer disappeared when the chief sub asked me if I was enjoying the new role.

'Yeah,' I replied.

'Why?'

'Because, unlike reporting you can come in every morning with a stinking hangover and you don't have to worry about being sent out to speak politely to morons.' Not the best way to engineer a career move. So it was back to reporting, at which I was astoundingly poor. Twice I failed my proficiency test because I burst out laughing during a staged interview with someone pretending to be a leading light in some non-existent town, telling me a non-existent story. There was nothing else for it – I had to jack it in.

Even the resignation in early 1983 typified how my life had

gone off the rails. The same day I asked Bert May for a job reference, I had to ask if he'd write a character reference for Uxbridge Magistrates Court where I was appearing on charges of being drunk and disorderly at Heathrow Airport.

Me and Billy were seeing Cainey off to New Zealand where he'd signed as a professional for a team in Auckland. Obviously the long goodbye had been a weekend bender. A bender of such magnificent proportion that Billy's Spiderman instincts kicked in and he decided we should bunk on to Cainey's plane.

We managed to get past customs, only for a security alert to go off, and the police to haul the pair of us back into the passenger terminal.

'Do you realize you've just left the country?' said a furious copper to Billy, who pulled a nonplussed face. 'Well, what do you have to say for yourself, then?'

'I wish you'd told us that a few minutes ago 'cos I'd have got my duty-free in,' was his reply. And off we headed to enjoy a night in the cells.

The gist of Bert's reference for future prospective employers said it all. After two-and-a-half years' work, this is the best he could muster: 'Brian is a fun-loving extrovert with a lively mind and an engaging personality. He is also a willing worker and has made considerable contributions in maintaining office morale during the gloom of recession which is currently hitting provincial newspapers.'

Nothing about talent or achievements (and who could blame him as none had been evidenced), just a public assertion of a private observation. He'd hired a fucking clown.

When his secretary asked what I wanted her to do with the £40 she'd collected from colleagues for my leaving present, I asked if I could use it to pay off my drunk and disorderly fine. It kind of summed up what a waste of space I'd been on that newspaper and was God's cue to move on.

But to what? Working behind a bar and on building sites in Reading was easy but not very lucrative. Bullshitting your way into reporting shifts in Fleet Street, which was only forty minutes on the train from Reading, was also easy and the pay was ten times better. So that's what I did. Freelanced on various national newspapers once a week, brought in a story once a month, and earned three times what I'd been paid at the *Reading Evening Post* to check on cats up trees.

Being in London once a week also meant I got to see a lot more of Our Vic, who was now within touching distance of literature's biggest prize – the editor's chair at *Whizzer And Chips*. We'd meet up at dinner-time in pubs around Waterloo Station and he'd rarely go back to work, or at tea-time and I'd rarely make the last train to Reading which meant kipping on his couch. He was a lot happier and settled than he'd ever been, mainly because his wife Chris had given birth to his son James in the October of 1982, and he was in the first flush of fatherhood.

Yet still, when we met, the main topic of conversation was Liverpool. Whether they could carry on being the finest exponents of the game these isles had ever witnessed, and if not, would his Orange father-in-law poison James's mind and turn him into a Rangers fan. There seemed little chance of that outcome in the spring of 1983 though.

The 1982–83 title was wrapped up ludicrously early. By 9 April we'd lost three times, picked up 80 points, and were so far ahead of the rest the team decided to spend the remainder of the season with their feet up, losing five times and drawing twice. Had they carried on their form prior to winning the title, they'd have chalked up 100 points. Giving the others a glimmer of hope, I suppose, before winning the title with ease the following season to record a hat-trick of English championships. And another European Cup. They weren't simply standing head and shoulders above the rest of Europe back then, they were standing head and shoulders on top of Mont Blanc above the world.

Vic was starting to become resentful at the big games he was missing and I was getting into. This was the subject of a heated row when we met in the Jubilee Tavern in June. He was still miffed that the last time we'd met for a pre-match pint was the League Cup (or rather the Milk Cup) final in March.

Neither of us had tickets, but I was going to chance my arm outside Wembley. He stomped off home saying he refused to pay touts' prices, I headed up there, paid £1 for a used stub which had been smuggled back out, and gained entry. By the 1980s Liverpool fans were world experts at ingenious ways of entering a stadium, whether it be wall-scaling, turnstile-hopping, forgeries or used tickets. It was just a case of going with the flow, finding out what method was working that day, and taking a risk.

If all else failed you could buy a takeaway, a stranger would have a wireless and although you were sitting on concrete North London steps staring at nondescript suburbia, technically you were at Wembley. Not that I ever had to take the wireless route. Fate always played its part in setting up a potentially happy outcome to the trip, and the players usually finished it off.

We beat Ron Atkinson's United that day 2–1, despite going one-down early on to a Norman Whiteside cracker. It was a particularly pleasing result, as it was the first time we'd beaten our most detested rivals in a cup final – which made Vic doubly gutted he'd gone home. Just as he was distraught at waving us off at Victoria Station in 1981 as we headed for Paris, and he staggered off incorrectly predicting his ticketless brother would end up in a French meat wagon, while he was watching it on the telly.

The row in the pub almost reached blows when I called him a spineless bastard, and smugly threw the SAS motto at him about daring and winning. The tension eased when he declared he was going to get into next year's European Cup final with or without a ticket because the 1983–84 season would mark his twentieth anniversary as a Liverpool fan.

For the next four rounds we talked of things, of cabbages (Sandy Brown, Malcolm Macdonald) and kings (Kevin and Kenny). We raised a glass to Shankly who had passed away months after the 1981 European Cup win. We picked our best and worst team, our highlights and low-lights, and time flew.

At seven o'clock I remembered I had to leave and take the train back to Reading to spend a final night with my girlfriend Cindy, who was heading off to Italy to work. Vic wasn't having any of it, demanding I stay until closing time. It was tempting but I had to go. He still had two-thirds of a pint, but unusually got up to see me off, calling me a traitor for deserting the rehearsal for his twentieth anniversary celebrations just to see a bird off on holiday. He walked outside with me, into the summer night, and told me I'd have to get over soon to see the baby. I said I would.

I walked about ten yards down Waterloo Road, and looked back. Vic was still standing there. Waving. He shouted 'traitor' again, and urged me back for a pint. I hesitated. Something was telling me to go back in. That he needed this. But I couldn't. I was half-cut already and I'd promised to take Cindy out for one last night before she went away. I mightn't see her again for months. But I'd always be able to see Vic in London. I told him to go and finish his pint and get home to his son, waved, and walked off.

It was late morning on 3 August and I was sitting in a Fleet Street pub with my mate Savo, another Scouser who had been at Warwick, after picking up a cheque from one of the Sunday papers for a story which wouldn't exactly be troubling the Pulitzer Prize judges.

Within seconds of the first pint being sunk I phoned Vic to see if he fancied swopping the cheque for an afternoon on the lash. The man's voice in his office was shaky. He wasn't in today. I'd better speak to his family. I rang his flat but it was engaged. I rang Sheila who was back up in Huyton by then, to see if she knew what was going on. My sister Karen answered it. She was in tears, and just blurted it out. Vic was dead. He'd had a heart attack that morning. He was only twenty-nine.

Me and Savo jumped a cab to his house in Wimbledon and arrived at a devastating scene. Chris was in a world of her own while ten-month-old James was crawling around the floor, oblivious. We sat there for a few hours not knowing what to do or say. It could have been worse. I could have been Reg travelling down to London on a train with Sheila.

It turned out Vic had been using a knife to rifle change out of the baby's piggy bank for his Tube fare when he'd keeled over and suffered the massive seizure. He'd been complaining of chest pains for a while, and gone to his doctor who told him it was indigestion. Meanwhile a blood clot was travelling through his veins which eventually blocked the major artery to his heart. He died of a pulmonary embolism. His body was brought back to Liverpool a few days later and he was cremated at Anfield, sent off by a nervous young priest who'd misread the script and called him Edward, his middle name, throughout.

I'd been in a form of trance from the moment I phoned my sister. A shield had gone up which refused to let the reality of the situation in. At the funeral I was all jokes and anecdotes with uncles, cousins and his mates. I was putting on a show. Enjoying being the butt of everyone's sympathy. Looking forward to the piss-up afterwards.

I'd never been to a funeral before, except as an altar boy to earn two bob off the chief mourner, and was thinking how it wasn't a bad day out. Then, after his coffin slipped behind the curtains, I walked outside. While everyone else was staring at the flowers, lighting a stranger's cigarette, sniffing into their Kleenex or simply looking at the ground to avoid eye contact with the close family, I walked alone to the end of the crematorium path and stared over at Stanley Park and up, past the football pitches to the structure that dominated the horizon. Anfield.

I thought back to 1965, how I'd chased him around the garden to find out what all the fuss was about when Reg threw the Bolton tickets on the kitchen table for his eleventh birthday treat, to the Taliban Wife years when I traipsed behind him with my stool, to Wembley in '74 dressed in my mum's coat, to the Bricklayers Arms after Rome '77 when we'd walked back up Putney Hill as proper brothers.

I remembered how he begged me to stay for another pint in the Jubilee Tavern to celebrate his upcoming twentieth anniversary as a Red, and how I'd turned him down.

And with wet eyes focused on the Anfield Road roof, I realized Our Vic would never see that anniversary. We'd never talk again of cabbages and kings, I'd never hug him when a Liverpool player made the net bulge.

It felt like an anvil had been dropped on my heart.

10

NOTHING TO SEE BUT THE SAND

2 JANUARY 1984 – MALINDI, KENYA

After Vic's death I lost the appetite to do cynical stitch-ups for the Sunday papers. When you experience that depth of hurt the last thing you feel like doing is inflicting it on others. Losing an older brother when he's still in his twenties puts life in perspective. It makes you want to sell off every material possession, throw yourself at risk and challenge the outrageously arrogant assumption that you have any future worth worrying about. It makes you want to do a legger from the banal expectations of adulthood.

So thank God for Savo, a mate with a permanent wanderlust, who sees life as one big checklist with boxes that need to be ticked. Savo is unlike any other Scouse male I've ever bonded with, in that he openly dislikes football. He'd tagged along to many a game, including Cup finals, but usually, after the pre-match session when we made our way to Wembley, he'd wander off to a Tutankhamun exhibition.

His indifference to a sport which had colonized the hearts and minds of virtually every other male Scouser was summed up in 1982 when he was teaching English in Sudan. On a trip to Khartoum he bumped into his old schoolmate David Fairclough who was over with the Liverpool squad for a showpiece game. Fairclough took him back to the team hotel and introduced him to Paisley, only for Savo to reply, 'Hiya Ian.'

Savo's love of Africa made him suggest, after Vic's death, that we attempt to backpack from Cairo to Cape Town. Normally I've got as much in common with backpackers as soap has with their armpits. But they weren't normal times. I had nothing to lose. So in October 1983 I threw an army kitbag over my shoulder and marched off to slum it the length of the African continent with no fears or reservations and no inclination to return to Blighty.

Egypt was a good laugh, especially after we'd pulled off a lucrative scam involving traveller's cheques and fat men who run back-street bazaars, which earned us enough readies to travel down the Nile in the style of Agatha Christie characters.

Sudan started off as a hoot too. I spent my twenty-sixth birthday riding through the Sahara sitting on the roof of a train with the locals, swigging illegal Johnnie Walker (this was a strict Muslim state) and teaching them the words to 'Poor Scouser Tommy', the one who'd been sent to a far foreign land where the flies swarm around in their thousands and there's nothing to see but the sand.

And then we hit a small town north of Khartoum called Shendi, where Savo had done his English teaching, and parked ourselves in a mud hut lent to him by an ex-girlfriend who'd run off with a member of the Sudanese Liberation Front. Within a day I needed liberating too.

If the universe does possess an arsehole, then it is called Shendi. And me and Savo were piles on that arsehole, enjoying an existence devoid of alcohol, proper food, TV, women, news-papers or other human beings to speak to.

The highlight of every twenty-four hours was the night. After we'd spent the light hours hiding from the 130-degree sun, we'd walk into 'town' and enter a shack marginally more upmarket than the one we'd spent the day in, for a 'meal' of leaves, beans, scraggy lamb and lentils, served up by a fella you'd just spotted washing his feet in a sink next to the counter. And if we were lucky, really lucky, we'd get a treat. A yoghurt (plain yoghurt, mind – don't get excited). Then order some black tea, saturated with sugar, and play a few games of draughts. Oh yeah, me and Savo were the Shendi brat-pack.

Throughout the evening, especially if it was the weekend, I'd be thinking about life back home. The Friday night pub crawl around town, a few in The Breck before the match, a few in The George on the way home. Quick wash then out again to eye up the gorgeous women in skimpy dresses who flocked to Plummers and Chauffers.

And here I was, playing draughts with a cup of black tea, looking behind Savo at four old fellas, each owning a face more wizened than an elephant's jaxey, sucking on their big brass bongs.

The lights had gone out in my life but I could have no complaints. It was my fault. My black mood after Vic's death had dragged me to the heart of the Dark Continent where there seemed no respite from a self-imposed bleakness. Until Saturday 26 November, when a man from a neighbouring hut lent us a radio which was tuned in to the BBC World Service, and neon blazed through my head on a Las Vegas scale.

Out came words, variations of which I'd heard hundreds of times over the years listening to Liverpool's away matches on a Saturday afternoon in my bedroom, which sent my soul soaring: 'And we welcome World Service listeners to Portman Road with the news that League-leaders Liverpool . . .' Words I'd always imagined were being addressed to soldiers on the Rhine, teenagers in Singapore, or tikka-tinged expats in South Africa being brought a G&T by their servant. Now they were being spoken to me. Cut off from civilization, desperate to hear an English voice, ecstatic that I was about to spend the next half-hour hearing every pass and tackle of a Liverpool game 6,000 miles away. Even when he finished his welcoming sentence with '. . . are trailing Ipswich 1–0'.

So what. They'd pull it back. Even if they didn't, I was about to experience a concept that had been lost during my time in this Sudanese prison cell. Excitement. They did pull it back through, who else, Dalglish. And the roar I could hear from the travelling

Liverpool support led to the rarest of connections. They were leaping around in a dingey old shed in East Anglia, I in a dingey mud hut in northern Sudan. But we were as one.

If I'd been back home listening to this on my couch there would probably have been mere relief at the equalizer, with a bollocking eventually screamed at the radio for dropping points. But here, in this grim shack, in these grim surroundings I felt a communion with those who'd trekked to Ipswich.

The game ended 1–1, but that half-hour commentary, and especially that Dalglish goal, had me buzzing. It made me realize how lucky football makes you. Because it's always there. You can go to the darkest dive in the most desolate corner of the earth and you're two batteries and a transistor away from a big, warm blanket. You can lose everything in life but you still have that.

I'd felt this glow of reassurance, this pull of an anchor dragging me back to my roots, in foreign places many times before. In 1982 I went to West Berlin and toured the Reichstag which was then a national museum, before walking towards the Berlin Wall. As I got closer I could see it was covered in graffiti, most of it either German or plain indecipherable. Staring at the middle of the wall, at a point where no other graffiti existed because it was directly under the noses of the Checkpoint Charlie watch-towers, I could make out an isolated word, daubed in red paint in two-foot capital letters on the virgin concrete. As I moved closer the daub took on a recognizable shape. It said 'LIVERPOO'. And after the second O a trail of red paint fell to the deck. Clearly the lad had been spotted by a guard and chased.

I wondered if he'd taken a bullet. Was he another casualty of this barbaric symbol of the imprisonment of the human soul? But my fears didn't last long. Ten yards down the wall the same artistic hand had picked up that paint and finished off his masterpiece: 'LIVERPOOL RULE OK'.

I drifted into a bar in San Francisco in 1977, looking for a bit of company, only to discover all twelve of the locals sat in pairs with handlebar moustaches. Just as my heels turned for the door

I glimpsed at the bar and saw a shrine to all things Liverpool FC. Eight hours of enthralling reminiscing later – even The Village People joined in with 'You'll Never Walk' when they realised it was from a Broadway show – and not a drink paid for, the exiled Scouse queen who ran the joint rolled me into a taxi and gave the driver ten dollars to take me back to the youth hostel.

OK, the stories aren't as good as the one told by an old mate who reckons he had his nose pressed up against the Wailing Wall, staring at all the little notes left in the cracks, when he read 'Kevin Keegan is God' on one of them, but they explain how following a team like Liverpool can be an almost Masonic experience. You're part of an exclusive sect, who dress up in the same funny costume, have the same ancient chants, attend the same meetings and know the same secrets as you. A sect spread worldwide which offers succour to its members in their hour of need.

Like the morning I tried to make it through Islamabad airport in 2000 when customs officers discovered a half-empty bottle of vodka in my coat, dragged me to a police room and demanded I be charged with trying to smuggle alcohol into the strictly dry Islamic Republic of Pakistan.

I had yet to touch a curry but my bowels were heading south as three policemen shook their heads. 'Why is it open?' asked the most menacing one, who'd clearly never spent eight hours on a booze-free Air Pakistan flight, desperate to anaesthetize the brain from the surrounding bedlam. 'I'm an alcoholic and a nervous flier,' I stuttered. 'It's like medicine really. But I didn't touch a drop over Pakistani airspace, honest.'

Thirty terrifying, *Midnight Express* minutes later, they impounded the Smirnoff and issued me a written warning. If found in possession of alcohol again the phrase 'going on the lash' would take on far more gruesome connotations. It was 4 a.m., I had two hours to wait for a connecting flight to Lahore and badly needed fresh air, so decided to walk outside the airport and take in the ambience of old Islamabad. I immediately wished I hadn't. It resembled a shanty town from the days of the Raj.

Very poor. Very threatening. Standing there in a cream suit I felt like a British army general who was keeping all the locals in abject poverty. I was the only white face in sight. A face now whiter than boiled excreta. I was tired, thirsty, convinced my suitcase was in Kazakhstan and slightly afraid that I'd walked somewhere I shouldn't have at the worst hour of the night. Through the chaos, I spotted a television, which I presumed had flight times showing. When I got there, I was gobsmacked.

It was tuned to BBC World, showing highlights of that afternoon's game between Liverpool and Coventry, where we dished out a 4–1 thrashing. I forgot that I was in a hotbed of Muslim fanaticism, my nationality, my colour and the neat vodka fumes pouring off my breath. I was unaware that an intimidating crowd had gathered around, staring suspiciously at my every punch into the air that hailed strikes by McAllister, Gerrard and Heskey (twice).

The highlights ended and I just stared at the telly in amazement, convincing myself that the BBC is indeed the finest broadcasting institution on earth. Until I remembered Jim Davidson and snapped out of the trance to see a menacing scrum surrounding me. I smiled but no one smiled back. There was a stand-off. I was frozen to the spot, fearing any minute I would be bundled into the boot of a battered Honda Civic, taken to an al-Qaeda training camp and tied to a radiator, where a camcorder would be set up and a scimitar sharpened for the decapitation shot.

After what seemed like an eternity the biggest one slowly opened his mouth and said, 'Liverpool, I like. Michael Owen very good, yes?' If I'd had a few more slugs of vodka in me, I'd probably have kissed him. Well, he did have a frock on . . .

It would be another three weeks of sobriety and misery, two of them spent in Khartoum where roughly forty-four mosques could be heard calling you to prayer at dawn, before we escaped from the Sudan. Civil war in the south of the country meant travelling overland was impossible, so we flew into Tanzania and took a bus to Kenya.

Within ten minutes of walking into the Hilton Hotel bar in Nairobi I felt like one of those suicide bombers who had reached heaven and was cashing in his chit for the seventy-two virgins. Everything about every second of those ten minutes was indescribably pleasurable.

I'd thrown two pints of ice-cold lager down my neck, been served a double cheeseburger and chips with HP sauce, read the sports pages of a day-old copy of *The Times*, and a Whitney Houston lookalike called Roxanne had draped her arm around me, rubbed the inside of my thigh and suggested we have a good time together in my room.

I had to break it to her gently that we were planning to stay at the local youth hostel, where having a good time in your room usually consists of sewing up a hole in your mosquito net, but she didn't mind. These girls were inventive enough to get around such obstacles for the price of a few beers and a tip.

I loved Kenya. We went down to Mombasa, then up the coast to a resort called Malindi, where we rented two bungalows for Christmas and New Year and expunged the hermit-like existence of Sudan from our memories. Apart from the memory of that Ipswich game. After that religious connection I made sure a wireless never left my side. The World Service isn't the best method of staying in touch with English football, as it's more concerned with the knock-on effects of the yam-harvest failure in Burkina Faso, but constant monitoring allows you to instinctively know when you'll hear commentary or round-ups.

Liverpool were doing OK. Winning a few, drawing one, occasionally losing, but accruing enough points (mainly thanks to a Rush–Dalglish partnership which had clicked into something special) to canter towards a third successive title.

On 2 January I lay on a beautiful, deserted white beach, clasping a cold beer in the late afternoon sun, thinking how good life was, when an uneasiness began to filter into my brain. Maybe it was Catholic guilt about living in a paradise where every pleasure was on tap but wasn't being earned by eight hours of grinding the nose into a mill. Maybe it was New Year resolution time. Maybe the month in Kenya had flushed the misery and disillusionment of 1983, when Vic had died and I'd left journalism, out of my system. But I'm pretty sure it was down to the radio that nestled next to me in the sand, and the commentary from Anfield on our game against Man United.

It wasn't a great match. We drew 1–1. But the atmosphere pulled on me like a giant *Tom & Jerry* magnet. I wanted to be joining in with the chants, part of the cauldron of fear and loathing, living on the edge of ecstasy or despair that goes with these all-or-nothing games. I didn't want to be in paradise. I wanted to be at Anfield on a bleak January day, warmed by the double Scotch I'd thrown down at ten-to-three before walking into the icy air, rubbing my hands ready for action, anticipating my return to the pub in two hours, where we'd dissect every goal and incident, before joining in a raucous sing-song. Preferably standing on a table. That was it. I was going home.

Savo was philosophical about it. He'd decided he was going to make it to South Africa and if he had to go alone then so be it. But there was no way he was heading home to January in England when he was on the south side of the equator, basking in real Africa. As he kept saying to me, 'What's the point of going home now? Why not wait until it's summer back home?'

But that's the thing about non-football lovers, they don't understand how the seasons work. How their sunshine-content is inversely proportionate to the pleasure they bring. There was no bleak-yet-beautiful Saturday afternoon pull on his heart, no hole in his life when it was absent. So I was going back to freezing Blighty and he was going on to become a modern-day Livingstone.

It was only when I landed in Manchester that I remembered how a British January can eat your soul. With nowhere to live or work I moved back in with Sheila and Reg in Huyton and signed on. It was all the rage in Liverpool in 1984, when Big Sister was at her vindictive best, having secured a second election victory on the back of liberating a barren rock filled with penguin-humpers in the South Atlantic.

'Just Rejoice,' Thatcher told us after defeating a rag-bag army of Argentinians, and all the patriotic flag-wavers, who'd been missing a good war and believed Churchill had been exhumed, rejoiced like there was no tomorrow.

Under Thatcher scores were being settled between social tribes. Boils were being lanced, and out of them poured a violent, ugly puss. Nowhere was this ugliness more manifest than in football. In the early 1980s football hooliganism had become a way of life at home and abroad, the only difference being at home we were tolerating it, abroad they weren't. Every England game outside our shores was turning into a national humiliation. Cities and stadiums were trashed, rival supporters attacked and locals abused. Sociologists claimed it was the rising up of the great dispossessed, but they only diagnosed a fraction of what was being termed the English Disease.

Professional, middle-aged men hankered after tanked-up violence, kids with nothing going for them at home sought robbery and adventure, fans of little teams with no prospect of foreign travel went along for the glory. Throw in an increase in nationalism brought about by the glorification of the Falklands War and a resurgent National Front targeting white, working-class football fans, and England's national side were permanently accompanied by a stench of xenophobia. Our own black players were subjected to the most appalling racial abuse, and foreigners were treated like a subspecies to the sons of Albion.

The reaction of foreigners was not surprising, especially in Mediterranean countries like Italy and Spain, where men historically slashed first and asked questions later. The locals defended their pride with knives and the police backed them up with truncheons, CS gas and the turning of blind eyes.

To stray from the mob following an English team abroad was to invite danger. The more the English fought, the more the police and locals fought back, the more xenophobia it unleashed, the more the ugliness made critical headlines all over the world and the more young men with empty lives back home were attracted to a release from their drudgery. But the violence and nastiness abroad simply mirrored what was going on back home as Thatcher viciously tore the nation apart for the benefit of big business and its dependants, glorifying in the callousness of her work. There was a heartlessness creeping into this once-tolerant country of ours. A cold-blooded contempt for those incapable of mounting the greasy pole. A savaging of life's chances.

Those men who had worked in the old industries like mining, dockworking and steel-making were cruelly abandoned, and with them went their families and their communities. Young people were told to get on their bikes and head south, to where all the nation's wealth was being accumulated. Loadsamoneys in the south, doleites in the north. And nowhere more than in Liverpool, whose factories closed at an unprecedented rate but whose people refused to lie down and take the slaughter.

Their livelihoods may have been stolen, council funding slashed, thousands of its people cast on life's scrapheap, but there was one field of excellence in which Liverpool stood untouched. Its football team. And Kopites wore their badge of pride with a mocking swagger. Their presence in Europe's biggest games, the increasingly moronic edge to fans who followed England's football teams abroad, the naivety of some countries and the hatred of others put us all on an inevitable journey towards the heart of darkness.

11

DANTE'S PURGATORIO

If an apocalypse had reversed the planet's axis and bestowed North Wales with such a rare beauty it was renamed Nirvana-on-Sea, you still couldn't compare Rhyl to a palm-fringed Indian Ocean haven. It would still be next to Towyn. It would still have an overpowering stench of chip fat on the front and a whiff of desperation down every side street.

But as I lay shirtless on its beach in the April sun, listening to radio commentary of a Liverpool game taking place in a distant land, I could have been back in Malindi. The pictures the words were painting inspired dreams of far-off places. Not a return to Merseyside but Rome. All thanks to a lad born down the road from Rhyl, Ian Rush, who had just scored his second against Dinamo Bucharest in Romania to send us back to a European Cup final in the Eternal City.

The Good Lord was still clearly an Anfield season-ticket holder and giving me a chance to repent for the biggest sin of my life. This time, skint or otherwise, I was going to Rome. Billy (the Evertonian Spiderman) was lying next to me, half-listening to the radio, half-shouting abuse at a shameless mingebag who was mine-sweeping the sand for stray pennies with a metal detector. He said he was going too. Well, Paris had been a good laugh, hadn't it, and with me being a doleite I'd need someone to buy the ale.

We were over in Rhyl because Billy had a couple of days off from supply teaching plus the keys to his grandad's caravan. Not exactly Richard Branson's Necker Island hideaway but it made a change from sitting in my boxroom in Huyton pretending to write telly scripts. If the *Reading Evening Post* experience had put me off plans to become the next John Pilger, watching *The Boys From The Blackstuff* had made me decide I was going to be the next Alan Bleasdale. Unfortunately every script editor in London had different ideas, as the brutality of their knock-backs kept testifying. But still I plugged away, convincing myself (if nobody else) that I did have a proper day job. All that was missing was pay.

I picked up the odd bit of work like cold-calling firms trying to flog them advertising space for police and fire service diaries (it's what Reg was reduced to, in between trying to flog *Encyclopedia Britannicas*) and Sheila wasn't taking housekeeping, so the dole stretched to a couple of nights out a week, plus Anfield.

Life wasn't bad, although going to the match had become a bit of a chore, so easy had winning the title become. I know. Appalling, but nonetheless true. During the 1983–84 season we witnessed fortnightly maulings handed out to teams like Notts County (5–0), Luton (6–0) West Ham (6–0) and Coventry (5–0) as Rushie poked home 32 League goals, with the rest of the players turning it on when they had to.

It showed in the attendances which, apart from the big games, were mostly down in the low 30,000s. The final game of the season summed it up. Norwich at home. The big send-off for Rome. The celebration of our fifteenth League championship. Meaning a historic third title in a row, and the second part of a potentially historic treble (the League Cup had been won against Everton in March).

The gate? 38,837. The capacity? 45,000. But it wasn't just Anfield that people were turning away from, it was football in general. Live games had just started being screened for free on telly. So why stand in some dilapidated stadium with facilities worse than a Turkish prison, when you could stretch out in front of your front-room fire?

Hooliganism had become such a central part of the match-day culture many dads had stopped taking their lads, and old fellas couldn't stomach what was happening inside and outside grounds they'd been coming to since the Second World War. More importantly, money in ordinary households had never been tighter. Thatcher was telling working-class families they should aspire to be middle-class. To buy their council house and fill it with hostess trolleys and fish knives in the hope they would view the world through her jaundiced eyes. But at the same time jobs in working-class areas were going down the swanee. Look at the facts. When she came to power in 1979, 24,540,627 people paid to watch Football League games. By the end of the 1984 season it was down to 18,358,631 and by 1985–86 it would be down to 16,488,577. As the Yanks say, you do the math.

Back at the Norwich game it was hard to stifle a yawn. I couldn't wait for the lap of honour to go past, so I could get my obligatory applause in then get to the pub. How arrogant it now seems. How many times during meaningless end-of-season games in the nineties and beyond would I think back to that Norwich lap of honour, and the shared boredom of fans and players as they paraded a trophy we hadn't had a decent challenge to for four years? And how difficult in those later years was the choice of whether to laugh or cry?

It was a lame, tame 1–1 draw (Rushie of course), with the players' minds on the Israeli training camp they were heading to, to acclimatize for Rome, and fans' minds on how they were going to pay to get there. My quandary wasn't how I was going to fund the trip but how I was going to pay Billy back for booking us on the Train To Hell (Part II).

Stories of the '77 trains to Rome were legendary. A six-day incarceration in infested cattle trucks, cooped up with thousands of other fellas who'd forgotten the notion of bringing along a change of clothes or a bar of soap. Well, they were only going to the match, weren't they? How were they to know there'd be no washing facilities, no unblocked toilets, nowhere to sleep, everyone else would reek and it would last almost a week? So many harrowing, hilarious tales entered Scouse folklore that Liverpool comic Alexei Sayle wrote a novel about the 1977 journey called, wait for it, *Train To Hell*.

Astonishingly, this time only one train was laid on and you could buy your match ticket as part of the deal. It had nothing to do with fans running scared of another nightmare trek through France and Italy, but everything to do with thousands of adults, either jobless, skint, or working away from home and unable to get time off work.

This was probably the most glaring indictment of how Thatcherism decimated income levels on Merseyside during the 1980s. In 1977, 30,000 Liverpudlians headed to Rome, days after the same number had been in London for the FA Cup final. In 1984 that figure was below 15,000 despite every fan knowing that a 3–1 win over Moenchengladbach in the most historic city on earth had been unquestionably the greatest night ever to be a Kopite.

Had there been 30,000 fans in Rome this time things would undoubtedly have been different, off the pitch at least – so different it doesn't bear thinking about. This time we'd all need a change of stained clothing, not because of the conditions on the cattle truck, but because our Roman hosts would treat us like lambs to the slaughter. Everybody knew at the time how utterly illogical and unnecessary it was to hold a European Cup final on the home pitch of one of the finalists. How many decent neutral grounds are there in Europe capable of staging such a showpiece game? Twenty? Thirty? But somehow UEFA had managed to organize the biggest club cup final in the world between Liverpool and Roma in Rome's Olympic Stadium. Where Roma played.

No desire to change venues was forthcoming when it became obvious what would happen. No explanation or apology. The canapés were ordered, the Pinot Grigio was on ice, the five-star hotel suites had been assigned and the club-class seats booked. Plus there was no way the UEFA officials were going to tell their little ladies they couldn't go on that shopping spree in the boutiques down Via Condotti.

Football fans were well used to decisions being made without their interests at heart. Indeed most of us assumed the old men in charge would laugh at the very idea that our needs and wishes should be anywhere near the top of their agenda. The Suits who ran the show were up for election every few years and needed votes. Consequently every big decision taken was purely political. Always has been, still is and always will be.

In 2005 it came as no surprise to battle-hardened Liverpudlians who turned up at Istanbul to see a ground almost twenty miles out of town, plonked in the middle of a wasteland which looked as though it had been used to recreate lunar landings, with no food or water on sale, and a two-hour coach journey back into town. Meanwhile the 'dignitaries' were wined and dined by sponsors in the shag-piled opulence of the executive lounges. Back in '84 UEFA had promised the European Cup final to Italy. To take it off them when it looked like a Roman team was heading for a Roman final would have upset an apple cart overflowing with prestige, freebies and the dolce vita.

Never believe anybody who claims elections equals democracy equals articulating the will of the people. Especially in football. In 1984 the desire of the authorities to ignore the well-being of the fans led to potential disaster. A year later the potential would be realized. Not one of them would suffer any injury or guilt. And certainly not blame.

We hadn't reached Runcorn before Billy was dragged out of our carriage by transport police for the heinous crime of swigging from a can of Skol. We'd thought all this talk of a dry train had been put about to keep the media and politicians happy, and been encouraged when the supposed body searches at Lime Street on Tuesday morning turned out to be nothing more than a cursory check of one Gola bag in every fifty.

But on board the British Transport Jobsworths were patrolling, and we'd had our stash removed a mile past Speke. We – that's Billy, myself and Mike – hadn't been clever enough. Coke bottles half-full of Bacardi, flasks filled with Stella, oranges injected with Smirnoff, that's how the veterans of the new Puritanism that afflicted the mass movements of football fans took their drink. The rest of us just attempted to get high sucking in their fumes.

The ferry was a different matter. Word must have reached P&O head office that a thousand football fans with tongues down to their shoes, and pockets bulging with cash, had boarded the ship in a mute and sober mood. Within minutes a friendly sounding captain was congratulating on us (a) reaching the European Cup final, and (b) appearing less tanked-up than a coach-load of Methodist pensioners en route to a Ribena-tasting convention in Salt Lake City, Utah.

Consequently he decided to declare the ship wet and invited us all to buy a drink. Two hours later, as mainland Europe loomed, he may have been regretting it. There wasn't a drop left on board, all of it either inside Liverpudlians' stomachs, coat-linings or bags. Most of it still to be paid for. Plus every table on board had a six-man gymnastic team performing a balancing act while screeching 'Arriverderci Roma' through already hoarse throats.

Now we were in the mood to party. Back on the train there wasn't a window that didn't fly a flag, there wasn't a local who couldn't hear 'You'll Never Walk Alone' ripping into the evening sky. Now we were properly on our way to Rome again. Those of us who'd missed out on that first great European Cup win convinced ourselves that this one would be even more historic. This time we would achieve something that would never be achieved again as long as a ball is kicked. A non-Italian side winning the European Cup against an Italian side on that Italian side's ground. Bring it on.

On the way down through France the talk was of the Roman promise to give us the kind of welcome emperors used to receive after kicking the lining out of the Gauls. Why had their pre-match overtures been so generous? Maybe it was guilt at being awarded a home draw for a European Cup final, perhaps a desire to offer the olive branch to perceived hooligans in the hope it would placate our violent tendencies, or maybe through a genuine wish to be amiable hosts. Who knows? But they promised us heaven. Especially those of us travelling on the notorious train to hell. We were to be taken to a piazza where free beer, free pizza, free music and free love would be handed out.

In northern Italy the signs looked promising. As we passed through the outskirts of Turin and the heart of Genoa train guards held up signs saying 'Go Rushie' and 'Forza Liverpool' while locals sold us beer and paninis and told us how badly they wanted us to triumph. At Livorno the station was decked out with Liverpool flags. We felt flattered and honoured, but quickly realized Italy is even more parochial than England and this swell of support was purely down to a loathing for all things Roman. As our train pulled in to Rome we realized even quicker that we'd driven into a loathing for all things Liverpool. There was a reception party all right. The type you'd expect to see afforded to the Ku Klux Klan if they'd booked Harlem for their annual conference.

It was Wednesday tea-time as we stumbled into Rome Central Station thirty-six hours after leaving Lime Street and a hush was descending. Something seemed wrong. Usually when you reached your destination for a Cup final or semi-final there was a sense of being welcomed to a grand occasion. You knew that soon you'd see the massed red-and-white ranks of your compatriots, taking over streets, parks, fountains and pubs, claiming squatters' rights on a little piece of earth that would be forever (or that day at least) Liverpool.

Pulling into Rome felt like an away game. But not just any away game – one which had whipped up half the city into a defiant frenzy. From every other window on the flats and apartments which hugged the sides of the railway line hung the yellow and red chequered flags of AS Roma and banners proclaiming them as *Campioni*. Locals who set eyes on us viewed us with disinterest or scorn. At best we felt like we had been reluctantly allowed in on a Roman celebration, to provide the necessary backdrop to their inevitable triumph. At worst we were the enemy.

As riot police, laden with guns and CS gas, herded us on to buses which had been assigned armed outriders it became clear into which category we'd fallen. And it wasn't the backdrop. So much for the free beer, free pizza, free music and free love. Over the next six hours all we'd get was free hate.

Speeding towards the ground a soon-to-be familiar sight greeted us. Youths with scarves covering their faces riding alongside us on Vespa scooters at motorway pace, flashing knives and making slitting gestures across their throats.

When we reached the Stadio Olimpico, and were dumped outside our entrance gates, there were no tents teeming with dusky Italian wenches opening bottles of frothing Peroni on their thighs. Just the odd vendor selling overpriced cheese sarnies and plonk. In the background coachloads of riot police looked on suspiciously, batons at hand, ready to teach us a lesson. Few Roma fans were in sight because they'd taken up their places on the other side of the gates hours ago, lighting their flares, singing their songs, awaiting their coronation as champions of Europe. It was eerie.

Inside the ground the atmosphere was toxic. Over on the notorious Curva Sud section, the hardcore Ultras hung their flags of hate and burnt Union Jacks. To the side of us, they let off their fireworks and hurled their missiles over the fencing. It seethed with hostility.

When a group of Liverpool fans rose to the bait and tried to charge the fence to get at their attackers they were beaten back by the riot police. The Romans, on the other hand, were given carte blanche to carry on baiting their guests. Little were we to know that this policy of non-interference between home fans and the local carabinieri is standard policing policy in Italy, even to this day.

Across our three-quarters-full end, bruises and cuts were being shown. Tales were being told of unprovoked attacks throughout the day in the city. Stories of innocents who'd been picked off and slashed from behind. This didn't feel like the balmy backdrop to the greatest night of our lives. The little piece of paradise where all Liverpudlian dreams had been realized back in 1977. Instead it was the poisonous cauldron described by Dundee United boss Jim McLean after his side were beaten 3–0 in the European Cup semi-final the previous month, when stomach-churning antics of fans, players and directors forced the Scots to crumble.

'The atmosphere was the worst I have experienced in my life,' said McLean. 'I would never want to go through it again. Their behaviour was outrageous.'

Press photographs backed up his words, like the one of a snarling pack of Roma players pursuing McLean and his assistant Walter Smith down the tunnel. One evocative photo showed a Roma player heading at McLean with a raised middle finger. Smith, meanwhile, was assaulted. But that was Dundee United and this was Liverpool, and whatever was happening off the pitch would surely have no bearing on what the most professional, most feared, team in Europe would do on it.

They didn't let us down. Souness was like a gladiator out there. This was precisely his type of game and he strutted his stuff, glacier-cool in the eye of the storm with an easy arrogance. We didn't know it at the time, but it was to be his last game in a Liverpool shirt before he'd take his skills to Sampdoria. How fitting that his last game, like Keegan's, should be a Herculean effort that won us the European Cup.

Brave, masterful and utterly magnificent, he completely ran the show. With the vastly underestimated Ronnie Whelan in the centre of midfield alongside him, Souness marginalized the famed Brazilian duo of Cerezo and Falcao. At the back Lawrenson and Hansen were rocks. In attack Rushie was the perfect line-leader. Dynamic in movement, shrewd in anticipation and a supreme opportunist waiting to pounce on every mistake. He ran them ragged.

After the obligatory quarter-of-an-hour spent taking the sting out of the home crowd, they took the inevitable lead. Craig Johnston crossed, Whelan jumped up with the Roma keeper Franco Tancredi, who lost the ball and Phil Neal was up there, sniffing, to tap it in. Roman players and fans threw a hissy-fit claiming Tancredi been fouled, hoping to sway the Swedish ref by outright hostility and sheer weight of numbers, but he wasn't having any. It stood.

The rest of the half saw sporadic Roma attacks but Liverpool were in control, playing the Italians at their own cagey game. And then three minutes before the break, Bruno Conti picked up a rebound, pinged in a short cross which Roberto Pruzzo cutely headed backwards over Bruce Grobbelaar, into the net. The stadium erupted. Their moment of triumph had finally arrived. Surely it was only a matter of time before they made their home advantage count and the crowning ceremony could begin.

I saw the second half and the half-hour of extra time through a blinding headache, brought about by two days on the train to hell plus the litre of cheap vino cacko I'd hurriedly necked in the short gap between being thrown off the coach and ushered into the ground. Even without the headache it wouldn't have been easy on the eye. Here was classic Liverpool containment. A side that had just picked up its third consecutive League title and its fourth consecutive League Cup and was in touching distance of its fourth European Cup in seven years, knew exactly what to do. Forget that you were playing in a European Cup final and remember you were playing in an away European Cup tie in Italy. Then play them at their own game. Suffocate them. Little surprise then that it became the first-ever European Cup final to go to a penalty shoot-out.

What I went through that night, and during the many penalty shoot-outs since has taught me what a vile process it is. Relief, optimism, fear, pessimism, panic. They're the five takers your head nominates. The knowledge of how close your are to achieving something coming a horrible second to the realization that you're one tame stroke, one reckless blast, one blinding save, one inexplicable choice of taker away from a season's work amounting to nothing.

And through a blinding headache and narrowed fingers I watched the first inexplicable choice meet the first reckless blast. Stevie Nicol. He was a kid. A defender. Not even a regular first-teamer and he'd come on as sub. So what was he doing walking towards the Italian end, ball in hand, placing it, turning away and blasting it way, way over the bar. This was criminal negligence. This seemed like certain defeat especially when di Bartolomei took two short paces and casually slipped in the first penalty for Roma.

The first sight I made out when the net rippled was dozens of blue-suited ballboys leaping in the air, and a thudding cannon blast of relief thundering down the pitch towards our despairing silence.

Down that far end, so distant you could barely make out which player was which, the red-and-yellow flags were thrashing around in a victory rehearsal. These devout Catholics had convinced themselves God had fated them the European Cup. That He would surely not be that cruel to inflict defeat on them, not now he'd helped them to the final, *their* final, on their own hallowed ground. Not now he had finally allowed them to take the lead over the heathens from the north.

Phil Neal, ever-focused, ever-reliant, stuck his away, before Conti walked up to complete the next formality en route to Roman victory. Then something bizarre started to happen, which only the TV viewers and the penalty-taker could see at the time. Bruce Grobbelaar starting walking round with a big manic grin on his gob. We were a goal to the worse and he was laughing, strolling off his line and pulling the kind of manic faces Rome would not see again until Gazza landed.

Why? What was that about? Only when Conti shot over the bar, and 50,000 Romans gasped and fell to their knees did we get it. The man the Italian press would later call the Monkey Goalkeeper, was playing Italian tricks in their own house. Doing everything, inside or outside the law, to influence the outcome. And it was working.

Souness stepped up. Bang. Liverpool ahead again. Alex Righetti made it neck and neck. Rushie made it 3–2. Over to 'Ciccio' Graziani, the veteran striker, who could see two things as he placed the ball on the spot and faced the goal. Tens of thousands of Romans with their heads buried in their scarfs and Brucie turning the floor show up to full-blast.

In front of that red-and-yellow wall of noise, below the clear Italian sky, alone with just his gloves, Brucie started to dance. Up and down the line. Legs like Shakin' Stevens, arms like Al Jolson. What was going on in his head? What was going on in Graziani's? Answer: fear, confusion, distraction and panic. Cue a wild punt into his own fans and a slump to his knees. Agony. Silence engulfing all but our screeching end of the stadium. Brucie skipping away manically, like Bez without the maracas. Liverpool one penalty away from immortality.

Who will it be? Kenny had been subbed, so had Craig Johnston. Maybe Michael Robinson or Ronnie Whelan. Hansen or Lawrenson. No. No. No. Oh shite. It's Barney Rubble. He's never taken one before, has he? Has he? Are we seeing things? Is it really Alan Kennedy. Has Joe Fagan gone mad . . . yeeeeeee-eeeeeeeeeeeeeeeeeeeeeeeeeeees!

He buried it.

The wine headache was now so blinding I feared I was about to pass out. Throughout 'You'll Never Walk Alone', the trophy presentation and the lap of honour it felt like a Michelangelo descendant had taken time off from Sistine Chapel II and was chiselling his way through my skull. But the pain was made almost bearable by the glorious sight below us, of players jigging with delight, and all around us the empty terraces were littered with discarded red-and-yellow scarves, flags and dreams.

At least it seemed like a glorious sight at the time. Had my head been functioning properly it might have asked where all those angry, bitter Romans had gone. Or worked out the answer:

to choose their weapons and await battle. They were ashamed at not winning on their own ground. They could hear the laughter rocking Milan and Turin. These Made Men felt as though they had been dishonoured in front of the world. And it was Liverpool fans who would have to bear the brunt of their anger. We got whacked.

As we left the stadium loud, ugly voices cut through the Roman night and spoke of 'death to English bastards'. The scooter gangs we'd seen earlier had multiplied a hundredfold and were now circling us, lashing out with knives at any available limb. Others broke up paving stones and lobbed them at us. My personal souvenir was a wooden crate. I didn't see it coming but I felt the gash in my scalp. It matted my hair with blood and left me dazed for a few seconds. The blow was a real old bowel-loosener but not half as terrifying as the look on the copper's face when I staggered towards him and asked for help. He snarled, raised his baton and pushed me back towards the seething mass.

I approached another in riot gear and saw pure hatred in his eyes. They weren't there to protect the innocent but their own. To gain collegiate kudos by battering the head of an English hooligan. Even though few if any of us were acting like hooligans.

Those of us who'd come by train were the fortunate ones. As the violence outside the ground escalated the riot police pushed us on to the waiting buses and sped us off to the station. The odd face that was stuck out of a window was cut as we bounced up and down bellowing *'campioni, campioni'* at our pursuers, but it was nothing compared to the cowardice being unleashed on fans attempting to make their way back to their city-centre hotels. The scarf-faced heroes on Vespas slashed buttocks, others hung from car windows and sun roofs, lobbing bricks, flares and coins. Many waited in mobs around subways and dark roads, attacking at random.

I later heard how a mate had a knife shoved into his guts; how an elderly man who was with him was kicked senseless and left in a gutter. The only assistance either of them received came from Lazio fans who joined in the battle, ostensibly on behalf of Liverpool fans, but mainly to lap up the blood of their detested rivals. As one right-on mate later told me, he didn't know what was worse, being battered by the Roma fans or saved by the self-confessed Lazio Nazis.

The appalled Roman press reported that this was not simply a reaction to the defeat, but that Roma fans had stowed weapons in their cars before the game, rushing to get them at the final whistle. Reporters from the Liverpool radio station Radio City saw the violence first hand and told how Reds fans had been attacked by Roman gangs as they approached the local bus station, and how drivers refused to allow them on board in case they were attacked.

Eventually, a volunteer driver agreed to take Liverpool fans on a bus through the city with police outriders at the front and rear, dropping people off at their hotels. Some fans were so scared they sought refuge in the British embassy.

Radio City's news crew made it on to the bus and interviewed fans who had been stabbed and beaten. But none of these bloody, unprovoked attacks received any news coverage in the UK national media. Not a line. The only paper to mention it was the *Liverpool Echo*, under the headline THE ECSTASY AND THE AGONY.

Back at Rome Central Station we'd lapsed into the Twilight Zone. That period that follows these emotional tornadoes, when the adrenalin rush fades and the body has nothing approaching an equivalent to put in its place. A condition that can only be successfully treated by getting howlingly drunk in a pub with like-minded souls, diving into the darkest recesses of your brain to dig out long-forgotten songs that unite past glories with the present. Instead we were slumped in a carriage with no lights on, thirsty and exhausted, awaiting the long two-day haul back to Lime Street.

Billy made enquiries with a Liverpool steward who said the train was scheduled to leave in two hours and a risk presented itself that had to be taken. Mike wasn't up for it. This wasn't a night for Frank Sinatra impressions down the Via Veneto. The drama and violence had taken its toll and he preferred to rest his head rather than risk it back on the Roman streets. But I had to have a drink, just one drink in a Roman bar on this of all nights. I had to have it for Our Vic. To recall that arm-in-arm walk back up Putney Hill in '77, when we were drunk on glory but with a sobering realization that we were 2,000 miles away from the centre of the universe.

We found a bar in a side street. It was small and smelt of espresso. The barman and his few locals viewed us with suspicion when they saw my Liverpool hat, fearing our presence might herald a full-scale Anglo-Italian war. They still served us two lovely litres of crisp draught Nastro Azurri.

A couple of Vespa kids came in. One had a red silk Roma scarf with the word *Campioni* next to a yellow European Cup. They didn't catch our eyes. We could hear more Vespas buzzing down the road, their buttock-slashing appetites no doubt sated, and decided it made sense to head back to the train.

I raised a glass to Our Vic, Billy smashed his against mine, and we finished them off. I went up to the miserable Roman who was attempting to drown his sorrows, and offered him my hat. He looked confused, unsure if I was taunting him. I pointed at his scarf and made a swapping gesture. He gave me a look that said he was grateful to offload an embarrassing reminder of what never was, and handed it to me. I put it on. He stuffed my hat in his inside coat pocket, well away from view. I wonder why.

The Nastro had cured the headache. I felt good walking back to the train on this warm spring Roman night. There was no fear, just pride and privilege that I was alive for this night when Our Vic wasn't.

Once again Liverpool hadn't disappointed. Once again they had proved they were more than just another football club. More than just the best team in Europe. They were an unstoppable spiritual force.

By winning their fourth European Cup against the champions of Italy on their front lawn they had come closest to living out that Shankly desire to build them up and up, until, like Napoleon, they became invincible, and conquered the bloody world. *Arrivederci Roma.*

Imagine crawling a couple of thousand miles on the back of a geriatric slug, and you'll begin to realize how slow the journey home seemed. France was the worst part. For some reason their national police force had managed to hear what 56 million people back in Britain hadn't – that the streets of Rome had been flooded with hooligans after the European Cup final.

The problem was nobody had bothered to explain what language the hooligans spoke. So naturally they assumed the violence had been down to the English. Which meant we were stuck for hours in sidings, under armed guard, for no other reason than they felt like punishing us. As though they were trying to drain any lingering violent urges from our fatigued loins.

They needn't have bothered. It was like a hospital train coming back from the Front, with its passengers bruised, parched, immobile and pining for home soil. By the time we reached the English Channel we'd spent four days on a battered old train, let out in Rome for a few hours under escort. We felt chained to a British Rail slave ship.

But oh, the sense of liberation when we reached Lime Street at Friday tea-time. The joy of walking into the evening sun and being cheered and applauded by strangers still high on Liverpool's victory. It was the shot of life our systems needed. We felt like triumphant foot soldiers returning home after another successful war. Which wasn't totally off the mark.

Dozens of us headed straight into The Crown opposite the station and finally, two days late, real celebrations could begin. Flags bedecked the walls. Pints flowed. Songs soared. And all around us smiling, welcoming faces, many glad of an excuse to draw out another night of revelry on the back of the city's most successful export.

It felt so good we needed to take it outside. A conga line was formed and we danced into Lime Street singing, '*Campioni, campioni, campioni* Liverpool.' The traffic stopped, the shoppers cheered and buses honked their support. It was a glorious release. The way it should have been in Rome had the authorities afforded their visitors the minimum respect.

Already the stories had spread around the city. Drinkers in The Crown told tales of cowardly ambushes and fathers on life-support machines. Of the shock and humiliation felt by fans who'd arrived home by air and road before us. An anger towards Italians was simmering away and in the minds of the worst affected someone had to pay.

In the end we all did.

12

DANTE'S INFERNO

29 MAY 1985 – BRUSSELS

'Oi lads, you got any spur terk-ets?' burred the fat yokel with a Union Jack knotted around his shoulders and a face like a smacked farmer's arse.

We shook our heads.

Two similar beauts, one wearing a British Bulldog T-shirt, were playing splits with a knife in the hard, dusty ground outside the bar.

'Where are you lads from?' I asked the ticket inquirer.

'Wess Cun-ree.'

'Are you Liverpool fans?'

'Sorrrd of.'

'How do you mean?'

'Well I likes 'em, 'cos they're the best in Europe and they're English, ain't they.'

'But why follow them all the way to Brussels with no ticket?'

''Cos it's an English team in a big game, innit. Good buzz.'

This breakfast-time conversation outside Ostend railway station was the first of many sights and sounds that didn't feel right about 29 May 1985.

The following week I'd be convinced I was looking at that smacked farmer's arse on my telly. On grainy video footage charging across a deserted terrace with dozens of others in Liverpool colours. A film which would be used as prime evidence in a Belgian court during a manslaughter trial.

Six of us had gone to this European Cup final, which in itself was unusual. Me, Mike (Sinatra), Terry (Poirot), Savo (Tutan-khamun), Steve Power (a De La Salle lad who had lived with us in Reading) and Roy (a no-nonsense centre-half from Bootle who'd nutted many a student in his role as lynchpin of the Warwick Scousers' defence). We were all up for a good crack plus the formality of watching Liverpool crowned European champions once again. Well, all of us except Savo, who'd heard there was an excellent dinosaur exhibition at the Belgian Museum of Natural Sciences.

We'd turned up to claim our destiny. A fifth European Cup, which would make us only the second team in the competition's history to keep it for good. Putting us up there with Real Madrid as all-time Invincibles.

We were sure of our superiority in every sense. In history, ability, character, spirit and support. We were going to beat the Aye-ties on and off the pitch. This time it wouldn't be like Rome. There would be no scarfed hitmen racing away on scooters as you tried to stem a bleeding buttock. This time they were a long way from home and outnumbered, just as we'd been the year before. This time if they started anything they'd better be sure they could finish it.

The journey over was more like The Love Boat than The Train To Hell. Coach to the Channel, ferry to Ostend, then driven a few miles to what had been billed as a small Olympic-style village but in truth felt like a massive YMCA. It didn't bother us. Spirits were high. Within ten minutes of rooms being allocated there was a match, which started as fifteen-a-side and grew to fifty-a-side, taking place on the piece of greenery at the centre of the complex. An hour later this was an Olympic village minus grass.

The first disturbing sights came that night in the bars of Ostend. Maybe it was to do with too many lads struggling to hold their Stella Artois, too many outsiders along for the ride, or too many young teenagers who'd managed to make the short trip to Belgium, had no money left and were simply on a robbing spree. Whatever it was, there was a nasty edge in the air. Trouble seemed a smashed glass or a misconstrued look away. It all felt slightly out of control.

The first weird sound was the unconfirmed report that the Juventus game was to be Joe Fagan's last, with Kenny Dalglish becoming the new manager. Laughter was followed by derision until a bar-room TV beamed up pictures of Uncle Joe next to Kenny and it didn't take an expert in Flemish to work out that this was more than a rumour started by the fella standing next to you who'd been told by his brother-in-law who's got a mate at Fords whose auntie is a cleaner at Anfield.

It still seemed too bizarre to be true. Fagan, who looked like one of your grandad's Capstan-wheezing, mild-supping mates, might well be calling it a day though ill-health, but Kenny had just turned thirty-four, and was still our best player. A footballing genius undoubtedly, but where did making him manager come from? And why let the news out the night before a European Cup final?

It wasn't the Liverpool Way, so most of us refused to believe the rumours, preferring to concentrate on the match in hand. It wouldn't be the first time in Brussels we'd think that way. Twenty-four hours later we were engrossing ourselves in a tense game, screaming abuse at a referee who had just awarded a clear non-penalty for Juventus, unaware that fans who turned up for the same game on the terraces alongside us were not going home.

It is a sobering experience finding out someone has died from a heart attack watching the same football match as you. When thirty-nine have died, with 600 injured, and they've been killed by your fellow supporters it leaves you feeling more sick and more dazed than an unexpected blow to the solar plexus from a professional kick-boxer.

But maybe we should have seen the blow coming. By 1985 Britain had become a nasty, violent country which was ill at ease with itself. Two million manufacturing jobs had disappeared since Thatcher took power in 1979 and there were three million people on the dole. For the first time in history Britain was importing more than it exported. We weren't being encouraged to make things any more, just to be on the make. As unemployment and crime soared, the problems highlighted by the 1981 riots refused to go away. Our inner cities were poisoned with poverty, heroin and anger, Northern Ireland still burned, the bloody miners' strike dragged on and jingoistic hooliganism was given a shot in the arm by Falklands War. Glory on some foreign penguin-dung heap being cynically exploited to distract attention away from a country whose fabric was being ripped apart.

It was every man for himself in Thatcher's Britain. The problem being, some men were better equipped to take advantage. Those who were already rich, those who wanted to get rich quick, those who lived in prosperous Tory areas, those willing to ditch the notion of society and look out for themselves. Those whom Thatcherites viewed as One of Us.

Liverpool and most of its citizens did not belong to that club. The decline of a port which faced the way of the old routes of empire, not the new ones to Europe, the decimation of old industries, the encouragement of bosses to relocate their factories not in places that suited the country, but their shareholders, and the almost spiteful refusal of a government to support jobs in an area that was politically hostile – all this devastated the city.

By 1985 unemployment in Liverpool stood at 25 per cent and it was much higher in the poorer pockets. In the first five years of that decade it lost 50,000 manufacturing jobs. That's 10,000 a year.

Its economy, like the port, was shrinking and inward investment stagnated. The population fell, men were told at forty they would never work again, and kids left school with little hope of a career unless they got out of town. Crime escalated, council coffers were hammered and social problems became chronic. It was reckless neglect by a government using Liverpool's free-fall as a lesson to others about what happens when councils become increasingly bolshie and trade unions refuse to dance to their employers' tune.

Memos leaked from Tory cabinet minutes showed that the

city, like the unions and the IRA, had become an enemy within. An enemy that was there to be fought in a battle for ideological supremacy.

Fortunately (or unfortunately, depending where you stood) Liverpool was more than happy to take them on. Politically the national swing to the right pushed Scousers to the opposite pole. The city council was taken over by a broad-left alliance with a large Militant Tendency contingent in control.

It took a stand against budget cuts, and in the first fiscal year, due to the Tories' fighting on too many fronts, the government caved in, and Liverpool kept its funding. But the triumphalist celebration of this victory, played out in the media almost as a personal victory for the council's dapper, megamouth, deputy leader Derek 'Degsy' Hatton over Thatcher, meant it would be a short-lived one. She decided Liverpool would never win again on her watch.

The victory galvanized tens of thousands of Scousers who had nothing to lose. Such was the simplicity of Militant's message: 'no cuts in jobs or services and build more houses'. Such was the loathing for 'that bitch' and what she was doing to them. Such was their pride that Liverpool, of all British cities, had possessed the balls to win a game of brinkmanship. So easily did the confrontation sit with a psyche based on casualization of the docks which instilled a belief that you can't lose what you haven't got, that there was no shortage of recruits willing to march behind the council's Militant flag.

I was one of them. My dad's brother Billy had moved to the States allowing me to look after his two-up, two-down in Wavertree as a rent-free caretaker. I was still trying (unsuccessfully) to write scripts while teaching English Literature at night school in Sylvester Street off Scotland Road, two nights a week, for the princely sum of £60. I was skint but I was having a ball. As Alan Bleasdale put it, the city was sinking like the *Titanic* but everyone was dancing on the deck.

There was a manic spirit about the place. Liverpool may have been perceived by a London-centric media as dying on its arse, but with both football teams in the ascendancy, its groups still dominating the charts, its writers churning out the drama that filled the telly schedules, and its leaders standing up to a vicious dictator, Scousers felt invincible, superior and amazed that the rest of the country wasn't with them.

Jealous, we called them. Lazy, self-pitying, whining, thieving bastards, they called us, tiring of a TV diet of *Bread*, Bleasdale, *Brookside* and Degsy. But we didn't care. I've never enjoyed as many table-dancing lock-ins, which lasted until tea-time or dawn, depending on when the door had been closed, as I did during the mid-eighties. In all-day drinking terms, the city was twenty years ahead of its time.

The best description of that era, actually the best-ever description of Scousers, was one spoken by Liverpool's Danish-born midfielder Jan Molby, when asked how he'd settled into the local culture so easily: 'Well, erm,' he said, in an accent thicker than Garston mud, 'when it's Tuesday night and you're out having a bevvy, no one's thinking about Wednesday morning.'

An air of joyful anarchy had descended, and nowhere was it more in evidence than following Liverpool abroad where lads, schooled over many seasons in the art of taking the piss out of naive, unsuspecting Europeans, had survival off to a fine art. The average scally, bored with life on the dole back home, lived for these adrenalin-pumping awaydays where a forged Transalpino ticket would get you to most destinations, ferries could be fleeced, bars and restaurants mugged, and boutiques relieved of their top designer gear.

I'd first noticed this air of swaggering superiority in Paris before the 1981 final against Real Madrid. Jewellers' windows were going in, Lacoste shops cleaned out, barmen doing Benny Hill chases after grinning lads armed with wine bottles, Spaniards being rolled for their tickets and wallets. Paris wasn't pretty that day, but it was Brigitte Bardot in her prime compared to Brussels four years later.

It was hot and sunny for a start, which never bodes well with Englishmen in cities where the lager is extra strong. Shirts were off, Stella was flowing and bottles were flying. It didn't feel good. In the late morning before the drink and the memories of last year's attacks in Rome had kicked in, the atmosphere between Liverpool and Juve fans in the Grand Place had been good. There was the usual banter, swapping of scarves, taking of photos with arms around each other, which happens at all our games abroad as we try to show how different we are from most other England fans. A show that says we hate those pricks who support nonentities back home, and whose only chance to gain a footballing identity is to follow In-ger-lund. It's a show of solidarity designed to send out a message. We're not England. We're not hooligans. We've got history and respect, knowledge and class.

The signs had been creeping in, though, that this might not be entirely the case. Especially at the FA Cup semi-final with Manchester United at Goodison a month before, when there was football hooliganism of the lowest order. Outside the ground running battles kept the police busy. Inside, flares, coins and golf balls embedded with six–inch nails, were pitched over the fences by rival supporters. It was a nauseous, disturbing day.

We drew that game, then got beat in the replay at Maine Road. Football-wise it summed up a woeful season which had no doubt made up Joe Fagan's mind to call it a day. With Graeme Souness transferred to Sampdoria and Ian Rush missing the first ten games through injury, we struggled badly. When Everton won 1–0 at Anfield on 20 October the European champions were 18th in the League. We recovered to finish runners-up but lay 13 points behind Everton.

The team headed to Belgium knowing if they won the European Cup they kept it, and if they lost, it would be the first time in a decade that a Liverpool side had ended a season trophyless. As the day wore on, the initial friendliness towards the Italians turned to suspicion then animosity. There were no running battles, just little confrontations kicking off. Scarf-robbing, square-ups, stand-offs, chases, verbals. But the longer the sun beat down, and the more lager that was being necked, the uglier central Brussels became.

Chairs were flying, bars were getting cleaned out, women on their way home from work had obscenities thrown at them, windows were going through, drunks were crawling on their hands and knees through fast-food restaurants. Locals tried to go about their day, shaking their heads at scenes which to Englishmen could be labelled Hogarthian. To foreigners who don't understand our drink-until-you're-legless culture, it must have looked like Hades at throwing-out time on a Saturday night.

I don't remember singing that day. I do remember wincing a lot, hearing older fans having a go at teenagers who were veering out of control, looking askance at a large group, many with Scouse accents, singing, 'There ain't no black in the Union Jack send the bastards back,' and Roy and Terry saying, 'Let's get out of here.' The police response was to close the restaurants in the square, round up the troublemakers and ship them off to the Heysel Stadium, where they were dumped. In the light of later events, how wise would that prove to be?

Built in 1930, Heysel was an ancient, dilapidated tip, with large parts of it, including the outside walls, crumbling. The bulldozers were so close to its door, no money had been invested for years in modernizing its facilities or upgrading its safety. No wonder Liverpool chief executive Peter Robinson urged UEFA to use another venue, on the grounds that this one was totally unsuitable for such a big game between Europe's two top sides.

In the weeks before the final he sent telexes to UEFA, the Football Association, the Belgian Football Association and the Belgian government, urging them to think again. Obviously he was ignored. Just as the previous year, when complaints were raised about the fairness of playing a European Cup final in one of the finalists' grounds.

Everyone who was present that night was incapable of believing why UEFA allocated this stadium for a European Cup final. This was veteran journalist Brian Glanville's take:

That Heysel was ever chosen for the game was a shocking commentary on the folly of UEFA and the idleness of its team that was meant to inspect the stadium. The word was that the day they came, it was very cold, and that they scarcely bothered to emerge from the warmth to see what should have been obvious to them – that this stadium was not fit to stage a game of such magnitude.

The result was that for the first time in my life I turned up at a ground to watch a game of professional football and there was no one to take my ticket. The only other time would come four years later at Hillsborough. Spot the link.

I'd become separated from the others during the afternoon and arrived at the stadium half an hour before the kick-off was due to take place. The first indication that something had gone badly wrong was a weeping teenager in Liverpool colours running past me, in a world of his own, yelling, 'What have we done? What have we done?'

Having seen so many distressing sights that day I put it down to too much Stella. Then I reached the ground, and laughed in disbelief at what I saw. Flimsy, eight-foot high breezeblock walls, the type you used to see around council playing fields, had been kicked down, so that a twenty-foot gap had opened next to the turnstiles. Actually the turnstiles may well have been kicked down too, because I couldn't see any. Just a man sitting behind the kind of table nerds pile garbage on at car boot sales.

Fans just walked over what was left of the wall, ticket in hand ready for inspection, with nobody to inspect. The few bored police who were around looked on, unconcerned. Well, they'd got the rabble out of the city centre, hadn't they. So job done.

There were three standing sections behind each goal, with grandstands running along the side of the pitch. Our tickets were in block X to the left-hand side of the goal. Block Y behind the goal was also for Liverpool fans, and to the right of that was Block Z, supposedly reserved for neutral Belgian fans. This was another catastrophic mistake, which Peter Robinson and his Juventus counterpart had lobbied UEFA to put right. They knew that due to a huge Italian expat population in Brussels, virtually all of those tickets would end up in Italian hands, via touts and travel agencies. They did. Effectively, with hooliganism at its height, and bad blood still coursing through Liverpudlian veins after last May's ambushes in Rome, UEFA managed to have no effective segregation in a ground that was not worthy of the most basic safety certificate.

What made the tinderbox situation infinitely worse, and showed how criminally out of their depth the Belgian authorities were, was the barrier they erected to separate Blocks Y and Z – a run of thin chicken wire, protected by five police officers. That and a no-man's-land behind the goal was all that stood between containment and war. If UEFA had been asked to set up a scenario which gave the yob full opportunity to exploit his own inadequacies, they could not have done a better job than they did at Heysel.

The ticketless who had walked in, the scallies who were there for the laugh, the fans out for revenge after Rome, non-Liverpudlians who wanted a bit of Gotcha!-style wop-thumping, and the plain drunk-and-disorderly made their way to the chicken wire. Thanks to the crumbling ground there was even a ready-made supply of concrete ammunition to be lobbed at the enemy. And how delighted were they to find Italian yobs on the other side of that non-divide, out to show the Brits that the Ultras feared no one?

I don't know who started the missile-throwing. Neutral reports say both sides were at it, just as they were at Goodison the previous month. But an hour before kick-off it had escalated into a pitched battle, with both sets of supporters expecting the riot police to march in and calm things down. But the police presence was lamentable, and once a few Liverpool fans realized how easy it was to rip down the chicken wire and advance into no-man's-land, dozens more followed. The Italians retreated in a panic which turned into a stampede to escape the infamous English hooligans. Caged in at the front to stop them invading the pitch, they cowered against a wall at the far end of the terrace, with brickwork of the same quality and state of repair as the exterior walls.

The wall collapsed, and so too did the Italians. Like a pack of cards. In five mad minutes thirty-nine innocent lives had been taken and the world no longer associated the word Liverpool with music and football, but hooliganism and cowardly slaughter.

By the time I found the lads at the back of X terrace, Block Z was deserted save for bags, shoes, coats and litter. They'd only been in the ground ten minutes, and like me, were unaware of the scale of the tragedy that had unfolded a few hundred yards away. Indeed nobody around us knew of the deaths. The talk was of a missile-throwing bust-up which turned into the kind of charging you used to see every week at the back of the Anfield Road. To be honest we didn't think anything of it.

Of far more concern was why the Italians had come streaming at us from the opposite end of the ground looking for trouble. One of them was clearly seen on the running track brandishing a gun. They looked insane, fighting the police with rocks and bottles. The situation had grown so serious that the police horses were called in to hold them back. That must have been what the Italian voice on the stadium loudspeaker was telling them. To calm down. That must have been why the kick-off was put back. Animals, we thought, and started yelling abuse at them.

That's how insane it was that night. We believed the Juve fans were trying to spark a riot, while we were the good guys. Throughout the now meaningless match, which should never have gone ahead, nobody around us knew the extent of the tragedy. There was the odd rumour filtering through about deaths, but nobody confirmed it. Nothing was said on the stadium loudspeaker, and in front of us a game of football was going ahead. How could anything serious have happened?

It was why, when the referee awarded Juve a penalty after Boniek was pulled down a yard outside the box, we erupted with fury. And when we were denied a clear-cut one which would have equalized the one Michel Platini put away, it seemed the world was against us. Little did we know just how much of an under-statement that was. But as we trundled out of the ground still moaning about the atrocious refereeing decisions that cost us a fifth European Cup, it started to sink in.

Radio and TV cameras were swarming all over us. Riot police were herding us on to coaches, any coaches, just to get us away, liberally using their batons to quell resistance. In the distance behind a line of police horses we could hear screaming and yelling in Italian. And then the blow that took our knees away.

We found our coach, which was as silent as a funeral. On the radio a BBC voice spoke of Liverpool hooligans killing dozens of Italians. As the coach drove back to Ostend, Belgium had closed. The streets were deserted. When any bystanders saw the colours on our coach they looked away. Some spat on the pavement. Nobody wanted to share the same air as the Liverpool killers. We went straight back to our rooms, having been told the police could not guarantee our safety. Not that any of us had the appetite to socialize. We sat on our beds, opened a bottle of duty-free whisky and got pissed in an attempt to numb the pain.

As we ran back through all those ugly images of the day, and all the ugly images that had escalated over the years, the consen-sus was that it had all been inevitable. That maybe it was all over. We would be kicked out of Europe for a long, long time. We would never recover from it. But when you murder other fans at a match simply for having the audacity to be standing next to you with a different coloured scarf on, then maybe we don't deserve to recover. Maybe it was time to give up football as a bad job, and find something else to love.

As we drove back to Liverpool the next day the shame grew deeper. Once again, on the roads, in the ferry terminal, on the boat, even on the way up through England, onlookers avoided eye-contact. We were all cold-blooded slayers.

It was the same on every front page in the world, ably assisted by our own Prime Minister who apologized to the Italian nation at a press conference in Mexico City, and attempted to defend Britain by telling the world's journalists to keep it in perspective. We were talking about Liverpool here, 'a city possessed with a particularly violent nature'. Thanks, bitch.

In those dark days, when we felt like lepers, no one was in the mood to point out that we had played in Europe every season for the past twenty years, and although our behaviour had not been spotless, the fans were generally acknowledged as a credit to the club. No one wanted to remind the world that 20,000 Scousers had just visited Rotterdam to see Everton lift the European Cup-Winners' Cup, with a police spokesman saying, 'The behaviour of the Everton fans has been marvellous. We have no complaints at all. They can come back any time.' Nobody had the will to fight back because we were so paralysed by shame. Shame about the dead, and shame about our reputation being buried in that mad rush across the Heysel no-man's-land.

We were in a state of shock and self-loathing, which neatly allowed the authorities to place all responsibility for the deaths on our shoulders. Which is exactly what happened.

On 30 May official UEFA observer Gunter Schneider said, 'Only the Liverpool fans were responsible. Of that there is no doubt.' Twenty-two years later, after booking another unsuitable stadium in Athens, they would use exactly the same words.

There was no official inquiry into the causes of the disaster, and after three years of legal proceedings not one guilty man at the top was forced to spend a second in jail. UEFA General Secretary Hans Bangerter was handed a three month suspended sentence and fined 30,000 Belgian francs (£500). The President of the Belgian FA, Albert Roosens, was given a six month suspended sentence, and Captain Johan Mahieu of Brussels Police three months suspended, and fined the insulting sum of 500 Belgian francs (£8.50).

English football in general, and Liverpool in particular, had to take the rap. Which was when the fightback began. We knew there were many complex factors at work that day, and it was wrong and dangerous to lay all the blame on a handful of pissed-up yobs. The club's chairman John Smith claimed he had proof that the BNP were behind the riot, producing a leaflet he said had been handed out in Brussels, and scores of fans backed him up, with thousands of Kopites agreeing there had to be some explanation as to how we turned into monsters overnight.

So in the months and years that followed, people like me threw the BNP into the mix, along with the ground, the police, the ticketing, the Roman ambushes in '84, the missile-throwing Juve yobs in Block Z, strong Belgian lager, unemployment which had forced disillusioned youth to seek kicks abroad, and the sheer probability that Liverpool were more likely to have outside hooligans attach themselves to their support in the eighties, because we were the team reaching all of the finals.

I would defend myself and fellow Liverpudlians because I needed to for my own sanity. I refused to be ashamed of what I was, or to betray twenty years of following this team around Europe.

But when ninety-six Liverpool fans died in another sub-standard ground with equally lamentable policing four years later, it changed everything. After Hillsborough, lies were told, blame deflected, guilty men concealed and a cover-up carried out. The people who suffered most were the families of the dead, because all the deception and the buck-passing stopped them being given the truth. Every time a culpable party tried to squirm out of taking responsibility, the families were dragged back to the beginning of their nightmare. They could never move on.

Suddenly, if you were to blame it seemed like an insult to the deceased not to hold your hands up and say 'guilty', and let the cowards in denial shuffle back under their rocks. It was to say that, ultimately, those Italians died at Heysel not because of poor policing or a derelict stadium, but because English hooliganism had been allowed to spiral out of control, and thugs with Liver Birds on their chests ran at a cowering crowd with no thought for their safety.

Of the thirty-nine who died, thirty-two were Juventus fans, four were Belgians, two French and an Irishman. I'd like to say I know as many of their names as I do the names of the ninety-six, but the only one I can remember is the Irishman, Patrick Radcliffe. Maybe it's time Liverpool honoured them as much as we honour those who fell in Sheffield. How right and fitting would it be if the new Anfield stadium saw the thirty-nine chiselled up along-side the ninety-six at the Eternal Flame? How right would it be to tell our kids to read these names and ages, and feel as much pity for them as we do for our own?

Rocco Acerra (29), Bruno Balli (50), Alfons Bos, Giancarlo Bruschera (21), Andrea Casula (11), Giovanni Casula (44), Nino Cerrullo (24), Willy Chielens, Giuseppina Conti (17), Dirk Dae-necky, Dionisio Fabbro (51), Jacques François, Eugenio Gagliano (35), Francesco Galli (25), Giancarlo Gonnelli (20), Alberto Guar-ini (21), Giovacchino Landini (50), Roberto Lorentini (31), Barbara Lusci (58), Franco Martelli (46), Loris Messore (28), Gianni Mastro-laco (20), Sergio Bastino Mazzino (38), Luciano Rocco Papaluca (38), Luigi Pidone (31), Bento Pistolato (50), Patrick Radcliffe, Domenico Ragazzi (44), Antonio Ragnanese (29), Claude Robert, Mario Ronchi (43), Domenico Russo (28), Tarcisio Salvi (49), Gianfranco Sarto (47), Amedeo Giuseppe Spalaore (55), Mario Spanu (41), Tarcisio Venturin (23), Jean Michel Walla, Claudio Zavaroni (28).

Rest in peace.

13

SPILT BEANS

10 MAY 1986 – WEMBLEY

It was a long, horrible summer of allegations and counter-allegations, shame and fury, guilt and denial, sorrow and anger. We all had different ways of dealing with it. Some, like Alan Bleasdale, made their inner turmoil public, announcing they would never go to a Liverpool match again, because if this was what football had been reduced to, then what was the point? How could you look your children in the eye and tell them this was a sport worthy of investing a lifetime's belief and passion when it had sunk to such depths?

Some tried humour. I lost count of the times people sidled up and said, 'I see the Pope's broke his silence and spoke out over Heysel. Reckons it was never a penalty.' And you laughed. Not knowing why. It just seemed normal, even though anyone cracking a similar joke about Hillsborough four years later would have taken the big white taxi ride to Accident and Emergency.

Most of us were defiant, and set about convincing the world (or was it ourselves?) that the blame for Heysel lay at the door of outside influences. Our logic was that Liverpudlians mocked that kind of rampaging boot-boy hooliganism. Our contempt for it put us above all those England fans, those Cockney 'firms', those Yorkshire woollybacks, who went in search of rumbles to give themselves and their club an infamous status.

Liverpool scallies robbed shops, rolled strangers, bunked on trains and boats and into grounds. It's what I called the Chester Zoo mentality. When you went on a school trip everyone was there for the taking as soon as the coach left the boundaries of Liverpool. They were slower than us, so rob them soft. It was all part of the day out. But cause a riot abroad? What would be gained, other than the police finding the Sergio Tacchini tracksuits and Adidas Trimm Trabs you'd nicked from boutiques when they raided your hotel room?

The NF theory was thus a popular one which garnered support. Witnesses came forward to say they'd seen the fascists handing out their propaganda and signing up naive kids on the Channel ferries. We all hoped they would appear at an Isle of Dogs press conference with balaclavas on and huge swastika flags behind them and claim responsibility, so we could finally wake up from the nightmare. But they never did, because they were not the major culprits. To call them so would have been to flatter the unspeakable. What an indictment it would have been on Liverpool fans, who had always given this Nazi plankton short shrift, if suddenly enough of us had been taken in by them to murder thirty-nine people.

And that's what it always came back to. We murdered thirty-nine people. Like it or not, we all had blood on our hands. What happened at Heysel (and the way it was being explained around the world) was totally alien and deeply hurtful to those of us who'd been following the club since the sixties. But what hurt most was our inability to deny it.

The *Daily Mirror* called the tragedy 'The day football died'. The Italian papers spoke of 'English murderers', 'Assassins' and 'Red Animals'. The British embassy in Rome was attacked.

The rest of the world, distanced from the eye of the raging storm, dissected our culture. And it didn't look pretty. Britain's male working-class was perceived as a bleak, hard-drinking lumpen mass spawned by the factories of the industrial revolution and aggressive colonialism, made even more brutal by Thatcher's jingoistic, right-wing government, and a tabloid culture which screamed for joy when young foreigners were killed for daring to evict us from their land.

White British youths were portrayed as savages and Liverpudlians the most savage of the savage. Across Britain people were starting to tire of the Scouse stereotype. The right had always had it in for Liverpool but now it was coming from supposed friends on the left too. When the city council threatened to send out redundancy notices to its workers in an attempt to defy setting a budget, Labour leader Neil Kinnock grabbed his finest, sorry, his only, political moment and lambasted the 'grotesque' situation that existed in Liverpool.

The *Sunday Times* packed esteemed writer Ian Jack off to Lime Street to compare the two cities involved in Heysel. It was a one-dimensional slap in the face. Turin positively glowed whereas Liverpudlians were pigs in sties, their home town a pitiful, modern-day version of Old Bedlam. 'Liverpool loves to sentimentalise itself into comic likeability, though this summer it has been hard for others to gratify the wishes of an errant child,' was one of his kinder observations.

Back in 1985 nobody in the national media wanted to listen to Scousers playing victims. To many, Liverpool was becoming a loud, whining argument that grated; and the floodgates now opened for all those who had a grudge against the place. It would build up into a tidal wave over the next decade, spawning Liverpudlian chippiness and paranoia. The only refuge for Liverpool fans was the phone-ins on Radio Merseyside and the letters pages of the *Echo*. They became confessionals for penitents. Here, among our own, we could defend and attack, admit and deny, and search for our own personal truth.

One letter in the *Echo* spoke to me like no other. It was from a teenager who'd been part of the stampeding mob, who saw what was happening, and broke down in tears on the terrace when he realized what he'd been part of. He explained how he'd had too much to drink, got carried away with the excitement, felt the adrenalin-rush when the chicken-wire fence came down, and ran like a crazed warrior at the enemy. His shame and torture raged across the page. It read like someone explaining their first bad acid trip.

I couldn't help thinking if it was that lad who'd passed me outside the ground on my way in. I also couldn't help thinking that if I'd been ten years younger, unemployed with nothing back home, unable to hold my drink, keen to show the leaders I was a true foot soldier, that maybe I'd have run too. The thought of the weeping lad on the terraces wouldn't go away. Yet in the weeks that followed, as I sat down alone, digesting newsprint and video footage, there were many images of Italians that wouldn't go away either.

The brick dust on all those faces which made them look like ghosts. Those small objects that were strewn across the empty terrace, which from my perspective on the day seemed like unbrushed litter, but turned out to be fine Italian leather shoes and bags. The panic as families, unaccustomed to terrace surges, tried to make it to the small gate that led on to the pitch that was locked to cage them in, due to the assumption that all football fans were beasts. The petrified men scaling the wall. The mustachioed Italian fat guy, like Tony the pizza man, helplessly sprawled amid his dying friends in the rubble, his hand held aloft in a frozen gesture of despair. The big mama lying there numb with shock, holding a flag that had *'Grazie Juve'* written on it.

Thank you Juve. Thank you for bringing me to this hell.

But it was the image of those young Liverpool fans rampaging across no-man's-land, a sight I had never seen before, that haunted me. Mainly because I was impotent to explain it.

I reread Shankly's biography and was drawn to the paragraph that told of his youth: 'There were films about Al Capone, true stories about violence, but I don't believe these films make people want to go out and kill people. You are only a rogue if you are born a rogue – nobody makes you one. You might be led astray sometimes to do something stupid, but in the end it's up to you.'

I trawled back in time to try and work out how we'd mutated into this. Right back to my first glimpse of a Liverpool fan in Bolton on that freezing day in February 1965. Another roofless midden just like Heysel, but how different were those fans. Jovial, genteel-mannered men, with their chants of Liv-er-pool clap-clap-clap, Liv-er-pool, clap, clap, clap.

I went further back to the vague image on my nana's black-and-white telly of men in suits and ties and Liverpool scarfs, marching through some foreign customs singing a popular advert of the time: 'HP baked beans, they're the beans for me, HP baked beans they're the beans for me, what's the treat we all love best . . . HP baked beans,' with the bemused officials killing themselves laughing.

What was that? When was that?

I checked it out. It was 16 December 1964. Liverpool's second-ever away trip in Europe, after beating KR Reykjavik in the first round of the European Cup. It was Brussels airport. They were on their way to the club's first big test outside Britain. Against the then mighty Anderlecht. At the Heysel Stadium. I hadn't been aware that we'd played there before. As I was digesting the link, UEFA announced that all English club sides would be banned indefinitely from European competitions. Those close to the decision said that if this ban were lifted (and it would be a long time before it was) Liverpool would face a further spell in exile. It was a UEFA version of being detained at Her Majesty's Pleasure.

So Heysel had staged our first big game abroad and our last for the foreseeable future. A route to my own personal catharsis offered itself up. I needed to write a play, which would undoubtedly be knocked back like every other script I'd written, but one that might help me sort out my head.

I called it *Spilt Beans* with the action taking place outside the ground, between the end of the rioting and the start of the final. The main character was a thirty-six-year-old called Harry Rimmer who, as a fifteen-year-old, had swaggered through Brussels customs en route to Heysel in 1964, brimming with optimism about a team and a city on the up.

Harry returns to Heysel in 1985 with his fifteen-year-old nephew Gary, loses his ticket, buys a spare in Block Z, and witnesses first-hand the carnage among the Italians. Dazed and stunned, he reels from the ground and sits outside trying to make sense of what's gone on these past two decades.

It's there he meets up again with Gary, who mirrors the story told by the kid on the *Echo* letters page, and a journalist who is there doing a piece on hooliganism. There then follows some fierce soul-searching as Harry ponders whether to go back in and watch his beloved Reds. Inevitably he does.

It took me a few weeks to write and I sent it off to the Liverpool Playhouse, expecting a refusal slip by return of post. I wasn't too bothered either way. It had helped me rationalize the nightmare and move on, and we all had to move on. Meanwhile the chance of a job came up as a press officer at the Greater London Council (Ken Livingstone's Red Republic) and I grabbed it. I'd never seen myself as a press officer or a council worker, but my twenty-eighth birthday was fast approaching. My coronation as a leading playwright was as far away as when my eighth birthday had approached, and they were offering three times more than the £60 a week I was getting for conning night-school students I knew about Othello's inner motivation.

Besides, it was a chance to fight Thatcher in her own manor. I was only offered the job because she had decided the socialist-run GLC would be abolished the following April, so all career-minded PRs had jumped ship. Ken Livingstone had decreed the council would not recognize abolition until it happened, therefore all staffing levels had to be maintained until the death. It meant the press office would hire anyone who'd seen the inside of a newsroom for more than a day and been on a march against Maggie.

What a fabulous job it was. Getting paid to confirm to reporters from right-wing papers that, yes, we were indeed funding a survey into the difficulties faced by lesbians using London Transport. And what the fuck are you going to do about it? It felt good being back in London with a few bob in my pocket too. I stayed with my old mate Billy (Spiderman) who was teaching down there, in his flat in Harlesden, and we got around the London grounds watching Liverpool and Everton just as we'd done during our time at Warwick. Merseyside may have been on its knees but football-wise it was still putting every other town in the shade.

The previous season Howard Kendall's side had won the League, the Cup-Winners' Cup and were only deprived of the FA Cup by a Norman Whiteside wonder-goal. Had Liverpool won at Heysel, we could easily have been looking at the first European Cup final between two sides from the same city. Instead we got a season-long battle between the pair for the domestic honours, which at the death could have seen the League and Cup Double end up at either Anfield or Goodison.

Having Kenny Dalglish as manager only added to the post-Heysel feeling of surreality. We weren't playing in Europe for the first time since I'd supported them, we were considered the worst hooligans on earth instead of the best-behaved supporters in the land, and match-day orders were no longer being barked by a wrinkled old man in a cheap mac, but from our number 7 out on the pitch.

Not surprisingly, Kenny had been refused a summer of frenzied transfer activity, as the bean-counters grappled with the consequences of the Heysel ban. He signed nobody. Then in September he paid £350,000 to Aston Villa for Steve McMahon, and finally we had someone who could begin to fill Graeme Souness's number 11 shirt.

It was us and Everton vying for the top place all season, and me and Billy were at each other's throats. With new-boy Gary Lineker banging them in, Billy's smug confidence was bordering on the kickable. And after a woeful, winless February, which plumbed the depths as I stood next to Billy on the Kop watching spawny goals from Kevin Ratcliffe and Lineker beat us 2–0, it appeared there was method in his smugness.

Then we went on one of those fabulous, steamrolling surges to the end of the season, winning eleven out of twelve matches. The one we drew was one of the easiest, away at Sheffield Wednesday. I don't remember much about the dull, goalless game, except this. I stood behind the goal in the Leppings Lane End, and I had never felt more susceptible, more aware of an unknown danger posed by the swaying crowd, since I was a kid on the Kop. But I was no kid. I was almost thirty, 13 stone and 5ft 11in. Yet so flat was the gradient of the terrace, I struggled to have a decent view, and went under a few times as the crowd surged towards a Liverpool attack. For the only time I could remember as an adult watching football, simply standing there triggered a mild, inexplicable panic. Three years later I realized it was a premonition.

The destiny of that season's League title, and more importantly a huge personal wager between myself and Billy, came down to Wednesday 30 April. Billy went to Oxford, I went to Leicester. Both of us needed a win or we'd go into the final game needing the other to drop points.

In theory Everton were still clear favourites to lift the title. In practice it was the night their smugness died. One of those lovely, old-fashioned nail-biters, ending in mass hugs, which owes little to what's going on in front of you and much to events from elsewhere.

Ronnie Whelan and Ian Rush ensured we were 2–0 up at Leicester and coasting after 28 minutes, so it was sing-song time. With half-an-hour to go, it was crane your neck to hear that fat fella's radio four seats behind you, to see if Everton could come from one goal behind. They didn't. And we danced out of our old bogey ground, convinced the title was ours.

Three days later it was. But there was a dilemma for me and Terry (Poirot). Did we go down to Chelsea to see them take the point that would win it, or did we go, as planned, to Glasgow for the following day's Kenny Dalglish testimonial? It was a tough one which hinged on where we wanted to be celebrating our sixteenth title. (At the time Arsenal had won 8, Everton 8, Man United 7.) In London, in Glasgow or in transit between the two cities. Sod it. It'd make a change to celebrate it in Dalglish's home city, and what an inspired decision it was. Down at Stamford Bridge Kenny scored the goal that won the game and the title, and that night we were hailing the great man not merely in his home city, but in his own pub, Dalglish's Bar, in Glasgow's East End. On the night Celtic were crowned Scottish champions for the first time in four years.

At one point I looked at the table and there were eight large Scotches lined up. Nobody in the green half of Glasgow was allowing anyone to stay sober that night. Especially if they were a devotee of King Kenny. By the end of the night, as the bouncers finally agreed to turn a blind eye and let me pinch the sign above the door which said, 'Kenneth Mathieson Dalglish is licensed to sell beers, wines and spirits,' we were all in agreement that Kenny wasn't just the best man to have ever played for Celtic or Liverpool, he was the best player ever to be born in Britain. (We were with Celtic fans so George Best was Irish.)

I'd love to tell you something about next day's testimonial at Hampden, but unfortunately (or rather, understandably) I can't remember much, apart from me and Terry standing with twenty new mates, singing a song we'd just taught them called 'Just Like Kenny' (to the tune of 'Just Like Eddie') which celebrated him becoming the first player to score 100 League goals in Scotland and England:

'Now players may come, and players may go but they're all two-a-penny, a ton in the north, a ton in the south, Just Like Kenny. Nah – na, na, na, na, na – na, na, na, na, na, na – DALGLISH.'

Ah, to be young and in love.

The Celtic boys were distracted throughout the game. They just wanted to go into city-centre pubs and rub their title into Rangers' noses. And who were we to argue, even if we'd been capable? So, on the off chance that a coach-load of Evertonians had broken down in Glasgow, we offered to rub our title into blue noses too. Actually we were so drunk we couldn't see anything happening on the pitch, and didn't really care what was happening once Kenny had withdrawn to save himself for next Saturday's FA Cup final against Everton.

It was supposed to be the day Everton gained revenge on many fronts. For losing the first-ever Merseyside Cup final in 1984 (the Milk Cup); for knocking them out of the FA Cup semi-finals of 1971 and 1977; for stopping them entering that season's European Cup by rioting at Heysel and for stealing the title off them the week before. This time, we heard, they were fated to put the record straight.

Nine of us stayed in Billy's Harlesden flat, five red, four blue. These were still the days when you could go to a derby together, have a drink before and afterwards, and not end up asking locals how easy it was to buy a gun.

The banter was good right up to kick-off time. The pubs around Harlesden and Wembley packed with mixed groups of fans. Not a spot of bother to avoid. But there was an air of apprehension from the Blue Noses as we split up at Wembley Way, arranging to meet outside a telly shop, after the game. With the Double. We started well but Everton took the lead, Gary Lineker leaving Alan Hansen for dead after a beautiful through-ball from Peter Reid. The ease with which Everton controlled the first half made many of us believe the day wasn't ours. Then Jan Molby took over, using Wembley's wide spaces to open up Everton and put their defenders on the back foot.

One of them, Gary Stevens, buckled under the pressure, hit a sloppy pass forward which Jim Beglin seized on. He played in Molby who swept it into Rushie's path and that was it. We were back in. Graeme Sharp had a fine header tipped over the bar by Grobbelaar, but the tide had turned. Craig Johnston and inevitably Rushie killed them off.

Another one of those emotional moments was hatched. A year to the month after the shame of Heysel, and question marks being asked about why you should bother with that bird on your chest, we'd won the Double for the first time in our history. With Dalglish as our manager.

We hailed Kenny for his astonishing achievement. The man who'd stepped into Kevin Keegan's boots and won the European

Cup final in his first season, had stepped into the Boot Room and become the first-ever player-manager to lead his side to the title, only the second manager (after Fagan) to win it in his initial season, and only the third man that century to lead his side to an FA Cup/League Double. That's why his name was chanted loud and long. And that's why when it stopped, red throats spontaneously burst into tribute to our last great Scottish manager, Shanks. The man who first made us sing about running round Wembley with the Cup in 1965 and whose last competitive game was also our last FA Cup triumph, in 1974.

When his name was sung to the tune of 'Amazing Grace' for a good five minutes, it was telling the world that none of this would have been possible without the great man who started it all. The man who said to Kenny when he joined: 'Two pieces of advice son. Don't stay in hotels because you'll put on weight. And never lose your accent.'

The emotion made me think of Our Vic that day. How we'd gone and pissed in George Best's pot-plants the last time we played in an FA Cup final. How we'd both tried to imagine, in our pit of misery in 1971 when Arsenal beat us at Wembley to clinch the Double, what it must have felt like to have both them cups. How it must have felt to join the real list of all-time greats. And that's when I felt genuine pity for Evertonians. We'd snatched both trophies from them at the death, and now they had to face us, and endure our ecstasy while they tried to cope with such raw agony.

We met up outside the telly shop. Liverpudlians were whooping, Evertonians bickering about what height they'd like to hang Gary Stevens from after attaching piano wire to his bollocks. They couldn't look at us. We found it hard to look at them. When we did, we were met with 'We should have had a penalty when Nicol fouled Sharpy' or 'Dalglish's arld legs were well offside when Johnston scored.'

There was only one thing to do – split up. They needed to drown their sorrows free from jubilant or, even worse, patronizing

Reds. We just needed to savour the Double. So we parted ways with few words spoken, then headed off to find the first pub that was rocking to Liverpool songs, and have six rounds of doubles.

A few hours later I phoned Billy to see if he was coming out. He was about to go to bed and suffocate in darkness, but I persuaded him to meet us in a pub in Harlesden. Bad move. No sooner had he walked in than *Match Of The Day* was showing a replay of Gary Stevens's mistake, with delirious Liverpudlians revelling in Blue misery.

Before the highlights had reached Rushie's second goal, Billy had set Steve Power's red-and-white flag on fire with his lighter and walked out the pub. I loved his honesty. He'd been with me in Paris and Rome and most First Division grounds and wanted a Liverpool victory. We'd been hammer and tongs at each other throughout this neck-and-neck season, and he was emotionally exhausted.

Such crushing defeat – the loss of the League and the Cup when they're in your grasp – is hard to take. Even harder when it's to your deadliest rivals, supported by your mates who are celebrating at your expense. When Gary Lineker left for Barcelona in the close season, saying he wanted to play the European Cup football denied him by the post-Heysel ban, Evertonian resentment started to border on pure hatred. Today they chant 'murderers' at us during every derby. But it's not the Heysel thirty-nine they're protesting about, it's the death of their own dream.

14

THE BLACK PEARL

14 MAY 1988 – WEMBLEY

The irony wasn't lost on me as I walked into Wavertree High Street dole office and realized the old building had been my school dinner centre when I was five. Where once there were wooden benches filled with noisy, expectant kids, now bored youths slumped on vandalized plastic seats staring at the ceiling, pondering the point of life.

Progress, eh? Beat kids around the head when they're five, telling them that they won't grow up to be healthy, rounded people unless they eat their vegetables, then twenty years later beat them again with the knowledge that they've turned into vegetables of no use to the country.

At least the staff seemed to understand: 'What are the reasons for your current status?'

'I was working for the Greater London Council until Thatcher shut it down.'

'Jesus Christ. Is there any place that cow hasn't closed down?'

I didn't bother telling her that the only reason the GLC had hired me was because it knew it was about to be closed down by Thatcher on 31 March 1986, so the old witch had actually done me a favour by giving me eight months of decent payslips. Even heaping ironic praise on Thatcher in Liverpool back then was enough to earn a flying head-butt.

It felt good to be back home – sharing my uncle Billy's house with Terry who had given up studying drunken sex in Northampton for a job as a sales rep in Liverpool – even if I was on the dole.

The sense of emasculation that accompanies signing on could have made the future look dark, but it wasn't hard to see a golden sky and smell the greasepaint.

In the eight months I'd been away considerable progress had been made on the Next Alan Bleasdale Front. Wasn't poverty, idleness and first-hand observation of deprivation the prerequisites of being a playwright? Oh yes, my luvvies. The Playhouse were so keen on *Spilt Beans* they were putting on a two-night rehearsed reading before an audience in June and if it went down well they would give it a proper run during the winter season. So pass me the smoking jacket and call me Noël Bleeding Coward.

One thing in the play's favour was that a year on from Heysel it was still very much a topical story. The ban on British clubs was a burning issue in football, chattering classes obsessed on why our young males were so uniquely violent, and most nights on the regional TV news there was a new twist in the drawn-out extradition battle.

British police had trawled laboriously through film footage and photo stills before arresting twenty-seven men on suspicion of manslaughter, the only extraditable offence applicable.

There was some relief that 40 per cent of those arrested came from towns and cities outside Liverpool as far flung as Aberdeen and Ipswich, and that some of them had previous convictions for football-related violence. But you can make statistics say what you want. And they still said that 60 per cent of those caught running at the Italians were Scousers.

When the case eventually made it to court in 1989, there was a five-month trial in Belgium, after which fourteen men were given three-year sentences for involuntary manslaughter. Half the terms were suspended. The Italians had every right to feel bitter about the lack of justice meted out to the culprits responsible for European football's darkest hour. Especially those at the top who escaped with the mildest of censures.

When my take on events played before 100 people in the Playhouse Studio, I doubt if I've ever felt prouder. Although it got off to a shaky start when Steve Power's mum and dad walked out after ten minutes in protest over the foul language. (Kenneth Tynan and The Sex Pistols, I know how you felt.)

Much to my surprise it went down really well, although on the second night, when all my mates and their families were absent and the Playhouse hierarchy cast their monocles over it, the applause wasn't quite so warm. There were areas to work on, they told me. That's why we have rehearsed readings, they smiled, but it's still compelling and relevant, they added. Four months later, just as dates were being finalized, they asked me to pop in and see Ian Kellgren, the artistic director. I donned my cravat, finalized my vision for the set and posters, polished my list of preferred journalists for the pre-play interviews, and went to a meeting that started with Kellgren telling me, 'We *really* think this is a powerful piece of new writing,' and ended with me telling him to stick Edinburgh up his arse.

Events had conspired against me. The theatre had blown its annual budget on a lavish production of *Chicago*, which had flopped, meaning tough decisions had to be made. The studio was to be shut for ten months, after which time, Mr Kellgren informed me, the Heysel play might have missed its slot. Why, he asked, don't I take it up to Edinburgh instead? Which was when I told him exactly how far he could stick his idea up his own slot.

So that was it. A piece of 'powerful new writing' ditched because too much cash was being lavished on a clichéd Broadway musical usually watched on Shaftesbury Avenue by Japanese tourists and pensioners from Halifax on a Weekend West End Lights Break.

As for putting together a cast and dragging it up to Edinburgh where it would play in some dingy room above a pub in front of three bored students who couldn't get tickets for Stoppard, I'd rather have set my genitals on fire. Or even worse, watched a street mime artist.

So much for British theatre's commitment to new writing. So much for me being the next Alan Bleasdale. If a play about

Liverpool FC couldn't make the stage then nothing I ever attempted would. It was time to end my lengthy sabbatical as a struggling artist and go back to newspapers, tail between the legs of my shiny Burton suit. So I sent local newspapers a CV containing more fiction than *The Beano* annual – instead of bumming around Africa and lying in bed for three years I'd worked on various unknown papers from Nairobi to Nepal – and the *Chester Chronicle* fell for it, offering me a job as a sub-editor for the princely sum of £8,000 a year. Well, I had a Kop season ticket to support now, so I bit their hand off.

Sadly the 1986–87 season turned out to be one of the most yawnful anti-climaxes for many a year. The Double success in Kenny's first season as manager had led us to believe we would survive our European exile by winning everything in sight back home, thus reminding UEFA what they were depriving the wider world of. It didn't go to plan.

We lost four of our opening twelve games, and never really looked like overhauling a Lineker-less Everton at the top. We couldn't get past Luton in the FA Cup Third Round, and even our annual weekend in London left a sour taste in the mouth.

We'd had some good banter with the Arsenal fans before the League Cup final, in a Willesden boozer, scoffing at their claim that they always beat us in Cup finals. They were right, of course. Billy Liddellpool were brushed aside by Joe Mercer's men in the 1950 FA Cup final and the pain of the wound carved by Charlie George in 1971 was still raw.

But this was the League Cup. The one we'd already won four times this decade. And we were Liverpool. And when Rushie was played through by Craig Johnston, hesitated, looked up, and hammered it past Arsenal's keeper John Lukic, the bogey had clearly been laid. Fate had decreed there could be no coming back for Arsenal.

Everyone knew the script. Whenever Ian Rush scored for Liverpool they never lost. And as he'd played more than 300 games, and scored nearly 200 times, a replay at the very least had been secured. Especially with that mullet-headed ponce Charlie Nicholas (who'd foolishly chosen London's nightclubs ahead of Anfield four years earlier) leading their attack.

So how could we explain the eerie happening that unfolded before our eyes, other than that God clearly wasn't taking the League Cup very seriously once it had been rechristened the Littlewoods Cup? Liverpool stopped playing, and George Graham's dour side scrambled two goals over the line that were even jammier than the ones United managed at Wembley in 1977.

More to the point, how could this scoreline be possible, bearing in mind everything we knew about the scorers: Liverpool 1 (Rush) Arsenal 2 (Nicholas 2). Earth had surely tilted off its axis.

I felt sorry for Rushie. No, make that for myself. A deal had been struck the previous summer to sell him to Juventus for £3.2 million. Some said it was part of the healing process between the two clubs, a peace offering of sorts. Others claimed that Rushie fancied the challenge of playing abroad. Either way it just didn't seem right. A bit like pictures of Rushie donning headphones and frowning forlornly as a Teach Yourself Italian tape flew miles over his head.

He'd given his all in what we believed would be his last season in a red shirt, scoring 30 League goals despite not having Dalglish alongside him. The prospect of a new season without either of them playing in front of a midfield short on pace and inspiration seemed frightening. Until Kenny pulled off a blinding series of masterstrokes, bringing in four of the club's best-ever signings – John Aldridge, Peter Beardsley, John Barnes and Ray Houghton – for a combined fee of £4.3 million. Or peanuts to you and me.

This was a level of business that should have won Kenny a Queen's Award to Industry. A quadruple coup which would surely have merited a knighthood had he been managing a side in red thirty-five miles down the East Lancs Road. These four gelled so magnificently with the core of the side – Hansen, Nicol, Whelan and McMahon – that they produced the most exciting football ever witnessed from a Liverpool side, playing gorgeous stuff, week in, week out, with a breathtaking fluidity.

Other judges, who are far more qualified than I'll ever be, went further than that. After a 5–0 mauling of Notts Forest, which really should have been ten, and was such an exquisite display of total football the BBC rushed it out on video within days, Tom Finney called it the greatest performance by an English side that he had ever witnessed.

And as Shankly believed Finney to be the greatest player of all time, this was the key assessment of what our eyes had been telling us. There hadn't been a better season to watch football at Anfield. It was as close as we got to the consistent footballing perfection seen by Real Madrid fans in the early sixties, and at Ajax in the seventies.

For years we'd watched Liverpool teams ruthlessly dismantle their opponents with a clinical efficiency, earning us the reputation of being a relentless red machine. Neutrals admired and feared us. On big European nights they would will us to win not because of the way we played but what we did to foreigners in the name of England. We were Germany – unloved but respected.

This sense of injustice, a perceived lack of appreciation, was at the core of our Manchester United envy. They were the nation's darlings, the romantics' choice, not simply because of the Munich Air Disaster but the way their team was built around individualism.

Think of the great Liverpool side of the sixties and you think of a collective expression of Shankly's passion and will to win. Think of United's and you think of Best, Law and Charlton.

Although Shankly's and Paisley's sides had at times played some beautifully expressive football that drew gasps of admiration from outsiders – think Shankly's demolition of Newcastle in the 1974 Cup final and Paisley's 7–0 rout of Spurs in 1978 – both managers distrusted players they would term 'fancy-dans'.

Their philosophy had been uncomplicated and effective. Be

solid at the back, defend from the front, pass-and-move, always find a red shirt, wear them down, keep it simple. And it had rarely failed them.

Dalglish changed all that with the Class of '87. He liberated them. The heart of the team beat the same simple, effective Liverpool way, but around the edges he let rip. In Barnes and Beardsley we had individuals like Best and Law who could transcend the team ethic. Talents who chose to take on people or pull a trick, when the percentages screamed play safe. It worked to glorious effect, and by a twist of fate I had a grandstand view of it. Terry's growth issues – it was clear now that the only way his 5 ft 8 in frame was expanding was width-wise – meant a move for me, him and Mike to the Kemlyn Road.

The prospect of deserting the Kop depressed me. It would be nice to hear an end to Terry's moans about not being able to see a bleeding thing, but the Kemlyn Road? That retirement home for Victor Meldrews at whom Tommy Smith used to throw the 'wanker' sign as they shuffled out of their seats ten minutes before the end to 'avoid the traffic'. What next? Taking a flask and a tartan knee rug and passing round a bag of Werther's Originals?

It may have been down to a morbid fear of my looming thirtieth birthday but life changed on many fronts in 1987. The *Liverpool Daily Post* offered me a job as a sub-editor, meaning for the first time in my life I had a proper, full-time job in my home city, and I married my long-standing (or to be more accurate, long-suffering) girlfriend Ann. Her best friend was married to my mate Dave (who like Savo found football about as interesting as tidying up his sock drawer but tagged along on away-days for the crack) and we'd been going out, on and off, for years.

Although she was an Evertonian (which would lead to tragic ramifications several years later), and a Catholic, she agreed to abide by the strict teachings of my religion: the wedding had to take place on the Saturday after the FA Cup final as Liverpool would no doubt be there (we weren't). The engagement ring was bought from a jeweller's in Anfield for good luck. And I proposed under the Shankly Gates, making it legal in the eyes of the Supreme Being.

Believe it or not (and if you don't, feel free to go and check in St Margaret Mary's church in Dovecot) but Shankly was present throughout the service. Jesus, up there on a huge cross, bore such an uncanny likeness to Shankly it had me transfixed throughout the ceremony. Someone asked if I was becoming a born-again Christian and I told them I was just getting a bit of a team-talk.

Back at the great man's spiritual home, the Kemlyn Road move turned out to be utterly inspired. With the seats a dozen rows from the front on the Kop side of the half-way line, it meant that for 45 minutes of every game we were in touching distance of one of the all-time great Anfeld sights – John Barnes in full flow. He was majesty personified. Forget about his underperforming for England, in a Liverpool shirt he was consistently awesome.

Paddy Crerand once remarked that when George Best went on a run he would twist the blood of his opponents. Barnes, at twenty-four, was the closest an English player had got to inflicting similar torture. I'd seen Peter Thompson and Steve Heighway, and at the peak of their dribbling powers their control at pace was mesmeric. But there was an added dimension to Barnes, an athletic guile that set him apart. He was like a matador, drawing a defender in, giving a little shimmy, pushing the ball through him, bursting past, doing it to the next defender, before whipping a cross in for Aldridge or perfectly planting it in the top corner. Plus we'd never had a player who tried (and often succeeded) to bend the ball around a wall like a Brazilian.

Many memories of Barnes that year stand out, not all for pleasant reasons. His finest match was against QPR in October when he scored two absolute pearls, one of which I'll never forget. He picked the ball up on the half-way line to the right of our seat, coaxed a defender on to the wrong foot then waltzed past him, threw the shoulder and shimmied past another, turned one inside out, then another as he weaved towards the Kop goal, and suddenly without looking up steered it across the keeper into his top left-hand corner. It was one of those goals which lead to a communal silence as 44,000 brains try to take in the information being relayed to them by the eyes. One of those moments when you know you've just witnessed a piece of pure genius that will never leave you. Forget the Maracana with England, this was Barnesey's greatest strike.

The feeling of euphoria that accompanied that goal was a stark contrast to my first sight of Barnes in a Liverpool shirt. In fact his debut on British soil (in a pre-season friendly at Celtic) left me feeling more depressed in the company of Liverpool fans than I'd ever thought possible.

When it was leaked that Dalglish was trying to sign Barnes, the vilest of graffiti was daubed on Anfield's walls. Once again we found ourselves playing the National Front card to excuse the ugliness of our own people. But the truth was there were rumblings of discontent among a very small minority of supporters over Liverpool's first black signing. And in that Parkhead stand that July afternoon I feared it was much bigger than we'd given it discredit for.

Liverpool's two big new signings were welcomed on to the pitch individually by an announcer. First Beardsley to warm applause. Then Barnes to equally warm applause from the mass of travelling fans, but also a storm of aggressive boos from snarling faces to my left. And then the chants started: 'Hello der man,' and 'Liverpool are white,' from dozens of throats.

Initially I couldn't believe my ears. When it became clear I hadn't imagined it, and could make out a flag with 'Liverpool are white' on, I felt shock, revulsion and an urge to be physically sick. Because I knew that if this carried on, if it was picked up and tolerated on the Kop, then my love affair with Liverpool would be dead. That if these people drove Barnes out of Anfield, I would be driven out with him, never to return.

As the game started the chants carried on. Whenever Barnes touched the ball boos rang out from this small section of hardcore racists, to be met with astonishment by many of those around me. I was angry and hurt, but mainly for selfish reasons. What if Barnes, who looked like he could be very special, sussed what was going on and asked for a transfer? What if the rest of the nation got to hear about this and we were branded a bunch of goose-stepping fascists?

Yet why was I so shocked? When the first black players broke into the English game in the early seventies Anfield had been as racist as every other ground, the Kop welcoming the likes of Clyde Best and Cyrille Regis with monkey grunts and 'get back on your jam-jar' chants. How could I overlook the fact that despite Liverpool having the oldest black community in Britain, only one member of that community, Howard Gayle, had worn a red shirt. And none had played for Everton. How few black faces you saw outside Liverpool 8. How Lord Scarman had delivered this stunning indictment in his report into the Toxteth Riots: 'Liverpool is a uniquely racist city.'

I remembered the heated row I'd had on the Kop the season before during a Notts Forest game, with a dad bearing his son on his shoulders, who kept yelling 'get that black bastard' whenever Des Walker had the ball. And turning round to confront a cretin who screamed 'kill the coon' when Jan Molby squared up to Viv Anderson. I don't know if working at the GLC had hardened my attitude to racism, but I knew I couldn't stand there and take it any more.

I would dread seeing black players run out for the opposition. I could feel my body tense up and my fists clench, sensing the bile that was about to be spewed, and how it would make me react. I remember thinking, when we got the Kemlyn Road season tickets, that it was probably a good idea because if I kept on challenging people who took out their inadequacies on black players I'd end up hospitalized.

Meanwhile, at Parkhead, Barnes's exhilarating bursts of pace were causing Celtic all sorts of trouble and leaving the vast majority of Liverpool fans drooling. The more it became clear we'd signed a new hero the quieter and less frequent came the racist abuse. By the time Barnes left the pitch to a raucous standing ovation it had stopped. And I never heard him racially abused again by Liverpool fans. But was that anything to be proud of? Or did it betray a disturbing truth which was even more shameful and unpalatable? If Barnes had been a failure and conformed to all the bigoted stereotypes about black players being too flash, lacking the bottle or the heart, unable to turn it on when the temperatures fell and the grass turned to mud, the racists would have won. Their warped idea of an inferior race would have been acknowledged and many undecided fans would have bought their view that Liverpool should indeed stay white. Had Everton signed Barnes, as they eventually signed Beardsley, it might have been Kopites throwing bananas on the pitch during derbies.

Almost single-handedly, and overnight, Barnes eradicated vocal racism at Anfield. It was still there but it was deemed unacceptable to scream 'black bastard' at an opposition player. Why? Because we had our own black bastard who we'd clutched to our bosom due to a genius for ball-juggling. So attack Remi Moses for the colour of his skin and you attack our Barnesey. Twisted logic or what?

I was too old for singling out heroes to worship, but after the Celtic experience Barnes was my man. We went down to Coventry for the second game of the season (having won at Highbury on the opening day) and ripped them apart, 4–1. Barnes didn't score, but his contribution was mouth-watering. And sadly, worse for wear after one too many pints before the game, I decided to let him know. Maybe it was a morbid fear of the return of the Celtic racism. Maybe I just wanted the Jamaican to know he'd won a place in our hearts. I can't be sure. But as the teams came out for the second half, I started a chant. Not the greatest chant, in fact I didn't even pronounce his Christian name correctly. But there from the back of the stand came the following din from my throat (to the tune of 'Here We Go, Here We Go, Here We Go'): 'Johnny Barnes,

Johnny Barnes, Johnny Barnes – Johnny Barnes, Johnny Barnes, Johnny Bar-arnes – Johnny Barnes, Johnny Barnes, Johnny Barnes – John-nee Barnes, Joh-nee Barnes . . .' (repeat ad nauseam).

By the end of the game the entire away end was singing it. Before the first home game of the season, the Kop had embraced it as Barnes's official signature tune. Rodgers and Hammerstein, Lennon and McCartney, Burt Bacharach and Hal David, eat your hearts out.

The League was wrapped up with ease, and a club record 90 points, nine clear of Manchester United, was established. The ludicrously underrated John Aldridge turned out to be the perfect replacement for Rush, hitting 26 First Division goals which made him the League's top striker. Here was a goalscorer who lacked elegance, pace and a left foot but who was blessed with such a footballing intelligence and natural scoring instinct, who possessed such heart and discipline and worked so hard at his game, his career totals elevate him into the highest company of British strikers. Aldridge scored 476 times in 889 appearances for his clubs and his country, Ireland.

Few were Goal of the Season candidates, but one that was came in the FA Cup semi-final against Nottingham Forest at Hillsborough, a peach of a volley that sealed a 2–1 win and sent us back to Wembley. I'd had a ticket for the press box that day, and another for the stand. Realizing I'd get plenty more opportunities to be in with the journalists, I gave it to Billy.

It was one of those perfect semi-final days. Spring sun shining, optimism oozing. We crossed the Pennines into Yorkshire, stopping for a few pints at a village pub just outside Sheffield, drove off, parked at the top of the hill and walked down to Hillsborough feeling good about life. But throughout a game we had dominated since Aldo scored an early penalty, I had an uneasy feeling in my guts. My eyes were constantly drawn to the Liverpool fans in the section of terracing in line with my seat, the Leppings Lane End.

I had an aerial view of the fear and discomfort I'd felt two years earlier standing there. They were packed tighter than calves in veal crates, and every surge had me wincing in sympathy with those being pushed up against the wall at the front. So bad was the crushing that kids, some clearly in distress, were being passed up above heads and pulled into the stand above.

It didn't seem right. Especially when you looked at the huge Kop behind the other goal and saw gaps among the Forest fans. Why had they been given a bigger ticket allocation in a bigger part of the ground when Liverpool's average home gate was double theirs? Why is that terrace, with its one-in-six gradient that so frightened me two years ago, being used to stage an FA Cup semi-final? The questions soon disappear. You take it. That's what you do, you take it. Because you have to as a football fan. It's all part of the package.

You win, and you walk away, back up that hill happy, forgetting about the rip-off prices for entry into a cow-shed where you couldn't get a half-time pie, where you pissed in a stenching Victorian bog. You forget the crushing, the fear, the distress, and the fact that no one in authority really cares how you are treated. Because nothing you can do or say can change it. You're just a football fan after all.

What can I tell you about the final that the scoreline, Liverpool 0, Wimbledon 1, doesn't? We filled two-thirds of Wembley to witness the formality of our second Double in three years. We were roughed out of it, Aldo became the first player to miss an FA Cup final penalty and the nation went ape as the so-called Crazy Gang pulled off one of the biggest shocks of all time.

This is what I'll tell you. That morning six of us walked into a William Hill's bookies in the centre of London, affronted that their chart in the window wasn't offering prices on a Liverpool win higher than 4–0.

'What's the odds on 6–0 mate?' (Cue superior smirks.)

'I'll go and find out.' (Cue shame at not having them to hand.)

'I can give you 100/1, sir.' (Cue a look that says 'you mug'.)

'Are we in boys?' (Cue nods and the writing of slips amid confident laughter.)

This is what that tells you. We were an arrogant shower of pricks who'd got carried away with all the hype and flattery surrounding the side. We'd believed our own publicity and forgotten the very basis of the Liverpool Way. We insulted Shankly's mantra about football being a simple game made complicated by fools.

And we deserved to get our conceited arses spanked.

15

HILLSBOROUGH

15 APRIL 1989

Just before 7 a.m. the radio alarm cut through my dreams with a Bangles song about an Eternal Flame. I'd hear it twice again that morning on the drive over the Pennines. The following day it would reach Number One and stay there for a month, providing a haunting soundtrack for dozens of funerals, and eventually a permanent epitaph for ninety-six lost souls.

Such a prospect seemed unimaginable as I opened the front door of my Wavertree semi to pick up the milk, felt the sun on my face, saw the glistening dew on the grass and looked up at a clear blue sky dissected by a thin white plume from a passing plane. I wondered, as I often did, where the passengers were heading. Wherever it was, I wouldn't have swapped places with any of them. I was heading to Hillsborough on this perfect day.

Mark Clinton – who dragged his gammy leg around a five-a-side pitch with us every week – gave Mike, Terry and myself a lift over to Sheffield, and it was agreed we'd stick to the same plan as last year's semi-final: a few pints in that village outside Sheffield, then park at the top of the hill above Hillsborough and stroll down in plenty of time for kick-off.

This year the traffic seemed a bit slower. Roadworks were causing congestion which wasn't helped by the South Yorkshire Police pulling us over once we reached the outskirts of Sheffield, checking to see if we had any booze in the car. We tried a joke about them having nothing better to do than pinch our ale, but they weren't in the mood. 'Less of yer Scouse lip,' one of them barked back. There was a history between us. Ever since the miner's strike (which was at its most violent in Yorkshire), whenever we'd played in Sheffield we'd given the coppers stick about being Thatcher's whores and sang songs in support of the pitmen.

At last year's semi-final, as we queued to get into the tiny Leppings Lane End, we taunted them about handing the Kop to Forest fans as a reward for all the Nottinghamshire scabs who'd defied Arthur Scargill and broken the strike. There was no love lost between Liverpudlians and South Yorkshire Police.

We called in on the same pub as the previous year, had three or four pints, went to the same bookies (I had us to win 3–1 with Staunton scoring the first goal), drove to the top of the hill, parked up, and started the walk down to the ground. And there the similarities with 1988 ended.

There were far more people about. It felt like being part of a crowd streaming out of the match rather than into it. Kick-off was half-an-hour away but some Liverpool coaches were only just emptying. Groups of agitated fans, mainly dads with kids, jogged past, clearly behind schedule and keen to get to the ground to soak up the atmosphere their sons had been promised.

I asked one of the men getting off a coach why they were so late and he said there'd been an accident on the M62 which had led to a long delay. Looking down the hill at the crowds I was convinced they would have to put the kick-off back. Turning off Leppings Lane, through the wrought-iron gates and into the area which was the entry point for all Liverpool fans, I saw human gridlock. Thousands of fans milled around – some bemused, many agitated – waiting to be filtered into queues that didn't exist.

For the second year running 28,000 tickets had gone to Nottingham Forest, whose average attendance was 20,000, while 24,000 tickets were handed to Liverpool where the average gate was 39,000. The police refused to listen to logic, claiming the ends had been allocated 'for safety reasons'. It meant all 24,000 Liverpool ticket-holders, whether in the Leppings Lane terrace, the West Stand above it, or like me, the North Stand which ran the length of the pitch, had to get through twenty-three turnstiles. Turnstiles we knew from last year to be so old they constantly jammed. At the other end, the Forest fans had sixty modern turnstiles to waltz through.

It was mayhem. The few police that were around, on horseback, had lost control. One of the horses was so scared it had a panic attack. Kids were crying, many being pushed up on to their dad's shoulders to escape the crush, and the mood was turning nasty. As the teams prepared to come out on to the pitch, fans were pleading with them to sort the situation out and get them inside. Then the big blue exit gate opened. A huge cheer came up. The police stood back and more than 2,000 fans poured in, many running to ensure they didn't miss the kick-off.

At the back of the Leppings Lane terrace, as the majority of fans headed into a tunnel with the word STANDING above it, I looked for a steward to find out whether I was heading the right way for the North Stand. But there were no stewards to be found. Like the police they had abandoned their posts and let the fans get on with it. If they'd been doing their job they would have cordoned off entry to the central pens and directed fans into the side pens which were far from full. But all control had broken down.

By the time I made it to my seat at the far end of the North Stand, just after kick-off, the first victims had begun to suffer asphyxiation, limbs had been broken, and a crash barrier given way under the weight of the crowd.

I don't remember any of the play because my eyes weren't looking at the pitch. Just like last year I was transfixed by what was happening behind the goal in the Leppings Lane End, but this time it was a seriously distressing spectacle. To the side of the two central pens there were clear gaps in the crowd. In the central pens there was no movement. It was just a mass of heads, packed so tightly you couldn't put a needle between them. This time there were far more people being helped out of the terrace into the stand above. They weren't calves in veal crates now, they were calves in the slaughterhouse.

Eddie Spearritt, who lost consciousness in the Leppings Lane and also lost his son Adam, later explained the exact nature of the crush: 'I've heard talk that there was a surge, but there was no surge. It was a slow, constant build-up of pressure. It was like a vice getting tighter and tighter. Until you couldn't breathe.'

As the game settled down you could make out what seemed like a huge muffled argument, interspersed with angry screams, coming from behind Liverpool's goal. A couple of fans broke on to the pitch and started remonstrating with Bruce Grobbelaar. At six minutes past three the referee led both teams back to the dressing rooms, and fans started spilling out of the cages.

To the left of us the Forest fans were booing and chanting about Scouse scum. In their eyes this was just another outbreak of hooliganism. I hoped they were right. I hoped that what I was sensing in my guts was wrong. I hoped helpless fans weren't going under, the way I'd gone under on that terrace three years ago. Because this time, with all those fans streaming in from behind, there was no way they were getting up.

The next hour is a blur. I remember dozens of police walking on to the pitch with dogs, forming a line facing the Forest end. I saw Liverpool fans, many of them lads, ripping away the pitch-side advertising hoardings to use as makeshift stretchers, running back to the heaps of bodies lying prostrate behind the goal, and ferrying them the full length of the pitch to a small exit down below me, in the corner of the East Stand.

When I saw two bodies being carried away on those hoardings with coats over their faces and tears streaming down the cheeks of the stretcher-bearers I knew my worst fears were being realized. In the seats around us a collective panic masqueraded itself as a dignified calm. With no information coming from the stadium Tannoy, many gathered around radios brought to keep tabs on Everton's progress in the other semi-final against Norwich, to find out the scale of the horror.

'They're saying there's deaths,' muttered one middle-aged man, and a woman screamed a name, followed by 'my son' and ran to the exits with her husband in pursuit. Most of us just sat there in a state of shock, surveying the pathetic scenes out on the pitch. Some clutched their heads into their hands and quietly prayed.

After about thirty minutes an ambulance finally made its way on to the pitch and headed past the line of police, to the Liverpool end, and I felt a surge of anger. Why had it taken them thirty minutes to get medical help in? Why weren't those fans let out the cages by police as soon as the crush became clear? Why did they open that gate? Why wasn't the game delayed? Why have I got a full ticket in my possession, just as I had after Heysel?

We hung around in our seats waiting for some direction from the authorities, guidance on what we were supposed to do. But all that was happening was fans acting as paramedics, ferrying the dead to a makeshift mortuary.

Eventually a sombre voice told us to go home because we wouldn't be seeing any football at Hillsborough today. At last some guidance and it was a relief of sorts.

As we left the ground and headed back up the hill, there was no one dominant emotion among the fans. Many, like me and Mike, were too numb to talk, others were hugging each other silently while some ran past yelling 'bastards' to no one in particular. There were a lot of angry debates.

I saw a big burly man butting the roof of his car and bellowing, 'No, no, no, not this time. You won't fuckin' blame us for this. You won't fuckin' blame us for this.' He was listening to an interview with the FA's chief executive Graham Kelly on his car radio, in which he said he'd been told by the police commander that Liverpool fans had kicked down the gate and stormed the terraces.

A crowd of men wanted to leg back down the hill and sort him out, such was their rage at the lie being perpetrated and the implication we had killed our own fans. One of them, who was letting out a primeval howl, had to be pinned against a wall and calmed down. You won't fuckin' blame us for this. You won't fuckin' blame us for this. But they already had, and it was leading every news bulletin in every TV and radio station in the world.

We met the other lads and drove to a pub to find a phone where we could get word back home that we were safe. It was a wasted journey. All the lines were jammed and nobody felt the desire to drink. As we drove back across the Pennines the sky was a dark sheet of gloom in keeping with the news from the radio. It was thirty dead, then forty, then fifty.

I looked at the cars heading in the opposite direction and wondered how many were carrying mums and dads from Liverpool to Sheffield to identify their sons' corpses. And I felt sick to the pit of my stomach. When I reached home I found it difficult to talk to Ann. The TV news was now saying ninety were dead and the number was rising. The police had let it be known it was their decision to open the gate. Which was good of them. I poured a large glass of whisky and stared at the screen with glazed eyes. I couldn't take it in. Then the anger spilt out, and I just started yelling at the telly. I screamed about kids being dead because they didn't count. Dead because the football fan was viewed as some moronic caricature and the people who ran the country were happy to play along with that image because it makes their cushy jobs even cushier. I shouted about the gaps I'd seen in front of me in the huge bank which had been set aside for Nottingham Forest fans. About kids turning blue, screaming to be let out of cages, and being ignored because the plods had been conditioned to view them as criminals. About Alsatians making it into the ground but not ambulances and doctors, nurses and oxygen machines. Because the instinctive reaction was to keep the animals segregated and in their pens. That way if there's any trouble the ones who'll get hurt will be their own kind. And they're only football fans. They're only hooligans. They don't count.

After twenty minutes of ranting I lashed my glass at the floor and went to bed.

Weeks later a counsellor told me that when we're present at such scenes of unexpected death the mind goes through four cycles. Shock, anger, guilt and grief. I'd moved very quickly from shock to anger, but the next day in work I reverted to shock. The *Daily Post* editor put me in charge of laying out the Merseyside edition pages, which meant sifting through dozens of Hillsborough photographs, many unused in that Sunday's newspapers on grounds of taste. There were bodies lying unattended on the pitch, close-ups of the dead and dying, pushed up against the cages, their faces mangled. Coppers looking away as fans pulled at them begging for help.

A debate was raging over which pictures we should use, and I was continually asked for input. But I didn't have any. My head was withdrawing to a distant place, and I found it impossible to switch it into professional mode. I kept going to the canteen or the toilet, shrugging my shoulders and walking away when people stopped to ask what I'd seen of yesterday's disaster. There was a numbness in my skull, a cold detachedness. At times I couldn't hear what people were saying, because my brain was shutting them out. If they laughed at anything to try to raise the spirits I felt myself wanting to hit them. I was withdrawing into a shell. The only person I could talk to was fellow sub-editor Mike Chapple who had been at Hillsborough and who I could see was suffering too.

Eventually the editor came up to me with half a dozen pictures and asked my advice on which ones we should ditch. I stared down at one of them, and saw a girl's face pushed so hard against the cages that her hair, which was drenched in sweat, had matted in the metal. And something hard and painful rose from deep within. I told him: 'I can't do this any more.'

He told me to go and have a cup of tea. Instead I went to a half-empty pub on my own and sat in a corner. Mike Chapple eventually found me, and said a researcher from *The Time, The Place*, wanted us to take part in a live debate from Granada's Albert Dock studio the next morning. He said he thought we should, that talking about it might help. Then we sat together on our own and talked, and talked.

I don't remember much more about that night other than having the worst sleep of my life in which I seemed to sweat out my body weight. A recurring dream started, which would stay with me for months, in which black figures shaped like Edvard Munch's *The Scream* were being sucked up to the sky. One after the other, going on and on. All gathering above, and looking down at me in total silence. I tried to climb up to them but couldn't.

Numbers were being counted in my head – 67, 68, 69, which kept rising relentlessly, and I would wake up shouting to find the bed covers and mattress drenched. I tried to sleep in the bed in the spare room. But I woke myself up with my own sweat again.

The next day I went on *The Time, The Place*. Mike Scott, a sort of Kilroy with class, was the anchorman, and did a decent job in shepherding out the rage with dignity. When I had a chance to speak I held up my unchecked ticket, saying this cost me £14. Fourteen pounds to attend a sporting event only to be treated like a convicted criminal. Caged in, denied rights and spat on by authority with contempt. In what other walk of life would that be tolerated? I asked.

The shock was receding now, and the anger was coming back, especially as noises were coming out of Sheffield seeking to pile the blame on the fans. Again I couldn't face work, knowing the only news story would be Hillsborough and I would be expected to offer a rational contribution to an office debate in which right-wing out-of-towners, who loathed football and Scousers, would be drawing parallels with Heysel, and asking me to accept part of the blame. I knew what kind of response it would draw and I couldn't be responsible for my actions.

So I sat round the house in a morose mood, playing sad, old songs. The grief and the guilt were kicking in now. My mum rang up with a 'pull yourself together' speech prepared, but I cut her dead by telling her I felt worse than when Our Vic had died. Which disgusted her. So I didn't bother trying to explain that I coped with Vic's death because, although he was only twenty-nine, he'd died of natural causes. But this I couldn't cope with. This was so unnatural it was alien to anything I'd ever experienced. It felt as though a juggernaut had been driven into my central nervous system. Complete lethargy hit my body. I didn't want to read anything or speak to anyone. I just wanted to be on my own with my desolation.

Peter Surridge, the assistant editor, rang to see how I was. I told him. He suggested it might help me recover by writing down my thoughts in a feature. I declined and he understood. Then I turned the radio on and heard the headlines on Radio City: 'UEFA President Jacques Georges has accused the Liverpool fans of acting like animals and causing the Hillsborough Disaster.' The Frenchman said he had the impression 'that they were beasts waiting to charge into the arena'.

I went to the spare room and wrote this for the following day's paper. They used it across the centre pages under the headline GUILTY . . . FOR BEING ALIVE. I have never opened myself up so much as a journalist and I doubt I ever will again.

I didn't want to write this article but I had to for all the people who were at Hillsborough on Saturday who are now feeling vicious mental wounds.

I am trying to type these words but there is no strength in my body. I have been listening to the radio and hearing social services' numbers and the thought of seeking medical advice has been going through my mind.

I'm 31 years of age. I have been a journalist for the past 10 years – working in an industry where the major currency is tragedy. But I have never felt anything like this.

I just tried my own form of therapy. I thought I would take a taxi over to Anfield and spend the afternoon sitting on the pitch staring at the Kop. On my own. With my thoughts.

But I hadn't gone 50 yards down the street before the tears started again. So I turned back. It feels like there is a 50-ton weight on my shoulders. I keep sobbing. Very heavily.

All I can feel is guilt. Guilt because I wasn't hurt. Guilt because I haven't looked anybody in the eye who has lost someone. Guilt because I shouldn't be feeling like this.

I have no one to focus my anguish on because I haven't lost anyone. I haven't got someone to throw my arms around. To push my face on to theirs so our tears form one river of love. For the dead.

My only focus is a crest of a mythical Liver Bird with something hanging out of its mouth. I'm sitting in a room surrounded by pictures of men with that bird on their red shirts. The same kind of pictures I've had on my bedrooom wall since I can remember. And I'm a married man.

I keep wondering what the mothers of the dead will think when they next go into a room to tidy up after their lad and realise he's not there. And look up and see those pictures.

You see, we are all big kids. Football makes you that way. You didn't really have any choice. It was something you were born with. Especially in this city. And I don't regret it. My love for this great game has never been stronger.

But I shouldn't even be thinking about it because I only want to think what the bereaved are thinking and they will feel hate for the sport. But then that's not surprising when you've heard the words of a French gentleman who's supposed to be the boss of the game in this continent calling you a beast.

Well don't be surprised by those words. In May 1985, the Prime Minister of this country, when pressed on the reasons for the Heysel Disaster at a Press conference in Mexico, said the citizens of her country who were present at that game came from a city notorious for its violence.

It's anger now. But I'm trying to control it. The moods keep swaying in and out of my head the way the Kop used to in the 1960s.

Why did we choose that beautiful anthem? That's all I could think last night as I stayed up until 5 o'clock watching a video – *The History of Liverpool Football Club.*

Why that beautiful ballad – plucked from a Rodgers and Hammerstein musical by Gerry Marsden – when the youth of Liverpool were producing 101 other, more joyful songs that expressed the optimism of this great city back in 1964? I hope it's fate. Because no other words than You'll

Never Walk Alone can express the feelings of people like me who were at Hillsborough and survived to those poor wretches who have lost loved ones.

I'll be alright. The dead won't. Dead because they loved football. Dead because they were not treated as people.

I will not put up with being treated like an animal ever again. I will not put up with feeling filthy as I stand in a cage on a wet Wednesday night in an empty stadium in Coventry or Middlesbrough waiting for police to let me out 15 minutes after another Liverpool victory.

Of course hooligans have brought about this disgusting attitude to one section of society. But why didn't authority ask US what we should do about it? Why didn't the government and the FA and UEFA talk to US about the problem?

I can understand you Monsieur Jacques Georges, when you said we were beasts. Beasts from a violent region of the world. I understand. Thank you. You have summed up better than anyone why those people died on Saturday.

Because just as at Heysel, the people inside and outside the game who were paid to know what to do, didn't.

Unlike Liverpool FC Monsieur Georges, I don't want your head to roll. A part of me wants to kick it the length of the Champs Elysées. I feel guilty about that too.

But that anger makes me feel a little bit better now.

I'd be embarrassed today to admit in a newspaper that I cried. But so raw was my pain then that I didn't care what people thought. I still cry, occasionally, when no one is looking. Not at anything as specific as the anniversary, or reading the names on the Eternal Flame that now stands outside Anfield in memory of the victims. I cry at random, unrelated things which remind me of that day. They come at you sideways, these little prompts, and catch you unawares. You don't see them until it's too late. And then, like the wind, they're gone. A sunny spring morning. A Bangles song. A digital clock showing 3.06. A 96 bus. Seeing the excitement on kids' faces as their pace picks up when the gates of a football stadium loom into view.

In September 2002 I was sent to New York to do a piece on the first anniversary of 9/11. At Ground Zero, the people, like the landscape, were still in a state of devastation. Flowers were being laid, prayers being said, people consoling each other. I looked up at the sky and it was clear blue interrupted only by a sharp white plume trailing out of a plane. I was dragged back to my Wavertree doorstep on the heavenly morning of that hellish day, and the tears started to flow. A big New Yorker next to me who'd been snuffling as he read the messages on wreaths, no doubt grieving for a loved one crushed under the Twin Towers rubble, put his arm around me and said, 'Let it out buddy, let it out.'

He wasn't to know my thoughts were nothing to do with New York and their appalling loss. But I let it out anyway. For all those young people we left behind in Sheffield – more than 80 per cent of the ninety-six were under thirty, and half of them were under twenty-one – and their families who've been saddled with such an awful burden ever since.

And I hope I always will.

16

PISSING ON THE DEAD

Liverpool and its people were on the floor. Which was the perfect position for the Establishment to do what it does best when its actions are questioned. Put the boot in. The police knew they had blood on their hands, but they also knew how little sympathy the world had with football fans in general, and Scousers in particular. Which is why they lied, spun, briefed, leaked and poisoned.

So it came to pass that before any of the corpses were buried the second Hillsborough tragedy was under way. The cover-up. Having denied the dead a chance to live they proceeded to deny them any chance of justice.

In Sheffield, politicians and media, keen to clear its football club and its police force of criminal incompetence, were only too willing to disseminate shameless propaganda. A local news agency and a Tory MP were fed lies by an unnamed Police Federation official, and soon a story that was copper-bottomed by officialdom was in the public domain.

Beneath the headline FANS IN DRUNKEN ATTACKS ON POLICE, the *Sheffield Star* reported, 'Ticketless thugs staged crush to gain entry, attacked an ambulanceman, threatened firemen and punched and urinated on policemen as they gave the kiss of life to stricken victims.'

They claimed 'supporters were still propping up the bars at 2.30 p.m. They raced to the stadium arriving at the Leppings Lane End at the height of the crush. Some of them were the worse for drink, others without tickets were hoping to sneak in. Hubble, bubble, toil and trouble . . . drunkenness and ticketlessness were now added to the equation.'

The *Yorkshire Post* stated, 'Thousands of fans began the fatal charge . . . thousands of latecomers tried to force their way into the ground . . .'

This outrageous slant on events was also given prominence on Yorkshire TV and local radio stations. Small wonder that when it came to the inquests, a jury drawn entirely from the Sheffield area went in with their minds made up.

It wasn't long before London, needing a new angle to move the story on from the stark images of horror, fell for the lies too. This was the London *Evening Standard*: 'The catastrophe was caused first and foremost by violent enthusiasm for soccer, in this case the tribal passions of Liverpool supporters. They literally killed themselves and others to be at the game.'

This was the *Daily Mail*, quoting a Police Federation spokesman: 'I am sick of hearing how good the crowd were . . . They were arriving tanked up on drink and the situation faced by the officers trying to control them was quite simply terrifying.' *The Times* reported an unnamed police source as saying, 'Drunkenness and hooliganism were a major factor in the Hillsborough Disaster.' Back on Merseyside, where Liverpool fans were still trying to come to terms with the enormity of the suffering and families were making arrangements to bury their dead, it felt like a knife was being forced deeper and deeper.

The struggle to come to terms with the reality of what we'd experienced left most of us with little energy to fight back. Especially when you knew the police had got their retaliation in first and no one in authority was going to take seriously the protestations of perceived hooligans, who only four years earlier had been responsible for thirty-nine deaths at Heysel.

And then, on the Wednesday, the shit hit the fans. It was the single costliest miscalculation by a newspaper this country has seen, and it pushed the people of Liverpool over the edge. Under the headline THE TRUTH the *Sun* cleared its front page to tell the world: 'Some fans picked pockets of victims; Some fans urinated on the brave cops; Some fans beat up PC giving kiss of life.' The words that accompanied it claimed that 'drunken Liverpool fans viciously attacked rescue workers as they tried to revive victims' and 'police officers, firemen and ambulance crew were punched, kicked and urinated upon'. One anonymous copper was quoted as saying that a dead girl had been abused, while fans 'were openly urinating on us and the bodies of the dead'.

The *Sun*'s editor, Kelvin MacKenzie, had willingly bought the Police Federation lies, dressed them up, and sold them on in a typically sensationalist style designed to steal the moral highground and sell papers. There was only one Truth. And it was the *Sun* wot pronounced it. And anyone who thought differently could stick it up their junta.

It was war. Scousers, regardless of their football leanings, were apoplectic. To accuse them of killing their own was bad enough, but to state as fact that they picked the pockets of their own as they were dying was a call to arms. A paper that was already regarded by many on Merseyside as loathsome due to its rabid Thatcherite stance, Loadsamoney tone and obsession with tits and bums, was now seen as the spawn of the devil. It had slandered an entire people. And it would pay.

Overnight thousands of copies were stolen and destroyed. There were public burnings. Delivery men refused to touch it, shopkeepers refused to stock it. From selling 200,000 copies a day on Merseyside it plunged to a couple of thousand. Nineteen years on that figure hovers around 12,000, and humiliations are still handed out when copies are spotted being read in public.

The *Sun* has tried many times to win back Scousers, and failed dismally, mainly because each attempt at rapprochement was viewed as a cynical ploy to win back lost readers. When Kelvin MacKenzie revealed in November 2006 that he had only apologized at the time because the paper's owner Rupert Murdoch ordered him to, it showed that Scousers had been right to boycott it all along.

I admire them deeply for sticking to their guns. For once a community showed that solidarity can deeply hurt a business which is trying to hurt you. But be in no doubt, 'The Truth' front page was really all about one man. MacKenzie.

There were decent journalists working on the *Sun* in 1989 who were as appalled at that front page as any Liverpudlian. In their book *Stick It Up Your Punter* (an account of MacKenzie's time at the *Sun*), Peter Chippindale and Chris Horrie described what happened that night:

As MacKenzie's layout was seen by more and more people, a collective shudder ran through the office but MacKenzie's dominance was so total there was nobody left in the organisation who could rein him in except Murdoch. Everyone seemed paralysed, 'looking like rabbits in the head-lights', as one hack described them. The error staring them in the face was too glaring. It obviously wasn't a silly mistake; nor was it a simple oversight. Nobody really had any comment on it – they just took one look and went away shaking their heads in wonder at the enormity of it. It was a 'classic smear'.

The reality is that every national newspaper had that story fed to it, but only MacKenzie chose to run it in the manner he did. A couple of others carried the claims as part of a report, and immediately retracted them when it was clear how false and offensive they were.

But MacKenzie revelled in it. He had a tale that fitted neatly with his prejudices. It was Our Boys in Blue, the same brave lads who had stood up to the scumbag miners, who had now standing up to scumbag Scousers. It was his patriotic duty to back them, regardless of The Truth. For years afterwards the hurt it caused, not simply to the *Sun*'s circulation, was incalculable.

Back then almost four million people were buying the *Sun*, meaning 12 million people were reading it, the majority of whom were probably believing all that they read. Despite Lord Justice Taylor's report denouncing the report as lies, Liverpool fans have literally had to fight against the slur over the years. I've had at

least three brawls with people who have argued that there was
clearly no smoke without fire. That our police would not tell a
paper such a story, nor would a paper publish it, if there were no
truth in it.

All down to the owner of one twisted mind, one gargantuan
ego, who to this day is convinced tanked-up, ticketless Liverpool
fans caused the deaths and is proud to admit, 'I was not sorry
then and I'm not sorry now.'

When MacKenzie eventually suffers the same fate as the
ninety-six, there is a line in Elvis Costello's 'Man Out Of Time'
which should be chiselled on his headstone: 'He's got a mind like
a sewer and a heart like a fridge.'

Meanwhile I was discovering from the comfort of my own
living room that the theory about tanked-up, ticketless fans
scaring the poor police into submission was the one the Establishment hoped would save its neck. Two officers from the West
Midlands Police – the force given the task of collecting evidence
for the disaster inquiry and investigating the South Yorkshire
Police – paid me a visit.

The CID men seemed nice enough for a force that had battered
false confessions out of the Birmingham Six. They showed cour-
tesy and sympathy as they bowled me a few soft openers. And
then they cut to the quick:

'Did you have a drink before the game?'

'Yes.'

'How much?'

'Well, there was four of us, and we all got a round in, so
probably four pints.'

'Four pints.'

'Yeah, is that a problem?'

'No, no. Your mates who were with you, did they drink as
much as you?'

'Apart from the one who was driving, who had a couple of
shandies, yeah.'

'Fine.'

'How do you mean, "as much"? Is four pints a lot?'

'We're not here to judge, sir. We're just asking the questions.'

'But you have judged? Is it suddenly a crime to have a drink before a football match?'

'We're just collecting evidence. It's for others to deal with that evidence.'

But it was clear what was going on. They wanted to prove we were all pissed-up yobs who couldn't take part in the day's proceedings without alcohol. What was that line the *Sheffield Star* used: 'Hubble, bubble, toil and trouble . . . drunkenness and ticketlessness were now added to the equation.' As though this was the first time that fans had decided to have a drink before attending an FA Cup semi-final. Imagine if police had stood by as a marquee collapsed at the Henley Regatta, resulting in scores of deaths, or a crush had killed dozens of tennis-lovers at Wimbledon. Would the main thrust of the police investigation have been that these people had deliberately drunk too much Pimm's or Bollinger? If they had opened a gate at Twickenham resulting in tragedy, would every chap be grilled on how many tots of brandy he'd had?

Suddenly 100 years of football culture – a working man finishing at Saturday lunch-time, having a few pints and watching his team – had been turned into an offence against society.

The bereaved families told me later of the horror of that night in Sheffield when they raced over to find out if their loved ones were still alive. How some police officers were treating their dead children as suspects in a criminal investigation. How they were asked how much their child had had to drink, how much *they* had had to drink. It later turned out every corpse had been tested for alcohol content, with little or nothing found in any of them.

The police also wanted to know what time I arrived at the ground. When I told them it was 2.30 p.m. one of them asked if there was any reason for that, as though I was inviting trouble by leaving it so late. I asked him if he knew what it said about arrival times on the back of the ticket. He said he wasn't sure. So I told him that the FA regulations stated all ticket-holders should be in their position fifteen minutes prior to kick-off. Meaning I, and the vast majority of those stuck outside the Leppings Lane End, had technically turned up early. It was police with their insistence on giving the club with the bigger following the smallest number of tickets, and Sheffield Wednesday with their few, decrepit turn-stiles, who had been at fault. And where do you think the men who run that club were at 2.30 that afternoon? Probably getting pissed in one of the executive suites, celebrating roping in more cash from mugs like me, who'd paid £14 (a lot of money in 1989) to risk my life in their nineteenth-century pig-sty.

They also asked if all my mates had tickets. I told them they did but asked if it was suddenly a crime to turn up at a sporting event without a ticket. If so, why aren't they carrying out arrests at Wimbledon every year, where touts openly flaunt their wares and their profits? Why aren't they outside every pop concert in the land?

Of course there were fans there without tickets, like there have been fans at games since tickets were invented. Why suddenly, at this particular FA Cup semi-final, did police and their apologists decide that trying to buy a ticket for an event on the day was a reason to smear everyone outside the stadium as potential murderers?

I went back to work on the Friday feeling part skiver, part nutter and totally paranoid. I'd catch people giving me inquisitive glances, thinking they were trying to see if I was still a crumbling wreck, and I cursed myself for writing that piece when I was in the depths of depression. It's not what a British man is supposed to do, is it?

In reality, no one had paid much attention to me or my mental condition. This was such a desolate time on Merseyside, when every day there would be half-a-dozen funerals for the victims, all of which had to be reported in the local papers, that virtually everyone was affected in some way, and just battled through. The question that had to be asked, but nobody wanted to ask, was what would happen to the rest of the season? It seemed an insult to the dead to even think about football, and for a fortnight, publicly at least, Liverpool FC and their players didn't. There were too many funerals to attend and too many tears to mop up.

After all, these players were a crucial reason the ninety-five as it was then (ninety-four were declared dead by the Sunday, which became ninety-five on Wednesday when fourteen-year-old Lee Nicol died, and ninety-six in March 1993 when Tony Bland's life-support machine was switched off) were no longer alive. Those young people had idolized Barnes and Beardsley, Aldridge and Hansen. It's why they entered Hillsborough early that day to be close up to their heroes, and bore the full force of the crush.

And the presence of these idols at the funerals did so much for the bereaved. It showed them that football cared. That this cynical, disgraced industry which had claimed their loved ones and shattered their lives, wasn't rotten to the core.

When it was announced that Liverpool's first game after the disaster would be a friendly up at Celtic, the *Daily Post* sports desk asked if I'd like to do the match report. I accepted and walked into an emotional hurricane.

More than 60,000 Glaswegians packed into Parkhead to raise £250,000, rally the spirits of the players and show solidarity with their Scouse brethren. As the two teams took to the field the entire ground sang 'You'll Never Walk Alone' with such an intensity of feeling I went cold and started to shake. The final strains of the anthem gave way to a cacophony of applause, and the entire ground chanting 'Liverpool, Liverpool' in broad Glaswegian.

Down on the pitch the faces on the players showed they were bowled over. Up in the press box, my chest was heaving so much I struggled for air. We battered them 4–0, and it had nothing to do with Celtic feeling sorry for us. The team produced some glorious stuff. They were men released, overjoyed at being able to leave the black suits at home and do the jobs they were born to do. To cease being social workers and get back to being footballers.

After the tsunami of loathing and the litany of lies, that afternoon was a godsend. Much of the faith I had lost in football, and people, was being restored. Many of the questions I had asked about the point of life were being answered. At one point I looked down at the pitch. This side of the white line fans were still throwing coins into the buckets to help the families. On the other side John Aldridge was scoring his second goal and jogging back to the centre-circle with a smile on his face. Ten days earlier Aldo, a Scouser who had followed the Reds all his life, said he was contemplating retirement. That he couldn't see any way he could put on another pair of football boots.

'It hit me very, very hard. To the point were I couldn't cope,' he told me on the tenth anniversary. 'Hillsborough weakened me physically, emotionally and mentally. The thought of training never entered my head. I remember trying to go jogging but I couldn't run. There was a time when I wondered if I would ever muster the strength to play. I was learning about what was relevant in life.'

So we weren't alone, all those men like me, who felt the life had been scooped out of our bodies and wanted to revert to an almost womb-like state of solitude. All those empty shells who felt no appetite for duty or responsibility.

There was Aldo, one of us, out on the pitch, scoring and celebrating and exemplifying the hardest truth of human existence. Life has to go on. No matter what.

But how profound had been the change we'd undergone? That shrine called Anfield, smothered in a blanket of flowers. That Liver Bird. Did we love it more now? Did we owe an unpayable debt to those who went to the same game as us with the same sense of destiny, only to die with the same scarf around their neck, while we had lived? That was for the future. Life had determined that the present would be about a return to football, even though the pursuit of another League and FA Cup Double seemed irrelevant.

My memories of the rest of that season are all about observing one minute's silences, starting at Goodison Park on 3 May. Looking down at my feet, battling to hold the emotion in, feeling guilty that we were all about to immerse ourselves in battle again so soon. Wondering what state the families would be in, knowing a game was going ahead that their kids would have been at, or listened to on the radio.

I remember little about the FA Cup semi-final replay at Old Trafford on Sunday 7 May. A carload of Mancs giving us stick, and not having the will to respond. Another silence, this one harder than the last. Aldo scoring two headers to faint applause. Aldo rubbing Brian Laws's head and grinning, when the Forest player put through his own-goal, and vaguely laughing. But mostly feeling ashamed that the FA Cup was still going ahead. That no one had possessed the decency or the bollocks to cancel it for a season in memory of the dead. It was just another example – or is it the most blatant illustration? – of how little football fans mean to the people who run the game. The dead, like the reasons for their deaths, were being swept under the carpet. Classed as collateral damage in a war of vested interests.

Well, we'd always had the FA Cup final at Wembley to bring the curtain down on the season, hadn't we? The general public expected all the build-up, the joshing down Wembley Way, 'Abide With Me', a member of the Royal Family lowering themselves to turn up and present The Cup that Cheers. How could we cancel that? Why should we cancel that? The FA had budgeted for it. Would it make any difference to the dead? Gutless pygmies.

Again, I don't remember much about the Cup final against Everton. Hearing Gerry Marsden out on the pitch trying to whip us all up into a false sense of Merseyside United. Seeing that the fences had been taken down, out of token respect for the dead, and asking anyone who came within earshot why they hadn't done that at Hillsborough.

I actually felt very sorry for the Evertonians. They were aching to avenge the 1986 FA Cup final, but felt on such an emotional day that they had been booked as the support act. That a nation was willing Liverpool to win it, and dedicate it to the dead, and Everton were there to make up the numbers.

It wasn't much of a game. Aldo put us ahead after four minutes and nothing really happened until the 90th when Stuart McCall equalized. Rushie came on, carried out his traditional torture on Everton, with two superbly taken poacher's goals, and we won 3–2.

Unforgivably at the end, dozens of Liverpool fans, either through a sense of deep relief, or even deeper stupidity, spilled on to the pitch to embrace their heroes and the team had to scrap its lap of honour. It summed up why the day was such a deep insult to the dead. The fences that had been put up at Hillsborough to stop fans running on to the pitch, and had been taken down at Wembley because their presence was deemed grossly insensitive. And there they were, a small minority of fans, dancing on graves. It was apt I suppose, because we were all grave-dancing that day.

Since resuming their footballing lives again, those same Liverpool players (there was no such thing as rotation back then) faced eight games in May. Eight games in twenty-three days, after a gruelling season and a horrendous post-Hillsbrough fortnight, to win or lose another Double.

After that draw at Goodison they ran up three straight League wins before lifting the FA Cup. On the Tuesday after Wembley they ripped West Ham apart 5–1 at Anfield, meaning three nights later, on the Friday, we only had to avoid being beaten by two goals against second-placed Arsenal to cap off what would be, under the circumstances, the most astonishing Double ever.

The game, because it was shown live on ITV (a rare occurrence back then), has gone down in folklore as the most dramatic ending to any League title race. I suppose to the neutral it was. Unlike Everton at Wembley, who had suffered under the emotional weight of the occasion, George Graham's Arsenal side were well and truly up for it. Nobody gave them a chance of winning 2–0 at Anfield against a Liverpool side which had gone unbeaten in all competitions since New Year's Day. Except themselves.

All of us at Liverpool – fans, players and manager – simply didn't know how much hunger we had left, how much fuel was still in the system or how to handle the night. Bizarrely for such an attack-minded team which had been pulverizing opponents, Liverpool seemed happy to let Arsenal do all the running, and play for a draw. The plan worked well until shortly after half-time when Alan Smith scored for the Gunners.

It meant we were one goal away from blowing it. As the game went into extra time, it looked like this collection of brave and battered men, who had given every ounce of themselves for the club and its people, had done enough to limp over the line. But when John Barnes lost possession down at the Kop corner flag, they had nothing left in their bodies to prevent a swift Arsenal counter-attack turning into a Michael Thomas goal that sent Arsenal and their fans into delirium.

If that had that happened with the last kick of any of the previous twenty-four seasons I'd followed Liverpool, it would have seemed as though my entire world had crumbled. The players responsible for not stopping the move would have been cursed to oblivion. So deep would my depression have been, every oncoming bus would have appeared life's best option. But I didn't even put my head into my hands, let alone accuse a player. Neither did Terry or Mike, or anyone around us in the Kemlyn Road. We just accepted it, albeit with a heavy heart, as our fate.

So what? We'd lost a game our exhausted players were physically incapable of winning. What do you do, other than applaud them all? For the first time in my life losing didn't hurt. Mainly because victory could never have dragged me to a state approaching happiness. The FA Cup win had seemed like drawing a Charity Shield. I couldn't even put a mental notch on the bedpost reserved for FA Cups. Why was this any different? How could you be sad about something so trivial as a player making a mistake in the final minute of a game, when there were mums and dads out there so grief-stricken they were unable to breathe?

So we stayed behind and applauded Arsenal and their fans,

just like we had Don Revie's Leeds twenty years earlier. It seemed
the right thing to do. Maybe Arsenal fans deserved it more than
us, because they were the only ones capable of experiencing the
orgasmic pleasure of being crowned the best team in the land.
And they'd waited eighteen years.

We left in silence. There was no post-mortem on the way
to the pub because there was no need or appetite for one. We
walked into The Breck where the atmosphere was like a wake.
The manageress had laid out trays of sarnies, but they stayed
untouched. Men nodded respectfully at strangers in recognition
of the shared, unspoken connection. Small-talk was made, there
were shrugs, nods of agreements, knowing smiles. People stared
into the distance a lot and laughter was absent, the jukebox mute.
Everyone just wanted to get drunk and forget. So we did.

We didn't drink to Arsenal. Or Liverpool. Or life. We drank to
despair.

17

THE TRUTH

8 APRIL 1990 – VILLA PARK

There are certain moments when, without a trace of narcotics in your bloodstream, you feel the urge to race into the street and embrace every person in sight.

Such a moment entered my life at 6 o'clock on Tuesday, 1 August 1989, when a wrong was righted so eloquently, with such certainty, and my faith in human nature restored so absolutely, that I fell to my knees in my front room, thanked the Lord and repeatedly kissed the telly.

I was doing nights on the *Daily Post*, and not sleeping well. I'd gone to bed mid-morning and woken late afternoon, dossed around, stared like a zombie at young Australians trying to act, and got up to put the tea on. Then, following the opening bars of the BBC News, a voice boomed out that the report into the worst disaster in the history of British sport had completely exonerated the fans and laid the blame squarely at the door of the police.

I stopped dead in my tracks as the major points of Lord Justice Taylor's interim report into Hillsborough were read out. I could feel the nails hammering into the hearts of the police, Kelvin MacKenzie, the Yorkshire mafia and every other bastard behind the 'tanked-up hooligans' smear.

I'd seen Lord Taylor walking around the Anfield shrine, in the week after the disaster, and held out little hope. I feared this bastion of the Establishment would deliver a cleverly worded whitewash, that sent few ripples, covered many backs and preserved the status quo. I couldn't have been more wrong. Taylor ruled that drunkenness, late arrivals and conspiracies to bunk in without paying were red herrings. That there was no evidence of any kind of hooliganism or yobbish disorder. That the fans were not to blame for the crush.

Instead, he described 'the dangerous congestion at the turnstiles', caused by police failure to foresee and plan for 'the concentrated arrival of large numbers' and the turnstiles' inability to cope with the influx. That was what led to the opening of gate C. About 2,000 people, said Taylor, passed through that gate 'at a fast walk'. Most of them, following signs, headed straight for the tunnel which led to the central pens. All the police had to do was shut off the tunnel, as they had done at the same fixture the year before, and direct the fans to the side pens, where there was plenty of room.

'The immediate cause of the gross overcrowding,' Taylor explained, 'and hence the disaster, was the failure, when gate C was opened, to cut off access to the central pens which were already overfull. They were overfull because no safe maximum capacities had been laid down, no attempt was made to control entry to individual pens numerically and there was no effective visual monitoring of crowd density.'

He hit out at the 'sluggish reaction and response when the crush occurred' and claimed that the total number of fans who entered the Leppings Lane terrace 'did not exceed the capacity of the standing area'. So much for the thousands of ticketless yobs intent on anarchy.

Taylor's strongest criticism was aimed at Chief Superintendent David Duckenfield, the police officer in charge on the day.

Mr Duckenfield's capacity to take decisions and give orders seemed to collapse . . . Most surprisingly, he gave Mr Kelly (Secretary of the Football Association) and others to think that there had been an inrush due to Liverpool fans forcing open a gate. This was not only untruthful, it set off a widely reported allegation against the supporters which caused grave offence and distress.

It is a matter of regret that at the hearing, and in their submissions, the South Yorkshire Police were not prepared to concede that they were in any respect at fault in what occurred.

You needed to be someone who walked through that Hillsborough gate that afternoon to know what a feeling of relief those words were. What a rush of exhilaration they delivered. How comforting it was to know that, finally, someone in power was on your side. It felt as though a miscarriage of justice was being righted. That you'd been granted a pardon and released from serving a sentence for a crime you hadn't committed.

Over the following years Lord Taylor would be criticized for laying the blame solely at the door of the police, because in doing so, he let other culprits off the hook. Such as the FA for choosing Hillsborough and agreeing with the ticketing arrangements, Sheffield Wednesday for the state of the Leppings Lane End, Sheffield City Council for allowing the club to operate without a valid safety certificate, and the woeful lack of coordination among the emergency services.

But at six o'clock that Tuesday night in August, those observations didn't matter. What mattered was that the charge of killing your own, which millions believed you were guilty of, had been shot down by Taylor. Here was The Truth. And it was the complete opposite to the one the police had convinced the *Sun* to portray.

You couldn't put a psychological price on that. So much had been written and said, as well as whispered and unsaid, about the guilt of us fans, that there were moments when I would seriously question it myself. Did I miss something that day? Am I wallowing in self-delusion? Am I so paranoid after Heysel that I can't bring myself to accept my part in more deaths?

But no. The main man Lord Justice Taylor, who would go on to become Lord Chief Justice, the highest lawman in the land, had backed up everything we had seen and castigated those who had tried to pervert the course of justice. It was like seeing your eight score draws come up (ask your dads, kids) then hearing you were the only punter who held a winning coupon.

I wanted to take his hand, grip it tight, and thank him from the bottom of my heart. Four years later, interviewing him for the *Liverpool Echo*, I had the chance. Yet the man (unsurprisingly a state-educated Geordie) told me there was no need for thanks. He had taken no side and shown no favour to the underdog, but merely reported honestly on his exhaustive inquiries. And it was one of the most black-and-white cases he had come across.

'It was quite simple, really,' he said. 'It all pointed to the one thing. There had been this delay outside, the gates had been opened and instead of diffusing where the people were going, they were all allowed to go down this one tunnel where it was already full.

'There was really no two ways about it, that's what happened. Although many people said I was too hard on the police they should remember the chief constable who sat with me throughout the inquiry was in total agreement with what I said. The evidence seemed to me to be almost one-way. It really wasn't a difficult case to decide what went wrong.'

The delivery of that report in August was a turning point in my life. A month earlier I'd discovered that Ann was pregnant with our first child, which we found out (through being too nosy) was to be a boy. Despite the obvious joy I had a lingering feeling of guilt. I couldn't help thinking about all those boys and men who didn't come back from Hillsborough, who would never get the chance to pass on the flame to their sons. And I feared this horrible guilt, exacerbated by the slurs that those who came back had somehow been to blame, would never go away.

Taylor's interim report was the therapy all us sufferers had needed. The slap across the face that told us to lift our chins off the floor, hold our heads up and move on. When the real Truth was delivered it felt as though all the slurs would be laid to rest, the families would receive justice and fitting compensation and heads would roll. That we could put the guilt behind us and take up life again. I had a son on the way. A future to provide. What's more, it turned out he'd been conceived on holiday in Jamaica. Which gave me a sliver of a chance she'd go for Barnes Reade.

What a season 1989–90 was for Barnesey. He scored 22 goals in 34 games and set up countless more as we won the title back in style, nine points ahead of Aston Villa. Yet despite becoming champions with ease, there were ominous signs that the foundations of the empire were starting to creak.

Two games against the same team, Crystal Palace, summed up the bittersweet nature of this season. At Anfield in September Palace were destroyed 9–0, a record First Division victory for the club and the most one-sided Liverpool game I'd ever seen. But what really sticks in the memory that night is John Aldridge coming off the bench to take a penalty, then taking off everything but his shorts and throwing them into the Kop at the end of the game. Aldo was off to San Sebastian against his will. A victim of Rushie's return and a short-sighted board, who were missing their European revenues and saw the chance to make a quick £1.15 million.

It was bad business and unLiverpool business by any standards. Over the next two seasons Aldo would hit 40 goals in 75 games for Real Sociedad. When he came back to England he scored another 174 for Tranmere. Five years later he would still be scoring for Ireland in the 1994 World Cup. And over the next seventeen years I and many other old-timers would lose count of the times we'd be looking at overrated, overpriced mediocrity in Liverpool's attack and say, 'If only we had an Aldo out there.' John Aldridge: Legend.

The second Crystal Palace game, in the FA Cup semi-final at Villa Park, went down as the day the earth moved. A 4–3 defeat which showed up defensive frailties that had been alien to the club for the past two decades, yet which would haunt them for the next two. This was Watford in 1969 revisited. For Barry

Endean, read Alan Pardew. The day an average, hard-working side showed Liverpool the direction it was drifting. A game that told everyone with an understanding of the club that a wind of change was blowing through Anfield.

We went one up through Rushie early on and we were 3–2 ahead with three minutes left on the clock, yet we couldn't see off a Palace side we'd thrashed 9–0 only months earlier. They'd sussed that our weakness was a creaking, vulnerable defence and just kept pumping high balls in. Four times they were successful. Another Double dream had died. But the performance, and the reality it exposed, was far more profound. We were looking at epoch-changing times.

At the end, as the Liverpool players slumped to the floor unable to fully comprehend how a side of their calibre and experience had repeatedly surrendered a lead, one face summed up the collapse. Alan Hansen. The symbol of class and coolness at the heart of Liverpool's defence stretching back to the 1970s. A colossal force at the heart of eight championship-winning sides and three European Cups. He looked lost. He looked like the original colossus, Ron Yeats, at Watford in 1969. A month later Hansen retired.

Three weeks after the semi-final, a John Barnes penalty against QPR would give us our 18th title. Our 13th in 26 outrageously successful years. Every other year it was ours. But never in all those years had we looked so much in need of rebuilding.

A fortnight later Manchester United would beat Palace to win the first major trophy under Alex Ferguson. The man who had famously said that coming to Anfield left him choking on his own vomit had now set his sights on his one burning ambition. Tae knock Liverpool off their perch.

18

THE HOLY GHOST

19 NOVEMBER 1990 – BOWER ROAD, WOOLTON

The Derby County steward approached me for the third time and, as his puce face hinted, diplomacy and manners were off his agenda.

'Listen pal, I've told you. You can't stand up. And you definitely can't stand up and start a fight. Last warning or I'm throwing you out.'

To be fair I was on dodgy ground. I was after all sitting in the area of the stand reserved for representatives of Her Majesty's Press, where the deal is, for a free seat you keep your emotions in check. But I couldn't help myself.

The piece of lard with the Noddy Holder head, sitting two seats away from the press box, kept bellowing abuse at John Barnes. At the top of his mongrel, monotone voice.

'Yer useless Barnes . . . yer fat lazy bastard . . . couldn't give a shit about England . . . I wouldn't give you house-room.'

It was September 1989. Three days earlier Barnes had played for England in a dour 0–0 draw in Sweden, the only high-point of which was Terry Butcher's bleeding head turning his shirt bright crimson, epitomizing our good old John Bull spirit.

Barnes, of course, was the whipping boy, as he always was in an England shirt. The ignorant hordes who support mediocre clubs accusing him of only ever turning it on for Liverpool. At the Baseball Ground the abuse was flying at him, the Noddy Holder lookalike lacing it with clear racist overtones. So I gave it back, telling him he wasn't worthy of Barnes, and how, thanks to inbreds like him supporting England, I'd rather wipe the Three Lions across my backside than place it on my back.

Our ding-dong had lasted for a good hour, during which time Liverpool had put three past Derby without reply, including a typically clinical penalty from Barnes, and the players had one eye on the taps in the club lounge bar. It was clear to the Holder clone that the only pleasure he was going to take from the afternoon was winding me up. He'd tried all the 'get back to your Scouse slums/go and have a dead rat for your tea' slurs, to little effect. So he played his ace.

'Will someone cripple that useless black twat.' That was it. I was over the side of the press box, trying to drag him out of the seat, being pushed back by Derby fans. Two stewards grabbed me and frogmarched me out. The one who'd been trying to keep me in check all afternoon told me he'd never seen such reprehensible behaviour from a journalist in twenty years of stewarding.

I told him he should visit the Cross Keys pub at the back of the *Liverpool Echo* building most Fridays, but he didn't get it, and the Baseball Ground gate was slammed in my face. I walked the streets of Derby thinking that if this is what happens on my first away assignment as a reporter for the *Daily Post*, I was probably in the wrong job.

Following my post-Hillsborough Celtic match report, sports editor Len Capeling offered me a job on the sports department's subbing desk, with the chance to report on Liverpool and Everton games most weekends. What more could I ask for? Paid to go to the match? Home and away? Was there a better way to earn a living? That was the theory. In reality I was simply a fan sitting in the wrong seat.

There were plenty of highs that season. Totally outclassing Man United at Old Trafford a fortnight after my son Philip was born in March 1990 – Barnes Reade stayed on the cutting-room floor of the Births and Deaths Office – and going back to Coventry for a glorious 6–1 destruction a week after the title was clinched are two that spring to mind. But for most of the time I was struggling to control myself, and it wasn't a pretty sight for anyone.

The Luton stewards had a serious word with me, my eyeballing of a Man United fan during the Charity Shield at Wembley led to complaints to the men in yellow jackets, and the rest of the press pack were not enamoured with my leaping up at goals, shouting at refs, swearing at players. I even joined in a song at Anfield once, after too many pre-match pints, and got a slap on the head from a Radio Merseyside reporter trying to do his match report.

Before every game I'd give myself a talking to. Today would be the day I'd act like a proper reporter. Controlled, unbiased, objective, calm, professional. But I was like a Tourette's Syndrome sufferer. The words that were popping into my brain just kept coming out of my mouth. 'Yeeee-es', 'Bastard', 'Useless wanker', 'Come on Reds, these are shite' -- they would be out before I knew I was about to yell them. My brain lacked a control mechanism.

All those years and all those hundreds and hundreds of games, felt through the same heart, filtered through the same one-track mind, had left me like a trained dolphin at feeding time. My reaction to every incident was predetermined. These were primeval instincts coming from deep inside. Resistance was futile – I could only act one way.

As a sub-editor who did match reports on the side I didn't have the ball-breaking task of staying on-message with the local managers – unlike the proper journalists, the ones who had a full-time job reporting the Merseyside patch. I wasn't very popular among them – not only did they feel I was a yob in the press box, but an even bigger yob in print.

Basically my view coincided too closely with the lowest common denominator on the terraces. I'd spend an hour before the game in the pub, plus an hour or so afterwards, and I was reflecting what they thought, not what those inside Anfield or Goodison thought. Which is often the case with reporters who need to phone up the manager the next day to get the inside track on injuries and transfers. They can't afford too much honesty.

It got to the point where the man from the *Daily Mail* phoned up Len Capeling to try and get me sacked. I'd written in the report of a dismal 2–2 draw against Luton that the only word being used in the local pubs to sum up Liverpool's home form of late was 'crap'. Apparently I was demeaning the noble profession. Thankfully Capeling had been at the same game, told the *Mail* man it had been crap and slammed the phone down.

At first, seeing the players close up, and breathing in the same oxygen as Kenny Dalglish during post-match press conferences left me awestruck. But soon you realize they see you, a journalist, as at best someone who can help their career when form and results desert them, and at worst the enemy. I would soon also realize, in a painful way, that the warning about never meeting your heroes is one you should heed.

At first though, I used my privileged position to engineer meetings with as many of my heroes as I could. December 1989 saw the thirtieth anniversary of Shankly's arrival at Anfield and I persuaded the *Post* to do a series on it. There were four people who mattered to me and I made sure I spoke to all of them: Shankly's first great signing Ian St John (I didn't have the balls to tell him about my playground seal impressions back in 1964); Shankly's greatest signing Kevin Keegan (he said 'Shankly believed in me, he made me, and a big part of me went when he died,' then demanded Anfield be renamed the Shankly Stadium); Liverpool's greatest-ever signing Kenny Dalglish (who claimed, way before David Moyes uttered the phrase, that Shankly had made Liverpool the People's Club); and Bob Paisley, the man who took the foundations and the walls that Shankly had built, added another storey and stuck on the roof. Then built a conservatory, just for the hell of it.

Fourteen years after strolling down to Melwood with Chris Hill to see God the Father, I was going to meet the Holy Ghost. He was a few months short of his seventy-second birthday, six years into his retirement, and living in the same Woolton semi he always had, with his wife Jessie. She ushered me into the front room where Bob was sitting watching the racing. He had a jumper that zipped up at the front, a loud striped tie underneath, black slacks, slippers and Brylcreemed hair he kept patting down unconsciously. He smiled shyly, got up to shake my hand uncomfortably, muttered about switching the telly off, then hobbled over to do it manually. It was like visiting your mate's house and finding his grandad had moved in.

The room was pure working-class, but with a thicker shagpile to the carpet, which was testament to the fact he'd earned a few bob more than his coal-mining father. Not that he was showing it. On every spare surface – the mantelpiece, coffee table, top of the telly – were school photos of grandchildren still in their cardboard frames, and knick-knacks brought back from family holidays, carrying the name of the resort above a view of the beach.

I thought to myself, this is the most accomplished manager in the history of British football, a man who gave forty-four years' unbroken service to the country's most successful club, yet he could be any pensioner in any house in the land. Looking back I'm not sure if that says more about the way football has gone, how men whose talent would struggle to be described as mediocre live like film stars, or if it says more about Bob Paisley. Probably the latter. Because he was normality personified. The most simple, honest, decent and modest of men. But nobody's fool.

Jessie went to make us some tea and Bob sank back in his old armchair and said 'So you want to talk about Bill then, because we'll have to keep it to that.' Before adding with the trademark chuckle, 'I can't be getting into no more trouble.' Bob had stopped doing interviews two years earlier, after he was quoted in the *Sunday Express* saying the First Division was not as good as in his day, and John Aldridge wasn't fit to lace Ian Rush's boots. From the board down to the fans, everyone at Anfield was taken aback. It seemed wildly out of character that Paisley would be so outspoken and appear so bitter.

His family claimed he had been lulled, conned and misquoted

but the reporter stuck by his story. Paisley just seemed perplexed by it all, apologizing, but claiming he couldn't remember what he had or hadn't said. It was the first public sign that all wasn't well.

The sad truth was that he was in the early stages of Alzheimer's Disease, and just over a year after our meeting it would be officially diagnosed. I was having a deep favour bestowed on me. The great man had stopped giving interviews, but felt it only right that he should contribute to a series marking the thirtieth anniversary of Shankly's arrival. It turned out to be one of the last times he would be capable of sharing his memories in public with any real lucidity.

When Jessie brought the tea in she was nervous, concerned about her husband's state of mind and what he might not realize he was saying. But equally worried that I might suss he wasn't the full shilling. I half expected her to sit in with us, so concerned were the family that I might be out to turn him over. She left, reminding him in a semi-serious way to be on his best behaviour, looking at me, and nodding knowingly back at him, as if to say, we're trusting you here son, don't let us down.

There was more chance of me turning over the Pope and selling my tale to *Orange Weekly*. I was here to talk about Shankly with the man who knew him best. That in itself was honour enough. Then Bob started talking and the doubts kicked in. The interview didn't seem to be going anywhere. He appeared to be struggling with the most basic of questions, mumbling back in broken sentences, looking away, coming back at them after a second. Going off on what I perceived to be disjointed tangents. He'd drift into asides, chuckle to himself, or just end a sentence with 'the doings'. Always mentioning 'the doings'. As in 'so-and-so could put it in the doings [the net]' or 'the other fella, now he had the doings'.

The longer I spoke to him, the more I got on to his wavelength, understood his patterns of speech, and realized there was something profound behind most of what he had to say. When I played the tape back, and edited out his 'erms', 'ahs' and 'likes', his 'doings' and 'ya knows', I'd never heard such clear footballing logic in my life. There was a clinical authority to his words. I'd mined pearls of wisdom.

How did he react when he heard Shankly was calling it a day? 'I tried harder than anyone to get him to stay. I'd say to him, "Bill, what are you going to do with yourself if you retire?" You see he was a real loner. He didn't knock about with anyone.

'Nessie begged me to get him to change his mind. And I did. I went on my hands and knees and told him he couldn't pack it in because it would kill him. And sad to say, it did.'

What made him realize when Shankly was going that he should take his job? 'I asked the players whether I should and they said yes. So I thought, well, a new fella wouldn't know how it worked round here, not properly. So I thought, go on then, I'd best do it.'

There was an aura about him. A calm serenity that was almost saint-like.

How would he sum up his relationship with Shanks? 'In the fifteen years we worked together seeing a thousand Liverpool games we never once had an argument. We may have disagreed but we'd just have our say and that was it. No arguing. Because I always gave Bill a straight answer and he respected criticism from those he respected.'

He even gave me a story I'd never heard before, which was a follow-up to that Shanklyism about squeezing a rugby ball into a football. A Paisleyism that would forever be mine to tell – and it was actually funnier than the Shanklyism: 'Bill was always encouraging all sorts of lads to come down to Anfield and get treatment for injuries. I'll never forget one day I was in my room and I heard him in the corridor telling this lad: "What you've got there is no problem, son. Bobby Paisley will sort you out. He's the greatest trainer in the world. He can fix anything. There's his room. Tell him I sent you."

'And this poor young fella comes in in a wheelchair. Just sitting there looking up at me, believing I could cure him because

Bill had told him I could. It was so sad. The lad was crippled. I couldn't do anything for him.

'But that was Bill. He'd think just by telling someone something it would make them believe in themselves. That was the mentality that rubbed off on lots of people and made them better players and better men.'

I also heard how he had spotted Shankly's weaknesses, and learned from them: 'If I had one criticism of Bill it was that he didn't break up the great team of the 1960s earlier. He was content with what he'd done and kept faith with the players. He was a very loyal man but I thought it was more important that we got back to winning ways again.'

Paisley had a cold ruthlessness that Shankly didn't possess, and which the wider world underestimated. He understood that Shankly's human failing had kept Liverpool in the wilderness for seven years at the end of the 1960s, and it convinced him there was no room for sentiment in the modern game. Alex Ferguson (I refuse to knight him), the only manager who can seriously lay claim to being as successful as Paisley, was equally callous, showing the door to big names the second he thought they'd outstayed their welcome.

I asked him the big one about why Shankly went, hoping after all these years the truth would finally be laid bare. Initially it seemed not even Bob Paisley could put us out of our misery: 'I must have asked him a hundred times what was getting him down but he wouldn't say, and I can't for definite tell you why he did, and I asked him more than anyone.'

Surely after all these years he must have had time to work out why he ended up inheriting Shankly's mantle? What it was that made him walk?

'If I was pushed I'd say maybe he was frightened of having another lean spell. He'd built a great side in the sixties which suddenly stopped winning things, and in 1974 he'd built another great team, which had won the League, the Cup and the UEFA Cup.

'I think at the back of his mind he may have been afraid of failure. I think he'd made his mind up to go out at the top like a class boxer. Because more than anything Bill was a boxer at heart.'

I've heard dozens of so-called experts put forward their theories, and even asked Shankly myself, but none struck me as being as close to the truth as Paisley's. Because nobody knew Shankly better than his old lieutenant. Not even Shankly.

Jessie popped her head in, and asked if he was behaving himself. I just grinned nervously. She said she was nipping out to work, that she had a bit of a part-time job, but I could stay as long as I wanted. I could sense Bob was getting a bit twitchy and wanted the horse-racing back on the telly, so I got up to leave with her.

She asked how it had gone and I told her fine. But what I meant to say was it felt like I'd just had an audience with Gandhi. That I had been in the presence of utter humility yet I'd never felt more humbled.

I told her not to worry. He hadn't said anything he shouldn't and even if he had I wouldn't write it. She breathed a sigh of relief and said, 'That's good,' her crumpled nose giving off an 'Ah, bless,' a nod to the way her old, beloved teddy bear of a man was fading.

Bob stood at the front door as me and Jessie left, looking about as uncomfortable as his carpet slippers-and-tie ensemble. He gave me a wave and I waved back, feeling utterly privileged.

There above that zipped-up jumper, on that ordinary doorstep, was the football brain who spotted Rush, Dalglish, Souness and Hansen and who converted Ray Kennedy from bustling target man to midfield artist. He was the great modernizer who decided there was no room for a traditional centre-half like Ron Yeats or Larry Lloyd in a team that wanted to win European Cups, so employed footballing centre-backs like Phil Thompson, Hansen and Mark Lawrenson. There was the innovator who played the split striker role to perfection with Dalglish behind Rush way before others saw how vital it was to unlock defences. The thinker who realized that if Liverpool were to dominate Europe they had to adopt the patient, subtle, cat-and-mouse approach of their continental opponents. There stood the most successful manager in English football history, at the door of his ordinary suburban semi, watching his wife going out to work, despite both being retired. This is what you get when you labour all of your life for love not money. A life like everyone else's. Afternoons in front of the telly watching the racing, with just the *Sporting Life* and pictures of your grandkids to keep you company.

There are many quotes that ensured Bill Shankly was elevated to the status of Anfield's all-time sage. And rightly so. But two of the most telling utterances, which shed light on how Liverpool maintained their supremacy for so long, came from Paisley's mouth.

When he'd travelled to judge a player, and had to separate the diamonds from the dross, one thought was uppermost: 'The first few yards are all in the head.' When asked to define the essence of the Liverpool Way, he replied, 'If you're lost in a fog you stick together. That way you don't get lost. If there's a secret to Liverpool FC that's it.'

Bob Paisley's Alzheimer's became so bad in the mid-nineties that he had to be put in a nursing home. When he died in 1996 Jessie said he had been so poorly towards the end he couldn't remember being manager of Liverpool, let alone any of those three European Cup wins, six League titles and four League Cups. Her heart-breaking revelation saddened me beyond words at the time, and has haunted me ever since. Her husband was a man, the greatest of managers, the most loyal of servants to Liverpool FC over five decades, who had given us fans so much pleasure.

So many great players, so many inspired decisions, so many glorious victories, so many fabulous nights of celebration, which will stay with us until our dying day.

Yet he had lost all memory of those moments. A crueller, more undeserving fate it is difficult to imagine.

19

CRACKING UP

It was one of those tumbleweed moments when silence descends and every face in the room stares at shoes, apart from the one who is dishing it out and the one who has no option but to take it.

'What's that?' growled Kenny Dalglish. 'I don't understand you.'

I felt lower than a flea on a pile on a limbo-dancer's bum. Dalglish was holding a press conference at Anfield the day before Liverpool's opening game of the 1990–91 season at Sheffield United. I'd asked a harmless question – 'Is it a problem facing a newly promoted team like Sheffield United because they're an unknown quantity?' – not out of any concern for the answer, but because, at thirty-three, I still got a stalker's thrill just talking to Kenny.

The problem was he didn't want to talk to me. A few days earlier I'd written a piece saying Liverpool might struggle to retain their title because they'd lost Alan Hansen at the back, Dalglish and Aldridge up front, yet hadn't signed anybody new. In fact Kenny hadn't bought a player of genuine class since those four spectacular signings in 1987.

These words clearly gave him further evidence that I was an impertinent and ungrateful little tosser who didn't understand the deal between a football manager and a local hack back then: he keeps your card marked and you deliver uncritical press releases on his behalf.

I repeated the question, and he deepened my embarrassment by saying he'd understood what I'd said, but not what I meant. My punishment was complete when he asked what type of club doesn't have the opposition watched and what kind of football reporter thinks Liverpool would sack all their scouts? It triggered relieved laughter from the sycophants as he stared at me triumphantly, his eyes saying, you asked for that you jumped-up little prick. The flea on the limbo-dancer's bum had now crashed through the floorboards en route to Australia. You have to have been publicly shamed by a man you've idolized for a dozen years of your adult life to know how crushed it leaves you. I felt small, stupid, angry and betrayed. I knew then that I had to get out of this job before it destroyed my faith in football.

They say if you get too near to the flame, you get burned. Well, I fell into a ring of fire, walking out of Anfield that day like Joan of Arc seconds after the sparks licked her tootsies.

I didn't blame Dalglish. It was my fault, not his. When it came to football matters he was the genius, not me. He held a view, always had, that the thoughts of journalists who have never played the game professionally should be treated with contempt by those who had. And maybe he's right. Who are we, who sit ample-girthed before laptops, to tell those who have done it at the highest level where they are going wrong?

Through my job I'd ended up seeing many footballers at close quarters and realized that idols are just normal men filled with human flaws. Some, due to a lifetime of being treated as something out of the ordinary, had allowed those flaws to become even more exaggerated than normal, to the point where they weren't very nice individuals. If I hung around them too long and allowed cynicism to peel back my eyes and see what football is really about, it would inevitably lose its spell. I needed my distance back. I needed to view it all from a position where you can say and think what you like, and your right to do so is made sacrosanct by the money you pay at the gate.

So how grateful I was when, in October 1990, the *Echo* editor offered me a general column on his paper, enabling me to leave the *Post*, hand back my press-box pass, return to my Kemlyn Road seat and never again have to confront a player who was about to shove past and throw me a look which told me where he'd like to stick my tape recorder. Sideways.

The move didn't keep me out of Liverpool's bad books though. Free to write a weekly column on whatever tickled my fancy, I'd inevitably return to football. In January 1991 it emerged that England might be bidding to stage the 1998 World Cup, with Anfield cited as one of the host grounds. Now here was a comic opportunity not to be missed.

I told the travelling fans what delights lay in store in the Kemlyn Road: 'Seats built for gnomes, an almighty crush as you make for the ridiculously small exits, the sight of people urinating against walls and in sinks because the queue in the toilets is five-deep, a ten-minute jostle at one of the few refreshment bars – only to find, once again, that all that's left is a cup of overpriced, over-stewed pee. It would be a sad reflection on our city if the Boys from Brazil travelled half-way across the planet to see their samba heroes – and couldn't even get a meat pie at half-time. It's bad enough getting a taxi from Old Swan.'

The next day a posh-sounding secretary rang, informing me that the chairman of Liverpool FC would like me to pop in and see him for a chat over afternoon tea in the boardroom.

'Will it be over-stewed pee?' I asked.

'Three p.m. sharp,' she replied, and hung up.

Noel White was charm personified. With a homely Lancashire accent and a hail-fellow-well-met manner you could see how he'd made a mint flogging sheet music and second-hand tellies around Greater Manchester.

As he showed me plans for the Centenary Stand they would build above the Kemlyn Road he talked of his love and ambition for the club he had recently been made chairman of after the retirement of John Smith. A few things unnerved me. Why was a man his age and position wearing a leather bomber jacket which looked like it had been bought in a pub? Why did he keep getting his facts about past players and dates about cup triumphs wrong? If he'd been a fan for so long, as he professed, why were there such glaring gaps in his knowledge? Most of all, how on God's earth did such a person, whose main qualification was running Altrincham Town for twenty-five years, make the quantum leap to running Liverpool?

Probably the same way he had climbed the FA's greasy pole – through his contacts (like his best buddy and Manchester City chairman Peter Swales), his charm, and his ability as an operator. Well he was certainly operating on me. He asked how the fans thought the season was going and I told him there were mumblings of discontent. That we'd started off well, but the past two months had been up and down. That the team had become negative, packing the midfield with full-backs, leaving out Peter Beardsley, and that overall we were a bit puzzled about why new players hadn't been brought in. That the Liverpool Way had always been to replace players before they lost it, not while they were losing it. That we needed an infusion of new blood and if the recently signed Jimmy Carter was the strength of it, then we may as well sign Jimmy Krankie.

This was weird. We're talking floating up to heaven and looking down on your body lying on an operating table, weird. Here I was, sitting in the Anfield boardroom, sipping tea from fine china, telling the club chairman where we were going wrong, and being greeted with sympathetic nods and laughter. It felt like I was having one of the hundreds of dreams I'd had about LFC since I was a kid. So much so that I half expected him to give me Kenny's big padded coat, tell me to go over to a tactics board and show him how we should be playing next Saturday. But what he gave me was far more spooky. He turned my observations on where the club should be improving into a whinge about Dalglish's team selection, tactics and recent purchases. Jimmy Carter was mauled. He lambasted his manager like the worst bar-room bore in town. Bonding with me. Letting me know that we were on the same wavelength, and after the same goal. Willing me, me his best new mate, to spread the word among my fellow Reds that old Whitey was a good stick. That while he ran Liverpool, nobody, not even Kenny Dalglish, was bigger than the club.

My back felt sore as I headed to the car park, due to too many slaps as we parted. My head felt angry. It is one thing for the man who runs a business to try to bond with his customers. Quite another for the man who runs Liverpool to show open contempt for such a legend as Dalglish to a stranger. Especially when the assessment is delivered by someone whose knowledge of the club's history, and thus its soul, was so lamentable.

I felt very uneasy about it, convinced things were wrong at the highest level. Gone was the loyalty that Shankly had demanded from every employee and the harmony that John Smith's reign had established. It chimed with stories I'd heard about unrest among some of the senior players. Camps were being set up, egos jostling for control. Chinks were appearing in the solid structure that linked Boot Room to boardroom, which had kept the club at the top for twenty-five years.

Three weeks after that meeting with White the empire crumbled. Dalglish walked out, citing ill-health through stress. We all walked too, into a trophy wilderness.

He made his decision to go the day after a 4–4 draw in the FA Cup fifth-round replay at Goodison. Many neutrals and Evertonians called it one of the greatest cup ties ever, but for Liverpool fans it was acutely painful. A microcosm of all that was going wrong and the writing on the wall, sprayed large. We couldn't defend with any cohesion, throwing away the lead four times. Some of the players looked past it. As against Palace in the previous year's FA Cup the sense of invincibilty was demolished by inferior opponents. There was clear division in the ranks, with rumours that Dalglish had been forced to bring back Peter Beardsley, and when he scored the opening goal some of the players appeared to gloat in Dalglish's direction. As rumours of anarchy among players in the dressing room after the final whistle spread, there was an air of bewilderment among the fans.

In the dug-out that Wednesday night was the ghost of a man who used to be Kenny Dalglish, looking haunted, pale and drawn, a good ten years older than the thirty-nine he'd lived through. The news of his resignation broke on the Friday morning to almost universal astonishment. Some said it was more of a shock than Shankly's bombshell. After all he'd been sixty while Kenny wasn't even forty. But what they forgot is that due to Heysel and Hillsborough, so much trauma had been packed into Dalglish's time as manager, it had made him tired and old. Plus the pressures he was under to remain at the very top of English football, pressure pumped up by his own towering standards as player and coach, were far more intense than in Shankly's day.

I was a stone-sub on the *Echo*, which meant working with the printers as they composed the pages. The front-page was dominated by one sombre image of Kenny, close to tears, his mind somewhere far away. Flanked by old men in dark suits, he looked like a shell-shocked dad who'd been cajoled by police to go before the cameras and appeal for the return of a missing child. This led many fans to believe he was simply going through a bad patch, and would be back in a few weeks, apologizing for a temporary loss of sanity and, recharged, would lead us to the Double.

Others were relieved. They trotted out the old chestnut about taking the team as far as he could. They thought it needed a fresh eye and an iron fist to knock them back into shape. I just kept thinking back to my afternoon tea date with White, believing that pitiful photograph of Kenny was the inevitable consequence of a proud man under pressure and realizing he had lost the support of his board. If White could be so disloyal towards Dalglish in front of a local hack, how much poison was he spreading around the board? And how much of it got to Kenny?

Twenty-five years later my fears about White would be confirmed when he slagged off Rafa Benitez to my *Daily Mirror* colleague Martin Lipton, claiming he'd bought badly, his team selection was poor and he wasn't the man for the job. The exact same sentiments he'd expressed to me about Dalglish. So a traitor all along, then?

Dalglish was still a young man, suffering from nervous exhaustion brought on by Liverpool's crippling demands for success, plus the emotional stress of Hillsborough which he had shouldered more than anyone at Anfield. A chairman who really wanted him to stay would have told him to take a six-month sabbatical, and would not have taken no for an answer. But Noel White let him go and the wheels came off.

He was letting go of quite a legacy. In the five full seasons as manager Kenny Dalglish had never finished below second, winning three League titles and two FA Cups; for one of those seasons at least, his side had played the most attractive football Anfield had ever seen. Only two freak defeats against Wimbledon in the FA Cup final and Arsenal at Anfield in the League had deprived him of three Doubles. He had guided them magnificently through the two biggest disasters to hit British football, left them on top of the League and still in the FA Cup.

Over the years many theories have been floated to contradict Dalglish's own explanation that he was suffering from ill-health. As with Shankly, a retirement so sudden and so sensational demanded one overriding reason to explain it. But life's not like that. And neither is football.

Shankly told me when I met him at Melwood: 'Sometimes I felt so mentally drained I couldn't think straight.' Dalglish told the Liverpool board he felt like his head was going to explode.

How many of us could even begin to understand the pressure he was under? A never-ending pressure. A pressure Shankly described thus: 'It follows you home, follows you everywhere and eats into your famliy life.' A pressure that increases, not relents, with success. A pressure that was cranked up every season as football began to take centre stage in the arena of national celebrity.

At a club like Liverpool the incessant demand to fend off failure is often harder to live with than failure itself. When you crack, you crack. You don't plan it for the end of a season and it's more likely to come in the middle of a cup tie when you're top of the League.

There was an added pressure for Dalglish. He'd never had a chance to stop after a long, gruelling playing career. He hadn't had a breather, enjoyed the family he had been separated from so often, and work out what he wanted to do with the rest of his life. He'd gone straight into managing the best club in Europe at the age of thirty-five. His ability as a player was queried by none but his ability as a manager was increasingly brought into question. As long as it came from the pack of journalists he treated with such contempt, he could cope. We were the enemy.

Even when it came from the fans he could still cope, because a football man knows he will never keep them all happy. When it comes from the senior players, some of whom are mates, you are struggling. But when it comes from above, from the men who employ you, and who are there to throw a protective shield around you when the pressure builds in the loneliest of jobs, you know your time is up.

So you wake up one morning, as Kenny did, in another sweat. You look at your wife's concerned face, you look in the mirror at a pale reflection of your youth, you realize that you haven't been listening to the kids for a week and you ask yourself why you're still in your thirties but feel like an old man. Then suddenly it hits you that you've given everything to a game that doesn't want to give you anything back any more. So you go 'sod it' and walk away like a little boy lost.

Who among us could blame him?

20

CHARLIE CHAMPAGNIA

The hotel cellar bar, an hour after the filming of the *Daily Mirror*'s Pride of Britain Awards, is a heaving mass of well-sozzled luvvies, daytime TV celebrities and journalist executives. I'd been working for the last five hours, owned a tongue so parched it was contemplating licking up the perfume spills on the red carpet, and was struggling to catch the barman's eye through a wall of outsized egos.

'Oi, Readey,' yelled Des Kelly, the paper's deputy editor, 'over here. I've got someone who's dying to meet you.' I can tell by his grin that this should be avoided, and motion that I'm trying to get a drink.

'I'll get it. Come here,' he says, pulling me towards the packed bar.

From out of the scrum of backs a stocky figure in an immaculate dark suit turns to show me his bronzed face and moustache, gives me a steely glare, grabs my hand, crushes it until it feels as withered as Jeremy Beadle's, then mutters in a sinister Edinburgh drawl:

'Ah, the bastard who got me the sack. I've waited ten years to meet you.'

Oh no. It's Graeme Souness. Now I really need a drink. Because if his memory is as good as it seems, pretty soon I'll be lying on a hard bed with the sign NIL BY MOUTH hanging above my head. Me and Graeme Souness had history.

I wouldn't go as far as to say I got him the sack. He made a good fist of that himself. I just tried, very hard, to ensure it happened. In fact I tried relentlessly in my *Echo* column for twenty months, from 15 April 1992 until the day he walked out of Anfield in January 1994. A walk that lifted my soul more than Nelson Mandela's stroll from Victor Verster prison four years previously.

It hadn't always been that way. When he was named as successor to Kenny Dalglish in April 1991 it seemed like one of the shrewdest appointments since Shankly. He fitted the bill to perfection. Hadn't the club been drifting since the 1990 semi-final against Crystal Palace? Wasn't there some truth in the rumour that the dressing room had been taken over by a clique of senior pros, who thought they only had to turn up to be handed the shirt? Weren't we crying out for a hardman to sort out the poseurs, weed out the dross, bang heads together and reinstate the most basic of Liverpool qualities: hunger?

Well, who better than Souness? An Anfield legend who never, ever gave everything but his all to the cause. A born winner who barred the words fear and failure from his vocabulary, who had gone into management at Rangers and turned Scottish football into a one-horse race.

Here was the ice-cool gunslinger who once made Sir Alex Ferguson declare, 'When he's in assassin-mode he makes me shudder.' The ballsy street-mauler who laughed at death threats when he signed the first-ever Catholic, Mo Johnston, for Rangers. The imperious gladiator who, in his last game for Liverpool, swaggered into Roma's Olympic Stadium and stole the European Cup from under Italian noses. Sure, we knew about the other side to Souness's complex character. That his burning professional desire to win trophies was matched by his love of the dolce vita. Bob Paisley once said of him, 'If he could, he'd toss for ends using his American Express card.' In Sampdoria his flash, aspirational persona earned him the nickname 'Charlie Champagnia' from his Genoese devotees. And he was so vain he'd been christened 'Chocolate' by his fellow pros. Because he had so much self-love he could eat himself.

But we overlooked all that. Here was a heavyweight prize-fighter with pedigree and bottle, who felt sure he would become one of the world's great coaches, and wanted to achieve that destiny at Anfield. Therefore many of us welcomed him like a returning prodigal son. Which is why, when everything went horribly wrong, on 15 April 1992, it hurt more than we ever imagined it could.

There, on the front page of the *Sun*, on the third anniversary of Hillsborough when the wounds were still raw and the anger still immense, under the headline LOVERPOOL, was a photograph of Souness kissing his blonde model partner Karen Levy in a private clinic where he was recovering from a triple heart-bypass operation. It felt like a blow from a blunt instrument on the temple, and every Liverpool fan forced to fight the smears perpetrated by a paper which had yet to apologize for its heinous lies, had their eye stung by Souness's spit.

On that bleak Wednesday morning, as Liverpool players and directors were preparing for a memorial service at Anfield where they would attempt to prop up families still on medication to numb the grief, Souness had allowed himself to be pictured hoovering up blood money.

For a reputed £50,000, he had sold them the exclusive story about his heart operation and his new lover – knowing Rupert Murdoch's henchmen were using him to cynically buck their dramatic circulation loss. The *Sun* had finally found someone connected to Liverpool who was urinating on the dead. It also emerged he had had a telephone conversation with Tory prime minister John Major, from his hospital bed. For the figurehead of the club, for the man charged with carrying Bill Shankly's mantle, his position was becoming untenable.

Souness had one shot at redemption, by offering a credible explanation as to why he picked up those pieces of silver on the Hillsborough anniversary, and delivering a deep and sincere apology. But his reasoning, and thus his apology, stank. He claimed he had no idea of the strength of feeling towards the *Sun*. His mitigation was he'd been up in Scotland at the time of the disaster and it had all passed him by. Which may have been accepted if a shareholder hadn't come forward to say they had written to Souness telling him of the war with the *Sun* and asking him to instruct his players not to have dealings with that paper. The shareholder then showed the *Echo* a signed reply from Souness saying he was aware of the issue and would ensure all his players were too.

It was a cut-and-dried case. Souness had sold his story to the *Sun*, knowing they would give him far and away the biggest pay day because they desperately sought approval from the Liverpool manager. In doing so he brazenly chose to ignore the hurt it would inflict on fans and bereaved families.

The single-minded greed and arrogance of the Man Who Takes No Shite had come to the fore. He later admitted he should have resigned that day, but he should never have had to because the board should have sacked him. Instead the weak men at the top let his long, lingering death carry on for another twenty-one dismal months – the thinking being that his side had scraped past Portsmouth into an FA Cup final, victory in which might placate the majority of fans until the storm died down, so it would be foolish to jump to any rash decisions. Besides they didn't have the cash to settle his contract.

Even though we won it, the FA Cup final against Sunderland was horrible. The sight of Souness hoisting himself prematurely out of recuperation, to walk slowly to the bench, stuck in the craw.

The Wembley crowd's reception was mixed. Plenty applauded him, mainly out of sympathy for what he'd been through, and relief that we were about to pick up a major trophy again, but many, like myself and my mates, refused to join in. I hadn't yet reached the point that I wanted Liverpool to lose games so he would get the sack – not when there was another notch to be put on the FA Cup bedpost. I simply no longer recognized him as a Liverpool man.

To me he was an outsider in charge of Liverpool not out of love for what that meant, but a love of what it could bring him: recognition, money, kudos and a stepping stone to even greater riches. But it wasn't simply over Hillsborough that Souness's appointment was shown to be woefully misjudged. Class players like Peter Beardsley, Ray Houghton and Steve Staunton were sold for peanuts with years of service left in them, and replaced with rank mediocrity. Training methods were overhauled and made more intense, under the gaze of his yes-man sidekick Phil Boersma, which produced a crippling injury list. The dressing room like the boardroom became a war zone. Even the famous Boot Room was bulldozed – an act of heresy, in Liverpool folklore terms, which was akin to the demolition of The Cavern. But then, what purpose did that great defining symbol of Liverpool FC serve, when the man in charge was intent on demolishing the philosophy on which it was founded?

The club's bedrock is a close-knit group of modest, working-class men like Shankly, Paisley and Fagan. A fraternal democracy, made up of equals, who forsake ego and pull together for the good of the club and its fans. That was never the Souness Way. Maybe it was fitting that the Boot Room should go when the umbilical cord between the manager and the Kop had been severed in one disastrous LOVERPOOL headline.

But Graeme Souness didn't care. A glittering playing career and a few domestic pots with Rangers had convinced him he was God's gift to football. That he was untouchable.

Instead of learning humility from his grave error of judgement, Souness became more emboldened. As Liverpool took up residence with all the other mid-table sides outside the top six, he turned from a bull in a china shop to a bull in a china shop with a red-hot poker up his behind. Phil Thompson was sacked and Souness publicly questioned the loyalty and commitment of great servants like Ian Rush, Ronnie Whelan, Steve Nicol and Jan Molby, who he claimed were only hanging around for testimonials.

The Big Time Charlie's attitude to anyone he perceived as being a Bigger Time Charlie than him was to hammer them into submission on the lines of 'Whatever you think you've done, I've done more. Whatever you think you know, I know more. So don't dare cross me, or you're out.' And who came in? Hall of Fame Legends like Torben Piechnick, Istvan Kozma (isn't it funny how the worst players' names always look like a Scrabble hand: think Salif Diao and Frode Kippe as well), Julian Dicks, Dean Saunders, Nicky Tanner, Paul Stewart, Mark Walters, Nigel Clough, Mark Wright, Steve Harkness and Stig Inge Bjornebye. I'll let him off with Michael Thomas. What he had done with the *Sun* showed a lamentable lack of judgement but to many fans that was almost matched by his assessment of players.

On the pitch the quality had gone, along with the camaraderie, the passing game, and the fear of playing against Liverpool at Anfield. By January 1993, I was openly appealing for him to do the decent thing and walk. Under the headline FANS DESERVE MORE HONESTY THAN THEY ARE GETTING, I wrote this in my *Echo* column:

This is a tale about professional loyalty.

It starts with a BBC Scotland cassette released when Graeme Souness was manager of Glasgow Rangers. In it a Souness impersonator utters: 'When I was at Spurs I was a Middlesbrough fan who always supported Liverpool, but I couldn't forget that as a boy in Edinburgh I used to sneak out of school to watch Sampdoria in Italy, yet as I watched them I couldn't forget that as a foetus I was a Rangers fan.'

The satirist's point was that loyalty to Mr Souness was a disposable item. This view was hardly destroyed when, as speculation linked him with the vacant managerial job at Liverpool, he declared in *Rangers News*: 'As far as Liverpool goes I'd be flattered by their interest, but I know in my mind I would never contemplate leaving Ibrox.'

Just over a month later he was strolling through The Shankly Gates.

It was reminiscent of a pledge Souness gave to Liverpool fans after the European Cup final in 1984, when he vowed: 'As far as I am concerned I'll still be playing here next season.' And two weeks later he was on the plane to Italy.

I mention this for those who are puzzled about why the most successful Merseyside enterprise over the past 30 years, Liverpool FC, is in crisis.

Well, manager Souness is in no doubt. In a phone-call to the *Echo* last week, the morning after his side's shameful FA Cup exit, he concluded it was all down to the disloyalty of his players: 'Too many of our players have no real love of the club . . . they don't see playing for Liverpool as the pinnacle of their career . . . it's about how much money they end up with at the end of the day.'

To say those comments were the most hypocritical and insulting I've ever heard from a Liverpool manager is putting it mildly.

Not only was he the one who handed outrageous contracts to the men he now accuses of the basest professional crime, he forgets how he encouraged them to see Liverpool as a stepping-stone to riches.

He forgets what he said to Michael Thomas when he gave him an opt-out clause allowing him to go to the first big Italian club that makes an offer.

How he lured Thomas to Anfield by passing on personal knowledge of how to fill your boots with Lire: 'My advice to him was to get back playing to attract the big teams in Italy and there is no one who attracts audiences like Liverpool on the continent,' Souness proudly proclaimed when he signed Thomas for £1.5 million.

So how can he now turn around and accuse the players of not seeing Liverpool as 'the pinnacle of their career'?

What must those players think when they are labelled gutless mercenaries as tea-cups are hurled around the changing rooms?

The truth is the men he picks to wear red shirts now look frightened, confused and resentful.

And what must stick in their throats is how Souness of all people can lecture about putting the love of money above all else.

The fans deserve more honesty than they are getting. The players' attitudes are not the crucial point here Mr Souness.

You signed them, you pick them, you organise them, you motivate them and you're paid handsomely to carry the can.

And if it's too heavy, do what you do so well with the buck. Pass it on.

By May, when another dire season was drawing to a close and the best we could hope for was to scrape in at sixth place, the situation was turning into a farce. In the week before the final game a crisis board meeting was held where it was decided that Souness had to go.

Leaks told the press that Tony Ensor, the solicitor who had skilfully guided the club through the legal minefield of Heysel, and who was Souness's major opponent, had succeeded in persuading a majority of his fellow directors to force his sacking.

The *Echo* ran a front-page splash headlined HE **IS** OUT, with polls showing almost 70 per cent of fans wanting him to go and Souness telling friendly reporters that he had days left. Joy swept through the ground on the final game of the season, when Souness refused to show his face. Liberation was universal. Spurs were thrashed 6–2 in a wonderfully uplifting, free-flowing performance, with Souness's two biggest dressing-room critics John Barnes and Ian Rush each scoring twice. The Kop was back to its best: full-voiced, witty, passionate, and booing every mention of Souness's name.

Everything in our L4 garden seemed rosy, until chairman David Moores called a press conference the following day to inform us his big buddy Souness would be seeing out his contract and hopefully staying on beyond that. Desolation. It was unclear if Souness had wanted too much money to go quietly, there was a lack of candidates to succeed him, or his mates in high places had dug their heels in. Whatever the reason, a mysterious U-turn had taken place, and Ensor and his faction, plus three-quarters of the fans, had been kicked in the goolies. Liverpool's board, once clinical in sorting out its problems, looked small, dithering, amateurish and dangerously out of its depth. Everyone with any knowledge of the club knew they had merely put off the day Souness would be history and allowed the club to drift further away from the summit.

I now trusted the people who ran Liverpool about as far as I could throw Souness's sunbed. I wrote in the *Echo* that 'I'd view their request to renew my season ticket as a vote of confidence in the management and do with it exactly what they seem intent on doing to Liverpool FC: Rip it in half.'

There it was. Out in the open. The boil had been lanced and there was no going back. The next time I would go to Anfield would be when the Souness regime wasn't leaving a stench hanging over the place.

I'd like to be able to write that I went through sleepless nights filled with panic attacks about giving up my season ticket and banning myself from Anfield for the first time in thirty years, but I couldn't have been more clear in my mind.

What was going on was a disgrace to everything the club stood for, and I couldn't be a part of it. Neither could plenty of other Liverpudlians, including Terry and Mike, who gave up their season tickets too. It may be illogical to deprive yourself of the thing you are most passionate about simply because you hate the man in the manager's seat, but who said there was anything logical about supporting a football team?

When we kicked off the 1993–94 season with a 2–0 home win against Sheffield Wednesday, I wasn't at Anfield, wouldn't listen to it on the radio and wanted them to get beat. It felt like I'd been mashed up in a car crash and had my vital organs replaced with someone else's. As though a hypnotist had put me under, read the score on *Grandstand* and told me when I awoke I would believe that the victory was a defeat.

The birth of my daughter Christie a week before the season started ensured my mind was elsewhere, and as Souness racked up another three wins in August, I'd begun to envisage years of future Saturdays spent pony-trekking with my little girl. But the loss of every game in September, including a derby, brought hope.

Hope that was increased by a defeat, four draws and dumping out of the League Cup by Wimbledon in December. Another typical Souness season was taking shape. The question was, would he survive it?

Clearly I wasn't the only one staying away, with home League gates plummeting to as low as 24,561 for the visit of QPR. I'd still meet with Mike and Terry whenever the Reds were playing at home. Obviously we told our partners we were still going to Anfield. Souness may have taken our Kemlyn Road seats from us but we weren't going to give up a guaranteed Saturday afternoon pass-out that was ours by birthright. We may have been taking a noble stand against an evil regime but we were going to stand there with a pint in our hand. So we'd go on a city-centre pub crawl hoping that when *Final Score* came on the telly, Liverpool had lost, Souness was closer to the door and Mike could climb on the tables and belt out 'Fly Me To The Moon'. It was a horrible, horrible feeling. Especially the Saturday afternoon when I bumped into Ann coming out of Marks & Spencer's and had to make up an instant lie about Terry losing his ticket and me and Mike feeling so sorry for him being turned away at the gate that we had to help him drown his sorrows.

A hard question I've asked myself since is: Would so many of us have stayed away if Souness had created a title-winning side that swept all before it? I'd love to think yes, but the truth is we'll never know. We're football fans after all. Shallow beasts who gorge on success.

But in all honesty I think the question is academic. It was never going to happen. Souness failed to build anything but a few mounds of rubble at Liverpool because he'd failed to embrace its spirit. He was a hugely talented football man but he lacked Shankly's ethos of communal effort, Paisley's quiet but brilliant cajoling, Fagan's jovial shrewdness and Dalglish's maturity and perception. His confrontational persona meant he was doomed from the beginning. When Dalglish left we needed someone with the talent and charisma to steer the ship back to calm waters, then gradually strip it down, before making it a sleek machine once more. Souness steered it into a rock, sparked a mutiny, then let it drift towards the breakers' yard.

It was with little surprise and stupendous relief that, three days after tiny Bristol City knocked us out of the FA Cup third round at Anfield, he packed his bags and walked the plank with Boersma. But not before pocketing a £400,000 pay-off.

I didn't get Souness the sack. Souness got Souness the sack. I told him so in the Hilton Hotel, but he wasn't listening.

'You two bastards at the *Echo*. You and Tommy Smith. You made my job impossible,' he said, still crushing my hand and moving his face closer to mine, making me think he was about to do an impression of his doppelgänger, Yosser Hughes, and lay the head on me.

Then he smiled and offered me a drink. And we talked. We discussed Liverpool past and present and it was clear he did have a passion for the club. He knew he'd made mistakes as manager, which he had grown to genuinely regret. I just think at the time he'd been incapable of not making them.

A decade had passed and he'd mellowed considerably. Until I told him, at the end of our conversation, that I'd seen him make his debut at West Brom in January '78 and watched him in his final game in Rome in '84 and throughout those six years he showed himself to be one of the greatest players ever to wear the shirt. That's when the charmer vanished and the snarler came back out:

'Awhh, do me a favour, will ya? Don't fuckin' patronize me. Every time I meet a Liverpool fan they tell me I was a fantastic player but a shite manager. And it pisses me off no end.'

I said nothing. I didn't need to because my eyes said it for me: 'But you were Graeme. You were.'

21

SPICEWORLD

11 MAY 1996 – WEMBLEY

After Hurricane Souness had passed, and we could rip down the makeshift shutters and emerge from the shelters, all we sought was calm. I didn't care who the new manager was or what was on his CV. All I cared about was that he didn't have the words Graeme and Souness on his birth certificate.

At any other point in time, Roy Evans would probably not have been the number one choice. There was plenty going for him. He'd worn the shirt and won nine trophies in eleven years as reserve team coach. Throughout the seventies and eighties he'd sat on that wise old bench throwing sponges in the air as the final whistle was blown on yet another silver-lifting success. He was solid and modest, loyal and Scouse, and in the thirty years he'd spent at Anfield soaking up all that knowledge from all those great leaders, he hadn't put a foot wrong.

His name may not have set the pulse racing, but in the early days of that cold, grim February we nodded in quiet approval. We were damaged kids being released after years in an abusive home, and we needed some tender care and attention. We needed someone we knew and trusted to take us by the hand again.

David Moores hit the right tone at the press conference when he said he was giving us 'the last of the Boot Room boys'. And Evans reassured us when he said, 'I don't believe in being hard for the sake of it, but if someone steps on my toes, I'll step on theirs.' By appointing Evans the board was trying to swing the pendulum back. After Dalglish they'd brought in a hardman to try to knock the players into line, but they'd miscalculated. Souness was a wrecking ball, who'd swung far too much towards confrontation. Uncle Roy would restore harmony, give the players a cuddle and get us back down to earth. And those young gems who were coming through – Steve McManaman, Robbie Fowler and Jamie Redknapp – would be allowed to grow in a climate of love not hate.

The only nagging fear was that after the scary teacher had put his strap away and left the classroom to be replaced by the nice guy who let everyone put their feet on the desks, would the pupils take the piss?

I lifted my self-imposed banning order and returned to the Kop for many of the remaining home games, but the season had become a write-off and apart from the odd flash of inspiration, including a 2–1 win over Everton, it was quite painful stuff.

We lost nine of the remaining sixteen games, and finished eighth in the league, our lowest position since 1962–63, the year after promotion from the Second Division. But nobody blamed Roy. We knew whose team this was, and not having him around was a form of success in itself. Besides, the prospect of what another wrecking ball was about to do to Anfield was focusing minds on a glorious past and an uncertain future.

April 1994 was the last month any Liverpool fan would watch a game on a seatless Kop. The Taylor Report had recommended all-seater stadiums, and we of all people were naturally willing to comply. Although as the day approached for the most famous football terrace in the world to be demolished there was an awful sense of sorrow. The reality of knocking down the Kop was a terrible, frightening wrench. We knew why it had to happen. Why, in memory of the ninety-six, we had to let go. But those of us whose hearts had never left the Kop were ripped apart at the prospect of losing it.

It must have transmitted itself on to the pitch because the four home games that April were four of the worst in living memory. We lost 2–1 to Sheffield United, lost 2–0 to Newcastle, and scraped past Ipswich with a Julian Dicks penalty.

Then we reached the goodbye game. Norwich at home. What a fiesta this would be. Oh, how we'd give the place that gave us so much joy a glorious send-off. I donned my Roma scarf – the red and yellow Roma one with the word *Campioni* on that I'd swapped with an Italian in the bar after the '84 European Cup win – queued for an hour and walked up the concrete hill for the last time, ready to feast on another slice of Anfield folklore. But St Etienne it wasn't.

Here's what I wrote in the *Echo* under the headline THE KOP'S LAST STAND:

The Kopites could have brought a Hoover the size of Latin America with them on Saturday but they still wouldn't have sucked in a goal.

To suck in a goal you first need a player to shoot. As the red hordes streamed away on Saturday they certainly wanted players to shoot, and if many if those faces are there next season, then shoot them they just might.

Pouring off that famous old mound for the last time fans spoke feverishly about something that has vanished. It wasn't the ability to stand on the Kop but a desire in the souls of the players that had been instilled in them since Shankly arrived in 1959. The desire to win.

That was the great shame about the Kop's last stand. A travesty of justice as someone might have put it, before threatening to dock his players' wages.

It's a sacred place full of sacred memories, many of them the most sacred memories of some people's lives. The Kop has been the backbone of Liverpool FC for generations and it was let down.

In the days of old the Kop's spontaneity and originality was sparked by those same attributes being shown on the pitch. But on Saturday it had to find its own spark and in the end it did a magnificent job. But it was always going to.

It was at its most passionate when the players were out of sight. In the packed pubs around Anfield from noon onwards and on the terrace before the game. At half-time, just before the players came out, at the end when the irrelevant mess on the pitch was terminated and then in virtually every pub from Breck Road to Lime Street right up to midnight.

They dragged out the old standards: 'We all live in a red and white Kop'; 'We love you Liverpool'; 'Oh when the Reds'. The *Dambusters* theme and 'Poor Scouser Tommy'.

The leaflets were out before the game, not campaigning against seats but reminding people to sing You'll Never Walk Alone the way it used to be. Slowly.

Ironically, it took Gerry Marsden in the flesh to get the tempo right, and when he was drowned out by the massed ranks, the neck hairs bristled, and for a few fleeting minutes you were dragged back to the great nights.

At least the Kop had a go, in song and in wit. At the end, when the players unfurled a large banner proclaiming: 'From the players of Liverpool FC: We'll Never Walk Alone' someone shouted that the well-heeled lads should change it to: 'We'll Never Need A Loan.'

You can't keep a good Kopite down. Not even when he's in a seat.

My last stand on the *Echo* was approaching too. That summer I was offered a job as a feature writer on the *Daily Mirror*, which meant living in London Monday to Friday and travelling back home every weekend. With two kids under five needing a week's attention in forty-eight hours, I had less chance of taking a seat at Anfield than Kelvin MacKenzie.

So it was Sky Super Sunday afternoons spent watching Andy Gray's white lines show everyone where they were going wrong, and scouring the fixture list with rosary beads, praying all our London away games were midweek. Astonishingly, in 1994–95 many of them were.

Which made a thirty-seven-year-old feel seventeen again. Sneaking out of the Canary Wharf office early (we were supposed to work until 7 p.m.) to get to Highbury, White Hart Lane, Loftus Road and Upton Park took me back to sagging school for midweek away games and queues for derby tickets.

But there the similarities ended. In some ways it felt more like being back in the press box. I travelled on my own, had a pint on my own, sat on my own, always ended up stuck next to alien voices. And was always a couple of grating shouts away from a row.

The Tottenham game in March summed it up. It was a largely uneventful 0–0 draw. (Of the five league games I saw in London that season we lost two, drew two and beat only Arsenal.) And I was stuck next to this loud-mouthed Grant Mitchell beaut screeching an incessant stream of ill-informed crap with a Kent twang. Let's just say he thought Neil Ruddock was the epitome of everything good about the side, and Steve McManaman, who was having one of his anonymous nights, symptomatic of the lethargy that held them back.

Ruddock was, in fact, as shocking and out of control as his weight. This was his first game back at Spurs since his move to Liverpool and the crowd were on his back from the off. To make things worse Jürgen Klinsmann was on his front, and Ruddock felt crushed from both sides. So he kept lashing out. The fourteen-stone oaf should have been sent off for a clear elbow on the German in the first half but got away with it. Ten minutes into the second half he held Klinsmann back in the area and the ref bottled it, again much to the home crowd's disgust. Anyone with half a brain could see what was coming with this weak ref, this hostile crowd and Klinsmann's experience. And it came with 20 minutes to go. Klinsmann, cute as ever, turned the oaf, ran into his back and won a penalty.

Cue Kent Man leaping to good old Razor's defence, screeching mouthfuls of utter garbage at the ref, churning out high-pitched verbals at Klinsmann as he strolled up to take the penalty, which David James saved.

Five minutes more of listening to his 'go on my san' whenever Ruddock clattered into a Spurs attacker and I'd had enough. There was no point in challenging him. He'd paid his money and all that. And my filthy looks weren't working so I sought ale to soothe a throbbing head.

I knew I'd never become a devotee of those London midweek games, stuck as I always was next to an *EastEnders* extra, staring forlornly at Ruddock's huge arse, defending McManaman's right to hold back in games and hurt the opposition when it mattered.

Ironically, two weeks after the White Hart Lane tedium, that is precisely what McManaman did. Torturing Bolton's back four in the League Cup final and scoring both goals in an easy 2–1 win.

Like Souness, Evans had won a trophy in his first full season. And like Souness it would be his high point. The low point would come a year later on FA Cup final day against Man United at Wembley. If the demolition of the Boot Room came to epitomize Souness's reign, the cream Armani suits worn by his players (and the empty performance that followed) was the symbol of Roy Evans's time in charge. That is a harsh indictment on a truly great Anfield figure like Evans, but it's true. The sight of a shower of narcissists joshing on the pitch beforehand, seemingly more concerned with how cool they looked than focusing on the massive task ahead, was effectively Roy's death knell.

As they strolled around in their matching designer suits and shades, half of them looking like they were trying to be spotted by a modelling agency, we just looked on in shock and amazement. Their get-up and their body language said everything we'd feared to speak about them. It said we want different things in life from you. When they did nothing over the next 90 minutes to stop United winning the Double, we walked away believing that those critics who'd labelled them the Spice Boys had probably got it right.

The most irritating factor about the consistent failure to achieve any consistency under Evans was how near they appeared at times to be to getting it right. That 1995–96 season had promised much. Stan Collymore linked well with Robbie Fowler, and between them they scored 42 League goals. At times the football they played was the best Anfield had seen since 1987, but it was all a cruel illusion.

The famous 4–3 victory over Newcastle, which to this day is

still seen as the most entertaining Premiership match Sky have ever televised, put us right back into contention for the title. Three days later they went to second-from-bottom Coventry, played like dross and got beat 1–0. Title challenge over. They had an even better chance the following season, going into January top, after a 1–0 win at Southampton. Man United soon reasserted their supremacy but we stayed with them, and in early April, Derby won at Old Trafford, meaning that if we beat Coventry at Anfield (this time they were third from bottom) we'd move above them. We went a goal up, then blew it 2–1.

The following home game was against United. Win that and we'd be back on top with three games left. We defended like strangers who'd just met up in the park after a twenty-four-hour drugs bender, and were outclassed 3–1. United won the League and we finished fourth. Once again they had bottled it.

My instinct, after helping to hound Souness out of Anfield, was to defend Roy Evans to the hilt and, like every other blind optimist, I'd mouth off every close season about how we were only one or two pieces away from the completed jigsaw.

The signings of Patrick Berger, Karl-Heinz Riedle, Paul Ince, Stan Collymore and Danny Murphy, added to Fowler, Mc-Manaman, Redknapp and Owen, made me dream, but I was soon rudely brought back to earth by the attitude of some of those signings and the unsuitability of others: Phil Babb, John Scales, Oyvind Leonhardsen, Bjorn Tore Kvarme, Mark Kennedy and Sean Dundee. It was all a mirage, summed up by one of Souness's last buys, David James, a goalkeeper who appeared to have it all, but totally lacked focus in the moments when you needed him to die for you.

In the mid-to-late nineties Liverpool played some wonderful stuff on occasions, but collectively they lacked heart. With a few notable exceptions – Fowler, McManaman, Barnes and Redknapp – they were the tin men of English football. Evans, desperate to dispel the memory of Souness, gave his players too much leeway, and they walked all over him.

The proof came not simply with United's dominance, but every time we took on half-decent Continental opposition and had our inadequacies ruthlessly exposed.

Closer to home the demise was more painfully exposed. Roy's four-year record between 1994–95 and 1997–98, against some of the worst Everton teams that century, made grim reading. They played eight derbies, drew five, lost three and won none. Whether it was Evans's fault for overindulging them, or the players' fault for lacking pride in their performance, one fact is indisputable. For the first time since Shankly arrived players took the piss out of their manager. And thus their fans.

The stories I was hearing from national newspaper reporters made me feel ashamed. Players having competitions to pinch the manager's car-park space at Melwood. Phoning him up in his office when he was doing an interview with a respected broadsheet journalist, urging Evans to call the writer a 'cunt'. Players telling reporters they were off to Dublin for a midweek night on the razzle, asking if they fancied tagging along. A hugely respected football manager telling how he'd been up at Anfield on a spying mission, left the ground early for his return flight from Manchester to London, only to find a handful of Liverpool players on the same plane, heading for Soho to rub up against Page Three Stunners at Chinawhite night club.

There was an apocryphal tale about David James having a modelling assignment in Milan which clashed with a training session. The story goes that he marched into Roy Evans's office, asked what the fine was for missing training, and when Evans told him it was a day's wages, wrote out the cheque and walked off whistling. James has since denied the story, and it may well be an urban myth. But Neil Ruddock cannot deny this one, because he told it live on Sky TV's *Soccer AM* in 2003: 'At Liverpool we used to play this game on the pitch. We had a pound coin you had to pass round and whoever had it in their hand in the 90th minute had to take all the lads out and buy the drinks all night. There was one game when we were lining up to defend a free-kick and it was being passed along the wall. We lost that one 2–1.'

So that was the game they were playing on the pitch and it couldn't be further removed from the game Shankly had taught his men to play – a game of honesty, loyalty, of giving your all for the working-class man who handed over his wages to watch you spill blood for him.

Looking back, Evans's League record appears far better than it did at the time, and he looks a far better manager. Finishing 4th, 3rd, 4th, 3rd was not exactly disastrous; had UEFA allowed the top four sides into the Champions League, Liverpool would have qualified every year. He was also a man who never shirked responsibility. Never became a sour-faced carper. Never shamed the club with anything he said or did. A gentleman who always thought, when he was pushed into a corner, how he could best serve the interests of the club he loved.

Years after Roy had left Anfield we were doing a TV show together, and one of the topics was Liverpool's best and worst transfers.

'Be ready, Roy, because it'll take me about two minutes to mention Sean Dundee,' I told him.

'Hang on, it's my turn now. If anyone's going to have a go at me for buying Sean Dundee, it's me. You've had your turn at slagging me off,' he replied, laughing.

'Did I give you stick, then?'

'Stick? You hammered me. I'd pick up the papers every week and think, 'ere we go, he's after me again.'

I could tell the criticism had hurt, and as I looked at him I regretted writing articles which claimed that, as decent as Roy was, managing Liverpool was too big a job for him. I tried to explain that when things are going wrong at the club you love, the harder it hurts, and the angrier you become. He just waved his hands.

'Eh, that's fair enough. You were doing your job. You didn't know everything that was going on though, lad.'

In the harsh light of day, teams and managers either have what it takes to succeed at the top, or they don't. And Roy's sides didn't. He was the ultimate nearly man, who deserved to be remembered in a kinder light for all that he gave to the club. Even that historic 4–3 win over Newcastle resonates in the memory bank as a triumph for Collymore, Fowler and the Kop. We visualize Kevin Keegan's dug-out despair before Evans's joy. In truth the epitaph for his four-year stint was that arguably the finest crop of home-grown talent the club has produced was handed to arguably the nicest man the club has ever employed. He failed to drill a ruthless discipline into the self-styled Guv'nors who surrounded that talent, and was walked over.

Nobody was surprised when, in July 1998, the club appointed Gérard Houllier as manager. For two years Arsène Wenger had been phenomenally successful at Highbury and the era of the foreign coach was upon us. English football was being swept along by a new way of thinking, and nowhere were fresh ideas needed more than at Anfield.

The only surprise was that Houllier had been made co-manager with Roy Evans. The board, bottling it again and unwilling to appear to be sacking a loyal servant, tried a comical compromise. It was a plan doomed to failure, primarily because the Frenchman had been brought in to apply radical new methods. Clearly they were waiting for Roy to do the decent thing and walk away voluntarily with no blood on their hands. It didn't take long. In early November, following a poor run of League results and a 3–1 dismissal from the League Cup at Anfield, Evans threw himself on the sacrificial pyre.

The loyal servant, a man who was sincere, honest and Liverpool to his fingertips, committed career hara-kiri for the sake of the club he loved. There was no bitterness or recriminations, no pointing the finger at Houllier and asking why it wasn't a case of 'last in, first out', no fury at the board for undermining him in a cowardly manner, no rage at the players for letting him down so badly, no posturing, leaks and demands for outrageous compensation.

Evans could have held the club to ransom. Instead he emptied his locker and quietly and with huge dignity walked away from a workplace he had first entered thirty-five years earlier as a scrawny apprentice, and to which he'd devoted his entire adult life. He sat ashen-faced at his final press conference, eyes red with the tears he'd cried that morning at Melwood saying his goodbyes to the players, and admitted he'd done his best for Liverpool, but his best had not been good enough. It was heart-breaking, like seeing your war veteran uncle weeping at a funeral. I felt sick to the pit of my stomach that it had had to end like this.

What a shame some of his players didn't share that feeling. Word emerged from Melwood that a couple of senior players had mimicked his tearful farewell, with others creasing up with laughter at the impressions. I hope in the years that followed, when Evans struggled to find a high-profile coaching job, that they looked deep into themselves and felt a twinge of shame.

But somehow I doubt it.

22

STORY OF THE BLUES

28 FEBRUARY 1998 – GOODISON PARK

Nothing can prepare you for that conversation with your son about the pivotal facts of life. No booklet, no film, no friend, no shrink, no wise uncle or problem-page aunt. You just have to take it in your stride and flounder.

'Dad,' said seven-year-old Phil, pulling back my duvet and interrupting a mind locked deep into slumber after a six-hour Friday night drive back from London. 'I've got something to tell you.'

I pulled him into bed, enjoying that warm blanket feeling you get holding the kids again after a week away. 'What is it, son?' I mumbled, my eyes still glued with sleep.

'I'm an Everton fan.'

My head froze.

'And I want the kit.'

My heart stopped.

'Can we go to the Everton shop today?'

My sphincter snapped.

There was a deathly silence that lasted long enough for my entire, miserable future to flash before me.

'Yeah, nice one Phil. Good joke.'

It was clearly a ruse he'd been working on all week. A little welcome home jab for his absent dad. Only it wasn't.

He'd started playing football at school, which I knew about. The majority of his mates were Evertonians, which I didn't. And they all had kits, which he wanted. A lifetime's loyalty to Everton decided in the five days I'd been down in London. A lifetime's sharing all of Liverpool's highs and lows lost for ever. Why did I take that job at the *Mirror* and overlook a father's most basic task of ensuring his son enters his faith? It was little more than I deserved. It wouldn't have happened if I'd been in Liverpool seven days a week, guiding him down the right path.

I'd tried to get him interested in football, but when he didn't bite I thought better than to push it on to him. There is no sight sadder, nothing more counterproductive, than a little lad in the park, decked out in a shiny new kit, looking longingly at the swings, as his dad does a knee-slide celebration after chipping him from ten yards.

So I'd played it cool. Assumed his love for Liverpool would find him as it found me. Such arrogance. Such stupidity. Such rampant neglect I should have been hauled away by social services with a coat over my head. As Shankly said to Paisley after ordering John McLoughlin to eat steak every day, only to discover he'd got his girlfriend pregnant: 'I've created a monster.'

Clearly it was all my fault. A reaction against a father who was never there during the week, and when Saturday came was either at Anfield or wishing he was. The lad's desire to kick a negligent dad where it hurt most was understandable.

It was Philip Larkin who wrote, 'They fuck you up your mum and dad, they fill you with the faults they had.' My lad had witnessed at close quarters the many faults of an obsessive Liverpudlian. That cavalier dismissal of any other side being mentioned in the same breath. The constant living in the past. The belief that you're part of God's Chosen Tribe, with any lean spell explained as the Almighty's way of giving the others a chance.

The framed photos of that old shaven-headed man, with a scarf round his neck and his arms held out wide below his Cagney face, scattered around the house. The anger and frustration throughout the nineties of seeing them fail and fail again. The refusal to accept it was affecting you. The depression you would force on the family when you came home from a defeat. The obscene abuse hurled at the telly or radio during match commentary, and at anyone else in the room who challenged your rage. The getting drunk of a Saturday night so you'd be in bed before *Match Of The Day*. Who could blame him? Especially when his mum and her family were all Evertonians.

When the shock had subsided I lay in bed thinking it through, trying to salvage something from the wreck that was my existence. It wasn't that bad. At least he liked football and that was something. It could have been worse – he could have told me he was a Man United fan. Or a Tory. I wouldn't have been able to look him in the face again.

I decided it was on a par with him telling me he was gay. I'm shocked and saddened now, at the inevitable future pleasures I'll be deprived of, but it might just be a phase. A scream for attention from a confused kid who's discovering new feelings he hasn't yet worked through. And the worst thing you can do is raise an eyebrow.

No, he needed my full approval and my full support. However painful it might seem, I was taking him to the Goodison Megastore that day and buying him a blue shirt. Even if he went for the double of kicking me in the bollocks and the wallet by asking for the name CADAMARTERI on the back.

Over the coming days and months I tried my best, I really did. I'd buy him packets of Premier League stickers, and allow him to plaster his wall with mugshots of legends like Craig Short and Andy Hinchcliffe. When I won a goldfish for him at a Sefton Park fair I let him call it Thomas, after Thomas Myhre, the goalie who kept them in the Premiership. It died the next day and he still blames me when it's mentioned, but as I tell him, the goldfish has yet to be hatched who died from a dirty look.

I took him around the Everton Megastore and although I'd buy him what he wanted, I couldn't help taking the piss out of the place – I told him it should be renamed the Everton Mug-a-store, as that's all they had on sale.

This was the danger. I couldn't change a lifetime's habit of being instinctively dismissive about anything to do with Everton simply because my son supported them. But it wasn't doing me any favours. He'd get a right sulk on, convinced my contemptuous tone was a ploy to embarrass him into changing allegiance. A wall was going up between us and I couldn't afford that to happen. I was back in Liverpool now, the editor letting me do two columns a week from home, but me and Ann had split up and I had the kids one night midweek and at weekends, in a small Sefton Park flat. So I had to make the most of anything we had in common, like a love of football. I had to be enthusiastic about Everton, or I'd risk turning him away. Even worse, I'd risk him turning into the bitterest of Blues.

It dawned on me that I had to start going to Goodison. So as an eighth birthday treat I took him and four of his mates down to the School of Science. It was a very interesting experiment, as I wrote at the time in my *Mirror* sports column:

I will remember this game as long as I am capable of watching football.

When others mention Hurst's hat-trick, Brazil's breathless destruction of Italy or Benfica succumbing to Best, I will talk of Everton vs Newcastle, February 28, 1998.

It's just a shame the football was about as memorable as watching Open University Physics after a dull, hefty, amnesia-inducing blow.

But that's a small irrelevance. This was the first time I'd taken my only son to a football game. A birthday present from a dad desperate to get his kid hooked on something that's brought him more joy than sex.

Okay so I'd advised against him being blue from birth. Ridiculed their misfortunes in nursery-rhyme form, bought red rattles, held the league table over his cot. I suppose that's the way the seed crumbles.

And as long as it stopped him dressing up in frocks, well there are worse teams to support than Everton.

On Saturday's evidence, there is Newcastle for a start, who played their part in this dreadful spectacle.

One word sums up the entertainment served up by two dozen

professionals who take their wages home in wheelbarrows for 38,000 fans who use the same vehicle for their season-ticket money: Non-existent.

A Keith Gillespie lob, a blast wide by Alan Shearer and a Gareth Farrelly volley was about it. A goal-threatening incident every half-hour.

But, as often happens at Goodison, the pleasure was to be found in areas outside the hallowed turf.

Mine was to watch a game for the first time in 33 years from the family enclosure.

The view is unique. At pitch-level, behind the corner flag, two rows from the front, face slated by hailstones, with all ten substitutes doing their stretching exercises in front of you.

I'd always thought Goodison was the home of the restricted view, but this was as ridiculous as it was welcome, so dire was the view they were blocking.

But the football didn't really matter anyway. At your first game you never watch the match. Just the floodlights and the tonsils of the man next to you. And the non-spectacle at least left five eight-year-olds with some hard questions to ask.

'Ey Philip's dad, why is Andersson wearing number 40? Does that mean Newcastle have 39 players who are better than him?'

'Er . . .'

'Ey Philip's dad, why do the Newcastle fans keep asking everyone else to stand up if they hate Sunderland when no-one does?'

'Er . . .'

'Ey, Philip's dad, why do Everton keep booting it into the air when Ferguson isn't playing and Cadamarteri's about as big as me?'

'Er . . .'

'Why, Philip's dad, do the Everton fans love Hutchison who used to be a Red and hate Speed who's always been a Blue?'

'Er . . .'

'Ey, Philip's dad, how much did these tickets cost?'

'Sixty-six pounds.'

'Is that a lot?'

'It depends. Slaven Bilic earned that in the time it took him to hoof the ball into the top of the stand.'

And on and on, asking Paxman-esque questions, until they finally got bored with crunching tackles, mis-placed passes, off-side flags and crosses that knocked the hail from the clouds.

'Ey dad, when can we go home?'

'That's my boy.'

Come on, let's get you measured up for that frock.

Bizarrely, Phil still wanted more even after that drab horror. The problem in taking him was I was looking after Christie every Saturday too, so chances were limited. I tried to take both of them once, to a pre-season friendly at Tranmere and of course Christie had to have an Everton shirt too, even though she was six and completely uninterested. Mind you, she soon caught on. After watching the players warm up, and joining in the applause back to the dressing room, she made for the exit saying, 'That wasn't as bad as I thought it'd be.' When I broke it to her that she had to sit through another 90 minutes of it, she almost cried. So at least I was finding common ground with one of the kids.

The point was I'd never been an Everton-hater, and I wasn't one then. I'd been to many Everton games with Billy and, if they weren't threatening Liverpool, actually wanted them to win. But these were bad, relegation-haunted seasons. The football was woeful, the atmosphere not much better, and anti-Red feeling was never far from the surface. I watched through gritted teeth, my mind focused on how Liverpool were doing. (I thought of taking a radio with me and listening to our commentary but somehow I don't think Phil would have appreciated it.)

At one point I was going to Goodison more than to Anfield, which hurt like hell. No, not hell exactly, more purgatory. But it couldn't have been easy for Phil either, having to put up with performances that were as depressing as my gob. This piece I wrote in the *Mirror* in 1999 summed it up:

Say what you like about football having a bad influence on kids, but it is turning my son into a classical scholar.

He has been visiting Goodison Park for more than a year now and has rarely seen a game end in anything other than a goalless draw. So philosophical is he about it, I caught him proudly using a felt-tip on an Everton flag which he has hanging above his bed.

Closer inspection showed he had changed the club motto from 'Nil satis nisi optimum' to 'Nil-nil satis nisi optimum.'

What a debt I owe the Blues. They may have turned him into an eternal pessimist, but at least they have him correcting Latin at the tender age of eight.

If Everton can carry on having this effect on my son, he will definitely get into Rugby. The game, not the school, that is.

I'd turned into a Bitter Red. A sign crashing down before my eyes whenever I walked up the steps of the Bullens Road into the sunlight, and looked down on the pitch: This Isn't Anfield.

Christ, I was homesick.

23

DIVIDE AND RULE

Due to 101 different conspiracy theories and sci-fi fantasies, generations of humans had been filled with fear and anxiety over the prospect of 1999. But for a generation of Liverpudlians there were ninety-six reasons to dread it. The tenth anniversary of Hillsborough, with the sorrow and anger that it would unleash.

We had reason to fear it because far from healing the wounds, the decade following the disaster had merely heaped contempt on the memory of the dead. The Establishment had played a blinder. When I look back on the nineties I don't think of Liverpool FC's barren attempts to win the title, I think of the Hillsborough families' barren attempts to win justice. Because I witnessed the heart-crushing agony at close quarters.

Despite Lord Justice Taylor placing the blame squarely on the shoulders of the police and Sheffield Wednesday FC, so many kicks made contact with the families' teeth, they were in need of gumshields. The inquests before a Sheffield jury and a coroner (who of course worked for Sheffield Council who were themselves culpable for not issuing Hillsborough with a valid safety certificate which left open thoughts of bias that should never have existed and were unlikely to be true, delivered verdicts of accidental death against the ninety-five (Tony Bland was still in a coma). The DPP threw out all charges against the police on grounds of insufficient evidence. Although Lord Taylor had said Chief Supt Duckenfield 'froze', causing 'a blunder of the first magnitude', no senior officer was prosecuted and a disciplinary case against Duckenfield was stopped when he took early retirement at forty-six on medical grounds, with a full pension. No legal, moral or financial compensation came the families' way, the majority receiving little more than funeral expenses. In contrast, fourteen police officers who were 'traumatized' by what they saw that day picked up £1.2 million. Astonishingly, their claims for compensation were based on the insurers accepting that their superiors had been negligent.

But still the families kept on fighting for some vague notion of justice for their sons and daughters. In the knowledge that when you bring a child into this world, the facts on the birth certificate are accurate. When they leave, the least you can do for them is ensure the facts about their death are accurate too. And so in October 1991, when two women from Liverpool City Council's Hillsborough Working Party, Ann Adlington and Sheila Coleman, contacted me with the harrowing case of Anne Williams, a Formby mum who lost her fifteen-year-old son in the Leppings Lane, I was more than willing to help.

Anne was trying to get the inquests reopened on the grounds that they were seriously flawed. The main bone of contention was that the coroner had imposed a 3.15 p.m. cut-off time, claiming that every victim would have been brain-dead by then, and ruling out any evidence relating to events after it. It was a very clever cop-out which automatically hauled the emergency services off the hook, making it that much harder to prove there had been criminal neglect. After studiously sifting through mountains of evidence, and months spent driving over to Sheffield to interview key witnesses, Anne Williams alongside Ann and Sheila found people ready to demolish the legality of the cut-off time.

This was her story, as told in my *Echo* column in December 1991:

There's a single word that bangs away at Anne Williams's skull in her every waking moment like a pneumatic jackhamer . . . 'Mum.'

It was uttered to a special woman constable by Anne's son, Kevin, who opened his eyes seconds before life drained from his 15-year-old body in a makeshift mortuary at 3.55 pm on April 15th 1989.

Half-an-hour earlier, at 3.32 pm, an off-duty policeman saw Kevin convulsing and tried to revive him. These facts were told to the Formby mother prior to the inquest into her son's death. The next day she was told the policeman had changed his mind and that the special constable's evidence was inadmissible.

Another young man, who was killed in the same incident, was certified dead at 4.35 pm. His mother asked to see police statements about what happened to him after 3.15 pm. She was denied access.

Remember the time . . . 3.15 pm. It's crucial.

According to 'medical experts' every one of the 95 people who died at Hillsborough died before 3.15pm. Even though some of the families have medical evidence to disprove it.

They were among 48 families who paid £3,000 each to be represented by ONE barrister at the inquests into the disaster. The public purse paid for EIGHT barristers to represent the police, Sheffield Wednesday, the ground engineers and Sheffield City Council.

The jury was from Sheffield and the coroner in the pay of Sheffield City Council.

One couple who made the 200-mile round trip to the inquests daily for four months heard their son's name mentioned once. At the conclusion when the words 'accidental death' were recorded.

A London barrister acting for a small number of the families is now applying to the Attorney General to have those verdicts quashed.

Yet many critics wish the families would disappear, and cry quietly in a corner. The families don't see it that way.

They believe everyone is entitled to have a proper inquest and they don't believe their loved ones have had one.

If they had been allowed to question the emergency services who tended their sons, daughters and husbands when they were still alive, they believe a different verdict would have been returned.

But when the coroner ruled that everything which happened after 3.15 pm was irrelevant to their cause of death, this made a proper verdict impossible.

The families don't just feel they were denied justice; they feel they were never given the chance to receive it. And the gaping mental wounds won't heal.

What makes it worse is the slurs: 'Why don't they let the dead rest in peace . . . they're just after spiteful revenge . . . haven't they had enough blood money?'

For the record . . . those parents who lost sons aged over 18 and out of work, were legally entitled to no compensation at all.

Token gestures of between £110 and £500 have been offered by insurers to keep them quiet, but the insult has by many, been refused.

Since Justice Taylor's interim report two years ago, every single legal ruling has gone against the families. And so has public opinion.

'Let it lie' is the common cry. Well, it's because of the lies that they can't.

Had their loved ones died in a road accident, British law would have given them the truth in graphic detail.

Because they died in a politically-sensitive disaster they have been denied the truth, and that has turned their pain up to an unbearable level.

I hope the Attorney General hears their voice now as clearly as Anne Williams still hears her Kevin's pathetic cry for his 'mum.'

Forty minutes AFTER British law says he died in an accident.

Anne had been told in the weeks that followed the disaster that Deborah Martin, a Special WPC, was with her son Kevin in the makeshift mortuary when he spoke. She had also been told that Derek Bruder, an off-duty PC from Liverpool, had given a signed statement saying he had seen Kevin convulsing at 3.32 p.m. He ran on to the pitch, tried to resuscitate him and felt a pulse in his neck.

Yet mysteriously both statements were retracted after visits from the investigating officers. PC Bruder said he had since been on a medical course and realized he might have been mistaken about the pulse in Kevin's neck. SWPC Martin made a fresh statement saying, 'My head had gone. I wasn't aware of what was happening or what I was doing. I felt like a zombie.'

These stunning reversals of fact fitted neatly with the legal decision that every fan who perished at Hillsborough did so before 3.15 p.m. But Ann Adlington and Sheila Coleman tracked down Bruder and Martin who said they stood by their initial statements.

Kevin *did* have a pulse at 3.32 p.m., said PC Bruder. He *did* call out 'Mum' at 4 p.m., said SWPC Martin.

In February 1992, despite some internal opposition, I managed to get Anne's story on to the front of the *Echo* after her MP, Tory Malcolm Thornton, wrote to the Attorney General calling for the inquests to be reopened. There was hope, but it didn't last long. Kevin Williams would not receive a fresh inquest. However, there was a momentum gathering behind the feeling that a major miscarriage of justice had taken place. Jimmy McGovern, the finest TV writer of his generation and an ardent Liverpudlian, was commissioned by Granada to tell the families' stories in a two-hour drama-documentary.

Researchers unearthed more evidence which undermined the police case, crucially that the CCTV camera trained on the Leppings Lane End, which they said had not been in operation, was working. The ground engineer swore an affidavit to that effect. Which proved they had been lying when they told the inquest jury they could not see the extent of the crush from the control box.

When the film reached the screen I asked the *Mirror*'s editor Piers Morgan to get behind it. He watched it in his office, wept, and pledged to do whatever he could to help them. On 5 December 1996, Hillsborough was back on the front pages of a national newspaper. This time the *Daily Mirror* splashed with a headline that told of THE REAL TRUTH, urging every reader to watch the drama on their TVs that night and do all they could to help the families win justice.

Thanks to the impact of McGovern's magnificent piece of television the public perception of the disaster changed significantly overnight. The *Mirror*'s phone lines were swamped with angry readers demanding justice, 25,695 adding their names to the paper's petition demanding that the Attorney General give in. Piers Morgan even sent me to address Liverpool City Council telling them that the *Mirror* would be behind any moves for a fresh inquiry.

Things were going well and, as D:Ream promised us in the

May of 1997, they could only get better. A young, fresh Labour government was elected, pledging to blow away the sleaze and corruption of the Tory decades, and rule in an open way for the majority of people.

It was also a government that owed favours to its heartland voters on Merseyside and its only ultra-loyal national newspaper the *Daily Mirror*. Pressure was applied on the new regime from both ends and within weeks of taking power Home Secretary Jack Straw appointed Lord Justice Stuart-Smith to scrutinize the new evidence to see if it merited a fresh public inquiry.

A pop concert was held at Anfield which raised a £400,000 war chest for any legal battle ahead. The families were ecstatic. It was surely only a matter of time before justice was theirs.

However, things didn't get better, but merely reverted to type. When Lord Justice Stuart-Smith came up to Liverpool in October to listen to the families, they knew before a witness had opened their mouth that they were walking into the latest brick wall. When there was a delay in starting the proceedings, due to the absence of some family members, Stuart-Smith turned to Phil Hammond, who lost his son Philip in the disaster, and said, 'Have you got a few of your people or are they like the Liverpool fans, turning up at the last minute?'

Back to reality with a bang. Straw may as well have sent up Kelvin MacKenzie to deliver a verdict. He defended himself by saying it was a joke. But it was like saying to a Dunblane mother, 'Hurry up dear, or you'll get me shot.' Or to an Aberfan father: 'Don't let all that stuff get on top of you.'

At best the man was simply an insensitive buffoon. At worst his mind was already made up about who had been the main cause of the disaster. Either way the families sensed another Establishment stooge had been sent up to Liverpool to patronize them and give them nothing. And they were spot-on. The following February, Jack Straw called them all to the Commons to tell them there was insufficient new evidence to deserve a fresh inquiry. The Labour government, like the legal system, was washing their hands of it.

I sat with the families in a room opposite the House of Commons and tried to comfort them in yet another hour of devastation. But there was no comfort to be taken. For nine years they had been put through a mangle and thrown on the floor like used dishcloths. For nine years their lives had been on hold waiting for the acceptance of blame from people who had been entrusted with the care of their loved ones.

It was now approaching a decade since their lives were stolen from them, after their sons and daughters, brothers and husbands had bounced out the door that beautiful sunny morning, brimming with optimism, never to return. Yet still nobody had the decency, or was it the capacity, to allow them their lives back.

Over the years I've been to most of the memorial services at Anfield. I've even had the honour of doing a reading at one. But none was as poignant, nor overpowered me with the sense of sorrow and impotence, as much as the tenth anniversary.

Here's how I covered it in the *Mirror* under the headline: WE ALL OWE THEM A DEBT:

You'd have thought there were no tears left.

That everyone there that day was all cried out by the countless minute's silences, the dreaded anniversaries, the snubs by the Establishment, the pleas by outsiders to move on. By time itself.

And then you hear 10,000 throats almost lifting the roof off the Kop with You'll Never Walk Alone, you look at 96 candles being lit behind the goal, you feel the hairs on the back of your neck go rigid and you realise how futile it is to try and fight your heart.

Let it out. Let it out and it makes you feel better they say. And it does.

Because when you look alongside you at the haunted eyes of people like Phil Hammond, Jenni Hicks and Eddie Spearritt, people you are familiar with merely because their dead children attended the same football match as you, you realise your tears are drips from a tap compared to the oceans they have wept.

So you shake their hand and look into those eyes and say nothing. But you feel how important a day like yesterday is to them.

How it buoys their spirits, comforts them, makes them feel closer to their lost ones. Closer to sanity. If just for a day.

They gathered at Anfield with members of every other family who lost someone at Hillsborough, with MPs and Bishops, fans who were there ten years ago and fans who weren't; with players and managers past and present; with mums who'd walked in from Breck Road with their babies after laying a bunch of flowers.

And despite the rain, despite the fact that ten years down the line no-one has been held responsible for the incompetence that wrecked their lives, despite it all, they were lifted. We all were.

From dawn, people had arrived at the eternal flame to pay their own private tributes. Behind it was the Liverpool flag at half-mast. In front was a beautiful sea of flowers, shirts and tributes from football fans as far afield as Canada and Australia.

Scarfs were tied to the Shankly Gates bearing the colours of clubs like Ajax and Sunderland, and more poignantly those deadly rivals Everton and Manchester United. It puts sporting hatred in its true perspective and shames you.

Throughout the day people milled around the ground in much the same way they had ten years ago, when Anfield became a focal point for a city's grief, the pitch a carpet of flowers, and the Kop a shrine. Occasionally a relative would arrive and stare at a name carved in marble next to the flame, then lay a wreath and cry a prayer.

One mother simply kissed her finger, rubbed it along her son's name then laid her bouquet, and walked away full of composure, as though she had just made a precious connection.

In the executive suites of the centenary stand the families thanked the players who were on duty that day in April 1989.

Young men who had turned from footballer to social worker, comforting the bereaved and attending more funerals in a week than most of us attend in a lifetime.

Players like Alan Hansen, John Aldridge, Ian Rush and Steve McMahon. All scarred for life by the horror of those dark days.

Alongside them were the young stars of today like Michael Owen,

Robbie Fowler and Steve McManaman. Men who have been through the Liverpool system since they were boys and know how it shook this great club to its very foundations.

At 2.30 pm players and families made a procession together in the rain, taking their seats in the centre of the Kop, which by three o'clock was virtually full.

The Love And Joy Gospel choir beautifully led the song that was sung over and over again ten years ago. The football hymn Abide With Me. The Bishop of Liverpool the Rt Rev James Jones, read out a message from The Queen, and then the clergy read out the 96 names, and lit 96 candles.

The reading took a full five minutes. And by the time the list had ended the rain had stopped.

Ray Lewis, the referee on duty at the 1989 semi-final walked to the penalty spot. At 3.06, the precise time he called the players off the pitch ten years ago, he blew his whistle.

It was the cue not just for Anfield but a city to stop. Inside the ground you could hear nothing but the odd baby's cry. Outside you could hear the church bells ringing out, a comforting sign to the families that an entire city had obeyed their wishes and come to a halt.

Just for a minute. To remember. As if it could ever forget.

And then it was time for Trevor Hicks, the chairman of the Hillsborough Family Support Group, to issue a poignant speech and a defiant message:

'Some people, many in positions of authority, politely say that we should let the tenth anniversary be the end of it. Others are more bold and say they are totally sick of us going on about it.

'I know I speak for many families when I say, we agree. At least to some extent. We are sick too. We want to get on with our lives, wrecked as they are. We look forward to some peace and quiet.'

And he explained why they have achieved neither peace nor quiet. How the initial joy of the Taylor Report when the cause of the disaster was cited as a failure of police control turned to dismay when the inquest returned an astonishing verdict of accidental death.

And then the crushing blow when the inquiry led by Lord Stuart-Smith concluded there was no fresh evidence but commented that a number of police statements had been altered.

'Jack Straw placed the documents in the public domain,' said Trevor Hicks, 'and we found 150 statements had been altered, many significantly. If that isn't wrong I don't know what is,' he said.

'I am sick of being asked "isn't it time to pack in?" My answer is simple. It is a matter for the families.

'We are definitely not going away and we will do everything necessary to conclude this unfinished business.

'But that is all for another day. Today is about remembering the 96 and how we wish things were different. We know that we cannot get them back and we try to come to terms, we try to understand, to seek answers, explanations, the truth, justice.

'I can think of no better way to restate the commitment to our justice campaign and to the memory of the 96 than to jointly sing You'll Never Walk Alone.

'And to sing it like we have never sung it before to show the faceless but ever-powerful Establishment that we do not forget the 96.'

They did. And it was indeed unforgettable.

It is something you never imagine will happen when, as a six-year-old, you pin your first picture of a footballer on your wall.

That one day you will stand in your own team's football ground, a decade to the second you watched 96 of your fellow fans die on a pitch in front of you, and feel numbness in every part of your body.

But then you never imagined that when you grew up fans would be herded into caged pens in a Victorian slum and treated with so little respect by authority as they gasped for life. And how in death they would be afforded even less respect.

And now our grounds have been made safe on the back of their corpses every football fan owes them a debt and society owes them a frank admission of what happened that day.

Just once that's all. Just once.

And then maybe we can lay it to rest with the ones who never came back.

I've always believed there were three Hillsborough tragedies. The first was the day itself, the second was the failure of the dead to receive any form of justice, and the third was the splitting of their families into two rival camps, amid bitterness and rancour. The Hillsborough Family Support Group (HFSG) led by Trevor Hicks, who lost his two daughters, was the public face of the bereaved and the focal point of the campaign for justice. Naturally, within such a group containing people who had nothing in common before they were thrown together by the deaths of their loved ones, emotions would run high and relations would be strained. Especially when you consider the circumstances, the stress they'd been under, and the fact that everywhere they turned, even though they played by the book, they were hitting brick walls.

It reached breaking-point when Peter Robinson and Roy Evans, after overtures from the *Sun*, tried to broker peace between the paper and the families. Hicks wanted to hear what they had to offer, believing that if they offered a full front-page apology and threw their weight and their cash behind the campaign, it might be worth considering. Most of the families, including John Glover, who lost his son in the disaster, wanted nothing to do with them. Hicks still met them and Glover was incandescent, telling the local media, 'It's no longer the Hillsborough but the Trevor Hicks Family Support Group. He's a Yorkshireman and so doesn't really understand the extreme feeling in this city.'

The bad blood was spilt in public, family loyalties split asunder, and a breakaway group called the Hillsborough Justice Campaign formed, pledging to ditch the HFSG's play-it-by-the-book approach, and go for more direct action.

It led to bickering, bad-mouthing and recriminations which persist to this day. It was inevitable I suppose, but heart-rending nonetheless. Because the families were handing ultimate victory to their enemies, those who had tried to break their will from the second they turned up at the Sheffield mortuaries.

The sadness of it all hit home to me during their final shot at justice. A magistrate had granted the HFSG right to privately prosecute the two senior policemen on duty that day. In June 2000 David Duckenfield and Bernard Murray went on trial at

Leeds Crown Court charged with the manslaughter of John Anderson and James Aspinall (there were sample cases) and the wilful
neglect of duty.

I went backwards and forwards to Leeds during the six-week
trial and loved meeting up, having a chat and a laugh with the
families, giving them support and convincing them that they'd
have their day. These were men and women whom I'd first
recognized only because their surnames tallied with those on a
memorial stone – Hammond, Spearritt, Hicks, Glover, Aspinall,
Carlile, Devonside, Joynes, Traynor, Tootle – and had become
friends. But now it felt as though I was walking a diplomatic
tightrope. If I talked for too long with families from the Family
Support Group I felt like I was snubbing those from the Justice
Campaign. I'd get comments about whose side I was on, and have
to listen to put-downs and malicious gossip about individuals.

It felt very uncomfortable. It was tragic that it had all come
down to this. As we waited days for the jury to deliver their
verdicts, I remember surveying the scene of the two 'camps'
outside the court and thinking how proud the British Establishment should feel about itself. True to history they had triumphed
through divide and rule.

It came as no surprise when the jury cleared Bernard Murray
of all charges. No surprise that they spent another day deliberating
on Duckenfield, and no surprise that the judge Mr Justice Hooper
called the trial to a halt, cleared him, and ruled there could be no
retrial. Especially after he directed the jury to ask if convicting
Duckenfield 'would send out the wrong message', even though
that message is not a jury's responsibility.

It was the final kick in the teeth. When the judge told Duckenfield to leave a free man, many of the women sobbed silently,
the men putting arms on shoulders, looking hollow-eyed into the
middle distance. As they slumped out of court, weary, drained
and beaten, there were eight armed police officers waiting to
escort them off the premises. It was heart-breaking to watch.
These people who had conducted themselves throughout all the

legal cases with such dignity, had never sought revenge, but just someone to admit there had been a cover-up from Day One. This would have enabled them to walk away and try to resurrect what was left of their lives.

It was summed up for me in the foyer of the Leeds court, when one of the mums approached ITV's court artist and asked to see the drawing of the public gallery. The artist obliged, then braced herself for a rant which never came. 'You couldn't do me a favour, love?' said the mother. 'Get rid of some of the lines around my eyes 'cos I look awful. I've been a bit washed out lately, you see.'

Although the legal system gave them nothing, their battle shed light on the truth about what happened that day. I salute them for that, in fact more than salute them. I thank them for teaching me something – that if anything ever happens to my loved ones, and the Establishment covers its backside with lies, I hope I have so-called 'whingers' like them on my side.

24

PARADISE REGAINED

25 FEBRUARY 2001 – CARDIFF

The harder the handful of Evertonians tried to get the chant going, the more I clamped my mouth and sucked in air through my nose to calm the stomach convulsions. I thought about Phil, about where I was, and bit my lip hard. But it was my ears that needed blocking, to muffle the noise coming from about forty mouths: 'You, You, You Ess-Ay. You, You, You Ess-Ay.'

So I used the trusted method when trying to distract myself from an imminent explosion in a moment of passion, and recited the 1965 FA Cup final team over and over again.

They still tried to get the chant going, even though it was only about a dozen of them: 'You, You, You, Ess-Ay.' The dam burst – I held the inside of my coat up to my face and howled. I didn't care what Phil thought any more. Well I did, but I couldn't do anything about it. This farce had gone on far too long, the discomfort had become intolerable and I lacked any desire to hide it.

It was FA Cup fifth round day in January 2000 and we were watching Preston outplay Everton, sat behind the Gwladys Street goal where there was less atmosphere than you'll find in a burst balloon on Pluto.

Late in a game dominated by the team from two leagues below, David Unsworth scored a free-kick, followed by an injury-time toe-poke from American Joe-Max Moore. Hence the swearing of allegiance to the Stars and Stripes. Everton were in the last eight of the FA Cup and their fans were streaming home content.

As always Phil wanted to stay to the end, and for once I was happy to oblige because I was finally enjoying myself.

'You, You, You Ess-Ay,' was now dying on its arse, but I was in my element. Maybe the homesick pangs were kicking in and I was missing Anfield more than I ever thought possible. Maybe I just wanted my son to know I could never be a part of this, that a lifetime's worship on the other side of Stanley Park made all of it totally alien to me. I can't be sure, but I knew I was in the wrong place. Nothing against Everton, it just wasn't for me. It was too late in my life to try to get it, especially when so much of their passion was spent on loathing the 'red shite'.

And I didn't care who knew.

I expected an elbow in the ribs from Phil, a 'shhh . . . you're making a show of me', and a look that could kill. But neither head nor lips moved. He just stared at the pitch. I felt bad. I said sorry. He said nothing. Until I added, 'Pop sucks eh, junior,' and I noticed his shoulders shaking. He was looking away from me but I could tell he was laughing. I sensed a breakthrough.

Nothing was said about it. I could have chipped away at the weakness, driven home the fact that he had been as embarrassed as me, but left it unspoken. I'd sensed through his lack of passion during that dreadful game that the flame might be going out. And when the sixth-round draw was made and I wasn't being begged to get tickets for the Aston Villa tie, I knew his heart was drifting.

As to where it was going I had no clue. Scouting? Skate-boarding? Goth-baiting? I was stumped. Until a fortnight later when I was stood on the touchline watching his Sunday League team warm up and one of his mates, Anthony Barton, spilt the beans:

'Have you heard about your Phil?'

'What about him?'

'He's a Liverpudlian.'

'What? Oh yeah. Like I wouldn't know.'

'He is, honest. The little traitor.'

John Ecclestone, like Barton, another Evertonian classmate, walked past and confirmed it via a withering look. I was rooted to the spot. A million thoughts rushing into my head. I saw myself hugging him at Anfield, jigging with him at Wembley, choking back tears of joy in Rome. I wanted to intensify my feelers for season tickets right there and then. But first I needed confirmation from his own lips.

Should I yell across the pitch to where he stood at centre-half? Should I run on and front him up? No, play it cool. Let him tell you in his own time. Make a fuss and you'll only alienate him and the next thing you know he's on Gay Pride marches dressed as a New York cop.

The game started, and within minutes Phil was dragged out of position by a tricky centre-forward and slid a tackle in, knocking it out for a throw-in, right under my nose. As he picked himself up ready to track back with the striker, I grabbed him by the arm.

'Are you a Red now?'

He frowned, pulled away, nodded and chased back. I just looked up to the heavens, and without any idea why, thanked Our Vic.

When the game ended, and I drove him home, I tried to find out when and why he'd undergone the conversion, but he didn't want to talk about it. He thought I was gloating, so I left it. Any hint of triumphalism might scar him for life and could send him on a vengeance mission straight into the arms of Man United.

If he had, who could have blamed him? That season they waltzed to their fourth title in five years, finishing 18 points ahead of second-placed Arsenal and 24 ahead of us in fourth. In the ten years since Liverpool last won the League, they had won it six times, as well as the European Cup. Fergie had well and truly knocked us off our perch.

Gérard Houllier was making solid if unspectacular progress though. He'd sorted out the defence by replacing the hapless David James with Sander Westerveld and pairing Sami Hyypia with Stephane Henchoz in front of him. The excellent Didi

Hamann had brought steel and nous to the heart of midfield, and local lads Jamie Carragher, Steven Gerrard and Danny Murphy were starting to exhibit the same kind of potential as Michael Owen, who'd found a new partner in Emile Heskey. Free-scoring show-stoppers were not on the menu. But this side could defend better than any other side in the Premiership and they had youth, discipline and unity going for them.

Houllier's first achievement had been to dismantle the Spice-world that had made Roy Evans's job virtually impossible. There was no more coin-passing on the pitch. No more tea-time flights out of Manchester to rub shoulders with pop stars at Chinawhite. No player could phone up the manager when he was being interviewed, asking him to abuse a journalist, because mobile phones had been banned from Melwood.

The man who took most umbrage at the new regime was the most high-profile casualty, Paul Ince. The self-styled Guv'nor was shipped off to Middlesbrough amid much public dummy-tossing and back-stabbing. Which in the fans' eyes only worked in Houllier's favour.

After the ill-discipline of the Evans years, Houllier was increasingly perceived as a leader with the strength and vision to make them a force again. When, in the summer of 2000 he signed Marcus Babbel, Nick Barmby, Gary McAllister and Christian Ziege, we were once more talking about the final pieces of the jigsaw.

Phil's switched allegiance had stood the test of time. His bedroom had become a shrine to Anfield (not that I dragged him down to the shop most weekends and gave him a blank cheque or anything, honest). All birthday money was being spent on kits, and I was constantly being pestered to take him to the game.

But it was full-house time at Anfield and finding tickets was rarer than finding Liverpool on *Match Of The Day* before midnight. For years I'd been pestering every contact, friend and relative who was likely to be of help, to get back the season ticket I'd thrown away in protest over Souness. Now I intensified the search. Barely a week passed that I wouldn't make enquiries about season-ticket holders being in danger of dying, emigrating or taking up Scientology. But none was forthcoming.

So it was friendlies, cup games and the occasional Premiership match. Still, after my two-year prison sentence at Goodison, they could have rationed me to dire 0–0s against Middlesbrough and Bradford and 3–0 thrashings by United and Arsenal and I wouldn't have complained. Taking Phil to Anfield, educating him about past glories (but toning it down after he told me I sounded like *The Fast Show*'s Ron 'jumpers for goalposts' Manager) finally made me feel like a proper dad.

For most men, separating from your wife, moving out of the house where your kids live, and only seeing them on an irregular, predetermined basis, isn't good for your self-esteem. Even though I saw mine every midweek and weekend my opinion of myself was often down in the gutter. I was a part-time dad. A paternal no-mark, derelict in the most important duty life can throw at you, failing the supreme male test.

So I seized every opportunity to bond, no matter how painful. I'd take Christie horse-riding every weekend, standing in cold, dung-smelling stables for an hour with a glazed expression that cracked into a smile and a nod every time she trotted past on her pony looking for approval.

I'd take Phil to his Sunday football game, listening to other dads bollocking virtual babies for not getting 'in the hole', playing it to feet, and my favourtie one: 'digging deep', which was always a cue for middle-aged men to suck their guts up to their chests and pull their hands up to their armpits while their faces turned blue.

We'd go to ten-pin bowling, the swimming baths, theme parks, the pictures, and watch WWF wrestling together every Saturday night (I even took them to a show in Earls Court). But it wasn't really bonding. It was 'quality time' supervision. It was filling the hours until I dropped them back at the old family home, which was now Ann's home, and they could climb back in front of their Playstations.

Bonding is about a shared passion. So when Phil embraced the only true passion of my life (I tried hard with Christie but she has stayed to this day an Evertonian) I finally felt, father-wise, that I served a purpose. I could encourage, enthuse and enlighten. As I did, I rediscovered the magic that drew me to football in the early sixties. Firing Phil's imagination reminded me why I'd become a total obsessive.

Most of the mates I'd been to the game with over the years had become too suffocated by responsibility, too cynical or too unprepared to clamour for a costly seat at Anfield when they could watch the action from the comfort of a bar stool. (Liverpool were rarely off the telly these days; Scandinavian and Arab channels would beam virtually every game into pubs willing to pay the fee and the only season ticket you needed was a pass-out from your missus.)

I drank with Terry (Poirot) every Friday night, and his son Tom had become a Reds fanatic, but he rarely got a chance to take him to the match as the season-ticket waiting list was now approaching 30,000-strong, and pairs of match-day tickets were gold dust. Mike (Sinatra) was a husband and a father and more worried about meeting big monthly mortgage payments than forking out £30 a week to fund multimillionaire pay packets. I'm sure Billy (Spiderman) would still have been making the odd entry into the ground via the roof if cancer hadn't claimed him just before his fortieth birthday. He died slowly, in his bed, and the ugly way he went shook us all. Towards the end he couldn't speak, would drift in and out of consciousness, and was so morphined up that, at times, he didn't know who he was talking to. If he summoned the strength to say something he'd motion you to pass him pen and paper and attempt to write a message. When I left him for the last time he called for his pen and, with hands shaking, evoked memories of that great year we had together in 1986 by scrawling: 'You should never have won that Double. Kopites are gobshites.' He went two days later. I still think of him a lot and his memory always makes me smile. Billy Birney, the best Blue Nose I ever met, RIP.

So one way or another, the old match-day mates had fallen by the wayside, but Phil had replaced them and educating him in the Liverpool Way turned me into a born-again fanatic. He was hungry for the buzz, scanning every line of the papers and fanzines, collecting the programmes, lapping up the gossip, learning the new songs, dancing with joy when we got tickets for the big games. For him, none came bigger than English football's first showpiece game at Cardiff's Millennium Stadium, the 2001 League Cup final against Birmingham – the first final we'd been involved in since Wembley's famous White Suit Final (not to be confused with the White Horse Final) of 1996.

The match itself was uglier than a moose on the loose in The Grafton at closing time. Memories include 6 ft 3 in Igor Biscan playing on the wing, my balls being frozen as wind whipped in from the River Taff through the open-plan wall behind me, Michael Owen not rising from the bench despite the game crying out for him, a peach of a Robbie Fowler long-distance lob after half an hour, Stephane Henchoz looking like he was about to concede a penalty whenever a Birmingham player broke into the box and doing so three minutes into injury time, which meant we had to suffer another half an hour's agony.

Birmingham outplayed us in extra time, Jamie Carragher (of all people) scoring Liverpool's winning penalty, Andy Johnson missing Birmingham's last, Birmingham boss Trevor Francis collapsing in tears, Liverpool players celebrating like they'd just won the European Cup, feeling sorry for the Brummies and thinking Cardiff was better than Wembley before getting stuck in a three-hour traffic jam trying to get out of the city.

All of those images pale into insignificance compared to the sight of Phil's face. From the moment he hung his scarf out of the window at The Rocket he was beaming. He loved all the banter at a Bristol service station with the Brummies, mainly because he sussed I was taking the piss out of them. He felt that knot in his stomach when the Millennium Stadium came into sight. He dived into the singing when we joined the mass of Liverpool fans outside the ground. He was euphoric when the captain for the day, Robbie Fowler, lifted the trophy above his head, half of the stadium turned red and The Hymn was sung.

He was hooked. I was a good dad. And a whole new dimension was added to the debt I owed Liverpool FC. The club that had given me most of the greatest moments in my life was now giving them to my son, and we were sharing in it. Was there any other glue on the market that could bond a father and son so gloriously?

Ten weeks later we were back in Cardiff to steal the FA Cup from under Arsenal's nose thanks to the genius of Michael Owen, and the following week in Dortmund the UEFA Cup was won against unheard-of Spaniards Alaves by the unheard-of scoreline 5–4. Houllier had won a treble, not a Joe Fagan treble or an Alex Ferguson treble, admittedly, but a treble nonetheless, and we partied like it was 1984, convinced not only that the UEFA Cup final had been the greatest Cup final since the invention of the ball but that the long-awaited renaissance was under way, and the League title round the corner.

It wasn't an optimism shared by most outsiders. Maybe it was jealousy, maybe fear that English football's greediest trophy-eater was getting its hunger back, or maybe honest objectivity. Whatever the true motives, critics still had their doubts about Houllier's side, and derided the treble as three flukey Cup final wins against weak opponents (Birmingham and Alaves) and natural justice (Arsenal had played us off the park).

The hatchet men painted this Liverpool team as a cross between George Graham's Arsenal and Harry Bassett's Wimbledon, churning out results with a jolly blond giant at the back and a baby-faced assassin up front. Johan Cruyff was even more brutal in his assessment: 'Liverpool play horribly and are incapable of putting three passes together,' he said, sticking his head firmly up the hole of the Barcelona media after Liverpool knocked them out of the UEFA Cup.

It was blatantly unfair. How many boring teams do you know who score 123 goals in a season? How many clueless, sterile sides survive 25 major cup ties on the trot while picking up every cup on offer? How many negative teams play all-out attack in a pulsating 2–2 draw against Chelsea on a Wednesday, produce that heart-stopping last 20 minutes in an FA Cup final on a Saturday, then come out on top in an extraordinary 5–4 European final days later? Not many.

What Liverpool showed in Dortmund, as they showed in Cardiff and against Manchester United, Arsenal, Barcelona, Roma and Porto that season, was that they were a young, resilient squad with the talent and spirit to vary their tactics, raise their game and get a result. If Houllier was over-cautious against some of those sides it was because he felt they were better teams than his own and he set about preventing a mauling which may have made his youngsters think that what they had achieved was a mirage.

What critics forgot was that when Manchester United did their treble in 1999 they had been picking up trophies together for half a dozen years and when Liverpool last did theirs in 1984 they had been hoarding silver for a dozen years. Yet Houllier's side was based around a nucleus of relatively inexperienced players, who two years previous where mostly total strangers.

But then the only people who really mattered knew that all along. The fans. We treated that treble as The Resurrection, because we'd been present at all the crucifixions in the nineties.

When you have witnessed your great European pedigree torn to shreds by French and Spanish nonentities, stopping Barcelona and Roma scoring on their home ground wasn't something we found horrible or boring. It gave us back our pride and, more importantly, the kind of magical night we had in Dortmund. A night when Liverpool's fans contributed so much that UEFA gave them an award for the sporting tribute they paid to Alaves.

Only those present at Heysel truly understood how much that meant.

For Liverpudlians to be able to hold their heads high, both on and off the field in Europe, after seventeen long years, was something more precious than any treble. And for Johan Cruyff to be there handing out gongs was the icing on a gorgeous cake. Sod what the rest of the world had to say. Our ship was coming in again. And I was back on board, with my lad as first mate. Could life get any better?

25

PARADISE LOST

I'd never seen my mum looking as bad as she did in that hospital bed on a bleak January morning in 2002. She was so frail, pale and old that at first I wasn't sure it was her. Then I handed her the *Daily Mirror*, she glanced at the back-page splash which said, BECKS: MY AGONY above a photo of a distracted David Beckham, and I knew it was still Sheila.

'When are you going to get a job away from the Daily bloody Manc,' she said, before throwing it down, grimacing and asking when they were letting her out.

Less than a fortnight earlier, on Christmas Day 2001, she'd been her usual boisterous self: joking, drinking, singing and giving someone who praised private health care such a violent tongue-lashing he almost ended calling the BUPA helpline. Then she caught a virus, went to bed, saw her stomach bloat and was taken to Whiston Hospital. An obstruction was found in her bowel and surgeons told us they would have to investigate.

On the Wednesday evening, hours after the surgery, myself, my dad and my two sisters were at her beside as she lay sleeping, waiting to hear what they'd discovered. We sat there for an hour and a half but no show. The duty doctor was busy in Accident and Emergency and couldn't guarantee when he'd be free. It was getting late, the lights were going out on the ward and the sister, sensing our anxiety, told us the consultant who had operated on her would be doing his rounds the next morning, so maybe we should come back tomorrow and speak to him.

My dad and sisters were unsure but I wasn't. Liverpool's game at Southampton was on Sky and the second half was just beginning. If we left now we could catch the last half-hour. So I put forward all the arguments in favour of legging it and coming back the following morning.

Fifteen minutes later I was sat with my dad in The Queen's in Huyton, yelling at the telly as the Reds abjectly surrendered to a painfully average Southampton. James Beattie had just scored a penalty, Emile Heskey was playing left-wing, and John Arne Riise was about to bullet a Sandy Brown-style header into his own net.

We'd only won one League game in the last seven. Once again any hopes of competing for the title had vanished weeks into the New Year. All around the pub it was inquest time, which me and Reg joined in, happy to be distracted from my mum's plight. I dropped Reg off, drove home and went to bed worried but positive. Surely if the surgeons had found what we all privately dreaded she may have, they'd have told us the minute she left the operating theatre.

At 6 a.m. Reg rang to say the police had just knocked him up to tell him she had taken a turn for the worse. By the time I reached the hospital a priest was giving her the last rites, and we were told she had hours to live. The doctor who should have seen us the previous night was white as a sheet as he told us the news he should have told us ten hours before. They'd found an aggressive cancer in her bowel, and the consultant had decided there was nothing they could do. It was the first time anybody had mentioned the word cancer in relation to my mum and now she was morphined up to the eyeballs, unable to make out our shapes or hear our voices. Dying basically.

I looked at her notes which said she had refused a blood test shortly before midnight. So she had been awake, with hours to live, and instead of being there to comfort her as she faced death, I'd been in the pub yelling at a telly for Vladimir Smicer to be taken off and put down.

'Why didn't you tell us this last night?' I bawled at the doctor, only for him to nervously stutter something about being too busy.

My dad told me to cool it and show some respect, the way his generation always do when faced with men in ties. But I was raging, and part of that rage was with myself. I knew if we'd stayed, instead of legging off to watch Heskey flounder down the wing, we'd all have had a chance to say goodbye.

But we didn't. And now all the four of us could do was hold her hand and watch the last traces of life drain from her. She was only seventy-four. Besides giving birth, this was the first time she'd been in a hospital in the past fifty years.

We all focused in on what this wonderful mother and wife had given us. I went right back to all the laughs and all the love, all the smacks and all the sacrifices. I thought of the big cloth Liver Bird and the outline of a number 9 she'd stitched on my first Liverpool shirt to try and make me feel like Ian St John. Only to be told she was a silly bitch for not supplying me with a proper number.

I thought of the forged letter I'd sent from her to Shankly begging for a 1974 FA Cup final ticket, and the bollocking I got for wearing her red maxicoat (her only coat) to that same final and bringing it home looking like a tramp's shroud. I silently asked her to forgive me for leaving her to die while I watched Liverpool's latest embarrassment, and I felt her smile. I could hear her telling me she was glad I'd gone because she didn't want anyone to see her in this state. That pubs were for the living, and geriatric wards in hospitals for the dying.

She was cremated at Springwood in Allerton and her ashes spread in Anfield next to Our Vic's. Reg organized a plaque with both their names on, which was placed facing Liverpool's ground. My only dying wish is that I share the same company and the same view.

*

Sheila wasn't alone in being rushed to a Merseyside hospital that winter. In October, Gérard Houllier had taken a funny turn during a home game with Leeds. Doctors at Broadgreen found a dissected aorta and he underwent an eleven-hour life-saving operation on his heart. It had been touch and go whether he would survive. He was out of the game for five months. Like Shankly, Fagan, Dalglish and Souness before him, the stress of managing Liverpool had wreaked havoc with his health, and many of those close to him, inside and outside the game, said that maybe he should forget about going back into front-line coaching.

His response? 'Maybe I should forget about breathing, too.'

In his absence, Phil 'Pinocchio' Thompson stood up to be counted, and did an excellent job, guiding them through their Champions League first-stage group with a notable win at Dynamo Kiev, and going on a nine-game unbeaten Premiership run until mid-December which kept them in contention for the title.

But come Christmas, domestically, Thompson was struggling. The club seemed in a state of limbo, awaiting the return of Houllier, who couldn't help but let it be known (whenever they won) that he was masterminding affairs from his sick-bed.

I was starting to see another side to Houllier. A vain side. Here was the man who had plastered a wall in his Melwood office with framed photos of some of the world's powerful figures, all shaking hands with Gérard Houllier.

It came as no surprise that when he returned to Anfield he did so with the timing of a Hollywood diva. Against Roma, with victory needed to take them into the last-eight knock-out stages of the Champions League, Houllier walked slowly to the dug-out, dressed all in black, after every member of both sides' playing and coaching staff had taken to the field.

Anfield exploded with emotion and Houllier stood there and sucked in the love. The players responded with one of their finest attacking displays of the season, the fans provided the best atmosphere since St Etienne, and Roma were flattened.

Although the UEFA team sheet said Phil Thompson was the coach, and although he had guided Liverpool past Borussia Dortmund, Dynamo Kiev, Barcelona, Galatasaray and Roma, the fans were being left in no doubt that it was Gérard Houllier and his miracle return to Anfield which had put their side on course for more European glory. When they were paired with Bayer Leverkusen in the quarter-finals Houllier left the world in no doubt that he had plotted an astonishing strategy from his hospital bed.

On the day after April Fool's Day (I think he'd forgotten to turn his calendar over), with five League games and five possible European Cup games left to play, he held his first press conference for six months and announced, 'We have double vision: to win the title and the Champions League. We are maybe ten games away from greatness.' He may as well have pulled out a chisel and started carving his epitaph there and then.

After a narrow 1–0 first-leg win at Anfield the Reds travelled to Leverkusen with Houllier's doctor strongly advising him not to make the trip. By the end of the game every Liverpool fan was wishing the quack had tied him to his hospital bed by the strings of his strait jacket. With half an hour to go, 2–1 up on aggregate, and Leverkusen needing two goals to win, Houllier dragged off the defensive shield Didi Hamann and replaced him with the flyweight Vladimir Smicer.

It was probably the most baffling (and certainly the most costly) Liverpool substitution I could remember. The defence was horrendously exposed and, three swift German goals later, so was Houllier's Muhammad Ali-esque prediction. They were now five League games away from winning as much that season as Everton.

To rub a ton of Saxa in the wounds, it transpired that if we'd got past Leverkusen we'd have faced Man United in the semi-final, who were below us in the League, we'd beaten them the last five times we'd met and they were missing their key midfielders David Beckham and Roy Keane. The most golden of opportunities had been blown in the most bizarre of circumstances.

The 'greatness' prediction and the Hamann substitution were

ominous signs that all was not well with the Frenchman's decision-making. Liverpool finished runners-up, their best position ever in the Premiership, but how much had that been down to Phil Thompson? Something had changed about Houllier. Something had happened on that operating table and during those long months of recuperation, which made him re-enter the working arena with an air of invincibility, a feeling that he could send any of his eleven chosen sons on to the pitch and they would drape themselves, and him, in glory.

The dodgy decision-making was further exposed that summer when he refused to take up the option to sign proven Premiership striker Nicolas Anelka, wouldn't lay out £15 million for Damien Duff, but instead splashed £20 million on three 'prospects' from the French League: El-Hadji Diouf, Salif Diao and Bruno Cheyrou. Or Curly, Larry and Mo, as devotees of The Three Stooges eventually christened them.

It wasn't all doom and gloom that summer though. In fact I was looking forward to the next season more than any other since the sixties. A mate had come up with a pair of Main Stand season tickets that were going spare, meaning I'd finally won back the birthright I'd surrendered in protest over Souness. What's more, I'd have Phil sitting next to me. A lifetime of happy Saturdays and undiluted pleasure lay ahead. Well, that was the theory anyway. In practice Houllier's men gave us the worst collection of home performances since the mid-fifties. They won only 9 out of 19 games at Anfield, and finished fifth. But it was the type of football played to attain those glum statistics that was the most distressing aspect of all. It was dire, one-dimensional stuff with no width and little craft. The team was only ever set up to play one way, on the counter-attack, meaning every opponent who came to Anfield camped on the edge of their own penalty area and got the deck-chairs out. And we simply topped up their pina coladas.

The summer buys were disasters, and the team was more reliant on Michael Owen than ever. Take away his 19 Premiership goals that season and we would have been below mid-table. We were going backwards.

Houllier's men crashed out of a weak Champions League group containing FC Basle and Spartak Moscow, and were totally out-thought and outplayed home and away by a Valencia side coached by a señor called Rafa Benitez. Celtic dumped us out of the UEFA Cup at Anfield, as did Crystal Palace in the FA Cup, both with emphatic 2–0 scorelines.

The gloom was lifted thanks to a League Cup final triumph over Manchester United. But it was a feeling of supremacy that lasted shorter than a crane-fly's lifespan, as they finished 19 points above us in the Premiership. In a rare outburst of Manc wit, one of their flags put Houllier, his hype and his squad into perspective: 'Thirty miles from greatness,' it read. Looking on from the stands it seemed much further than that.

There had been better times to introduce your son to a full season's offerings at Anfield. Virtually any time actually. As our seats were down by the Anfield Road End corner flag, he spent most afternoons engaged in hand-gesturing banter with the away fans. And I spent most of mine boring him about my weekly Annie Road confrontations back in the sixties.

As a veteran of the Walter Smith Goodison years, Phil knew all about football that crushes you into submission, so naturally he was less critical than me. But only slightly. Journeys home from the game would be spent re-analysing the brain-numbing tedium we'd just had to sit through, listening to irate fans on phone-ins calling for Houllier's head and former players like Ian St John savaging his style of play.

The way they were playing was summed up by the great John Peel in this emotional outburst on his radio show in early March, which chimed uncannily with my own feelings. 'Someone stopped me to talk about football earlier today and I had to tell them that I wasn't interested in football.

'Liverpool don't seem to be interested in football, so why should I?' asked the lifelong Reds fan.

'I shouldn't keep going on about Liverpool and I should be more sympathetic. But it is so depressing. When they play as badly as they did against Birmingham and Crystal Palace, I have a kind of negative, diabetic reaction to it and have about two days of feeling really quite ill afterwards because I get so angry.'

Houllier knew this type of football was unacceptable. In the summer he promised more attacking football and bought in Harry Kewell as evidence that he would achieve it. But after a bright start he reverted to the gormless, long-ball game which had been sussed by opponents after the treble season two years earlier, and which everyone but he agreed would take them no further than Roy Evans.

After a particularly gutless surrender at Portsmouth in October, there was mutiny among the players: 'It's simply not good enough,' said new captain Steve Gerrard, following a shambles where players were second to every ball and the coaching staff looked on like clueless zombies. 'Liverpool should be challenging for major honours. Nothing else is acceptable.'

It was empty rhetoric and the genie was out of the bottle. This side was going nowhere. Houllier, meanwhile, descended into a form of madness, blaming everyone from ex-players and journalists to referees, and everything from the fixture list to the length of grass, for Liverpool's slide towards mid-table.

Like a crazed professor, he would spend hours after games poring over statistics, not to show the players where they were going wrong, but to twist and hurl at critics to prove he had the most attacking team in the land. How can you say we're not playing like Brazil, asked an eye-spinning Houllier, when we're winning more corners than any other side? Small wonder he earned the nickname Toulouse Le Plot.

The vultures were circling, and a paranoid Houllier was drawing in his wagons, adopting a siege mentality and lashing out at anyone who dared to criticize him. Myself included, but I couldn't hold back. It was clear that when under full anaesthetic, Houllier had dreamed about leading Liverpool towards the Promised Land, convincing himself that he was The Way, The Truth and The Light. That like the Son of God, he had been put back among us mortals to perform miracles.

Yet when you spend way over £100 million on the likes of Frode Kippe, Daniel Sjolund, Bernard Diomede, Igor Biscan, Eric Meijer, Titi Camara, Rigobert Song, John-Michel Ferri, Antony Le Tallec, Djimi Traore, Abel Xavier, Salif Diao, El-Hadji Diouf, Bruno Cheyrou, Gregory Vignal, Florent Sinama-Pongolle, Alou Diarra and Carl Medjani, the only miracle you need is one that keeps you in a job.

Fortunately for Houllier, he had David Moores as his chairman and nothing short of a prolonged open revolt on the terraces would stir him into decisive action. Or so we thought.

At the end of another woeful season of unwatchable football and chronic underachievement, in which Liverpool scraped fourth place on the final day, to everyone's shock Moores decided that Houllier was ten days away from the dole.

It felt like the fall of Souness all over again, as though a huge burden was being lifted. I didn't care that Moores had only acted because he knew his position was under threat or that he'd given Houllier and his staff a colossal pay-off that would land the club in deep debt. I just knew he had to go.

As a journalist mate who worked closely with him (and grew to loathe the size of his ego) put it: 'They're going to need one hell of a removals van to get all of those framed photos of him out of his Melwood office.'

I did feel a tinge of regret. In fairness to Houllier, he brought much-needed discipline to the club, modernized the players' training, preparation and lifestyles. He was a dedicated workaholic who tore the lining of his heart in pursuit of reuniting the words Liverpool and glory. And for five very special days in May 2001, he did precisely that, and made us happy again.

But when you're in charge of a world-famous sporting institution which for two years has been sliding backwards, there comes a point when you have to carry the can. Houllier could never do that. It was always someone else's fault and he had the statistics to prove it. But statistics, as the Frenchman frequently reminded us, rarely lie. And these were the ones which ultimately mattered. He took over a team in 1998 which had just climbed from fourth to third, lying 13 points behind champions Arsenal, and he promised the Premiership within five years.

Six seasons later he'd not only failed to achieve that, but overseen Liverpool's removal from the top three, and left them battling for fourth place, 30 points behind Arsenal, which put them closer to the relegation teams than to the champions.

Houllier's clever, time-buying five-year-plan had become his managerial suicide note. As he left, demanding a long presidential address to the world in which he rewrote history, he implied that it was pressure from media critics and former players which got him the sack. It wasn't – it was the fans.

They remembered his declaration when he signed: 'Liverpool finished third last season, and that would be considered a good achievement by many. But not by us. We have to improve the team and reach out for top place.' They contrasted that with his words in his final match-day programme, that finishing fourth was a 'massive achievement'. And it didn't add up in their heads.

They watched an unadventurous, uninspiring style of play, far too reliant on Steven Gerrard finding Michael Owen, and deemed it so unacceptable Anfield ceased to attract full houses. Older fans brought up on winning football played with fluency, speed of thought, passion and movement, were watching losing football bereft of those qualities played by too many men unfit to wear the shirt. The gloom was deepening to the point where had Michael Owen not equalized against Newcastle in the season's final game they would have recorded their worst home record since relegation in 1954.

When the Kop started to register their frustration, by chanting 'attack, attack, attack', Houllier committed the fatal error of attacking them. 'Supporters should support,' he said. 'I don't know why they were moaning.' It was a diversionary tactic too far. Houllier was not just questioning the Kop's loyalty, but its knowledge of football. And that's when most of the hardcore minority who still fought his corner threw the towel in. In the final reckoning it wasn't Houllier's utterances but his poor judgement of players which did for him. He bought too many heartless journeymen. Worse than that, he stubbornly persisted with them, refusing through vanity to move them on, when it was clear they weren't up to scratch. And therefore, ultimately, neither was he.

C'est la vie, monsieur. Merci.

26

CHATTING TO GOD

On the eve of big sporting events Sky's publicity department sends out little gimmicks to tease our journalistic imaginations. A rubber cricket ball before the Ashes, a gumshield before a big fight, a box of Kleenex before the Olympics beach volleyball final (only joking Sky, but worth bearing in mind).

In August 2004 I opened one such package to find a miniature European Cup with red-and-white ribbons attached. I didn't know if Sky were sucking up to certain journalists by sending them their preferred colours, if red was all their gimmick department had left, or if they'd realized three of the four English teams in that season's Champions League wore red so were thus playing the percentage game. But there it stood proudly on my desk, its silver face so clear I could stare into its curving body and see a podgy Eamonn Holmes lookalike staring back. And my mind lost itself in the sheen and headed back to all of those big European nights which now seemed further in the past than puberty.

When it reached Brussels I returned the brain to the depression of the present and my laptop. On the Press Association sports pages was a file marked 'Champions League Odds' which I opened. Chelsea and Man United were 10/1 or less. Arsenal were fifteens, and Liverpool limped along with the also-rans at 33/1.

With memories of London, Paris and Rome still departing the subconscious, my instinct was to smack the laptop for delivering such heresy. But instead I pulled the punch, stared back at the little trophy and convinced myself, the way only desperate football fans can, that it was an omen. Why had they sent it to me today of all days? Why did I see those red ribbons, and sprint down Memory Lane minutes before opening a file that would show such insulting yet tantalizing odds? What was it trying to tell me?

I started talking up our chances. This new manager Rafa Benitez won last year's UEFA Cup and two Spanish League titles with Valencia when no one gave him a chance. He'll take time to settle in domestically, but he'll know the European scene well, as will the Spanish players he's brought to the club, and he'll be desperate to make an impression. The group of Monaco, Olympiakos and Deportivo La Coruña wasn't that daunting. Get past them and who knows.

Coat on, down the bookies, £20 on the nose. I didn't expect to see that note again, but it made me feel better about the Reds anyway. You can't beat convincing yourself about names being on cups, can you?

It hadn't exactly been a mind-blowing start to the season. In fact, away from home it had been disastrous, drawing at Spurs and losing at Bolton, United and Chelsea. Knives were being sharpened, with critics already dismissing Benitez as Gérard Houllier in disguise. An over-hyped one-trick pony who had simply replaced poor Frenchmen with poor Spaniards.

Alan Hansen went as far as to label his team 'the worst Liverpool side I can remember'. A quote which I hoped would come back to embarrass him as much as his warning to Man United that they'd win nothing with kids.

I was very defensive of Benitez because I liked the cut of his jib. Not only was he carrying off the Herculean task of coaxing life out of some of the men who had gone AWOL under Houllier, but it was clear from Day One that the odds had been severely stacked against him. As he would later confide to a journalist friend, had he known the mess he was walking into, he'd have thought twice about going through the door.

Benitez began life at Anfield like a Judaean baby with Herod hovering over the crib. He was promised a fortune to bring in the three world-class players that would keep Michael Owen and Steven Gerrard happy, but never received it – mainly because the settlements with Houllier and his backroom staff had been vastly over-generous considering how long was left on their contracts (the figure bandied about was £11 million but a director later told me it was even higher than that), and because the club had pledged £14 million to Auxerre for Houllier target Djibril Cisse, who would go on to make about as much impact as Houllier's first signing Jean-Michel Ferri.

With at least £25 million spoken for, and the club already deep in debt, Benitez was told he had to sell to buy. The problem was, Danny Murphy apart, nobody's services warranted serious interest. The confusion wasn't helped by having to persuade Gerrard and Owen to stay, situations which should have been well sorted out before the Spaniard had arrived, but weren't. To the club's eternal shame they had let Owen's contract run down to its final year, meaning he was within a few months of claiming a Bosman, and like Steve McManaman, leaving on a free transfer.

Unsurprisingly Owen had itchy feet, his agent was fuelling that old desire for 'a bigger stage', Liverpool weren't nailing him down to a new deal, and with days of the transfer window remaining, he did a runner to Real Madrid. In exchange for an insulting £9 million and a reserve winger called Antonio Núñez, who crocked himself in his first training session.

The promised new investment at Anfield looked nowhere near materializing and Benitez was told he couldn't recruit any of his old Valencia players due to a contractual dispute with the club. This might have made some men blame a wife unable to shop in the Liverpool rain as an excuse to scuttle back to Spain, especially when many of his critics demanded to know why his revolution wasn't complete by the end of August.

Instead, Benitez declared he was here for the long haul, took the stick, and got on with the job. He spent what money he had on Xavi Alonso, Luis Garcia and Josemi. The first two paid him back with goals and performances, and the third, eventually, returned his cash. This was a crucial difference between Benitez and his predecessor. The Spaniard wasn't afraid to own up when one of his signings wasn't up to it. And when he moved them on he nearly always got his money back.

Away from home we were abysmal, no two ways about it. Losing eleven times with too many abject surrenders either side of a Champions League game. But it was a joy to go to Anfield again. I may not have possessed a fraction of Hansen's footballing brain, but for someone induced into comas under Houllier, it didn't feel like watching the worst team in living memory.

If the football wasn't exactly vintage 1987, occasionally it approached it. Teams were getting brushed aside 3–0, spectacular goals were being hit (mainly by Luis Garcia and Gerrard), and we could once again recover from going a goal behind at half-time.

We'd switched our seats away from the corner of the Anfield Road/Main Stand graveyard to the Kemlyn Road (or Lower Centenary as I refused to call it) on line with the Kop penalty spot. And the pleasure I was getting from going to the games again was a revelation.

It wasn't just because the father–son bonding thing was nearing completion. I'd started to lose the faith under Houllier, just as I had with Souness, and it was a horrible, depressing situation. I'd decided, no matter what happened, I wasn't going to go down that soul-destroying path again. I was desperate for Benitez to succeed. He had to make it work and we had to help him get there. Drift backwards again, almost fifteen years after our last title win, and we would be in serious danger of free-fall.

In terms of the Premiership the decline was going unarrested, but in Europe the team was blossoming. And the first real sign that Benitez was a special coach came when he pulled off a 1–0 win at Deportivo.

Then a flukey defeat in Monaco meant the survival of my £20 bet rested on us beating Olympiakos by two goals at Anfield in the final group game. When Rivaldo threaded a free-kick through a poor wall after half an hour, we looked dead and buried. When they traipsed off at half-time needing three goals to survive, and I looked at the subs bench to see who could be added to our one-man Milan Baros attack, I saw the following: Stephane Henchoz, Stephen Warnock, Josemi, Salif Diao, Sinama-Pongolle and Neil Mellor. It doesn't get much more unimpressive than that. Throw in the fact that Núñez and Traore were in the starting line-up and you have a task which would have forced Hercules to throw a sickie.

Within a minute of the restart Pongolle replaced Traore, scored with his first kick, and suddenly the Kop sensed the most special of European nights. The noise picked up, the pressure mounted, Gerrard who had been telling the press he needed to see improvement in the side or he would be off, took it upon himself to bring about the improvement single-handed, and chased every lost ball like a loon on acid.

With 12 minutes to go Mellor came on for Baros and banged in a rebound. Now we had a real European night on our hands. Now we had a test of how deep this team could dig, how badly they wanted what their driven manager demanded. And with three minutes left, and the Kop baying for victory, Mellor nodded one down into Gerrard's path, he caught it beautifully with his right foot and, from 35 yards, drove it straight through the net and into the history books.

From that moment onwards, the critics changed their tune. They still doubted Benitez and mocked his every defeat, but they had to concede there was something about him which defied their pessimism. Grudging respect was starting to be paid.

Gerrard's superhuman stunner was not merely one of the finest and most dramatic Champions League goals of any season, it lanced a boil of frustration and taught them to believe again. Players and fans no longer feared the impossible, or any team who tried to stop them achieving it, as Bayer Leverkusen found out in the next round, battered 3–1 home and away. Houllier's ghost of two years previous had been buried. This time they genuinely felt themselves to be five European games away from greatness.

But first there was a Cup final and a dilemma. My private life had changed dramatically. My divorce from Ann had come through and I had a new partner, Carol (a *Times* journalist I'd met in London), and a new daughter, Lucy. At forty-seven I was a dad again, reliving all the joys of fatherhood. And boy did my back, head and nose feel good first thing in the morning as I crouched to change another dirty nappy from a babe who could out-howl and out-dump Robbie Savage.

The miraculous conception also meant I was no longer living on my own. Carol moved up from London and I moved from Wavertree to a bigger house in Aigburth, where Lucy was about to be christened on Saturday, 26 February. (As is the modern Catholic tradition, a huge all-day bender at our place had been arranged to set her on her path towards Jesus.)

Here was the problem. On the Sunday Liverpool faced Chelsea in the Carling Cup final and Phil demanded our attendance. Now Carol is an understanding woman. She's a northerner from Burnley way, feigns affinity to Manchester City and is rightly wary of non-gay men who have no interest in football. When we were married in September 2006 on the same afternoon Spurs came to Anfield, she allowed us to wave our guests on to the coach outside Liverpool Registry Office and nip over to The Exchange pub (carrying her bridal bouquet) to watch fifteen minutes of the match before jumping a cab to the reception. But if I'd risen at dawn the day after the christening and pecked her on the cheek, leaving a bomb scene, a hungry baby and my mates farting away in various beds as I headed for Cardiff, she'd have pecked off more than my cheek. So I paid for Phil's coach trip and tidied up Beirut.

Well, it was only the League Cup, wasn't it? And he had a great time without me, even if Liverpool were defeated, one of

Chelsea's goals being by a Gerrard own-goal which unfairly handed his detractors all the proof they needed that his heart really did lie in Roman Abramovich's wallet.

Strangely, I was visited with the type of menopausal feeling that descends on middle-aged mothers when a child grows up and leaves home. Phil's first solo away game filled me with sadness, pride and envy. I desperately wanted to be there with him, to share the ecstasy of Riise's first-minute goal, and the agony of defeat, yet couldn't. He'd outgrown me and flown the nest.

But I'd done a good job, hadn't I? I'd saved him from sinking somewhere between the Red Devils and the Deep Blue Sea. I'd fed his appetite for the game, applied no pressure when he strayed off the path of righteousness, welcomed him back to the true faith, nourished his beliefs, and made him strong enough to fly. Jammy bastard.

Oh, how I wished it was me heading out on that great journey of discovery. How I ached to go back to those early 1970s away-days, full of wonder, risks, laughs and rushes of pure pleasure. It wouldn't be the same now, of course. Phil would probably never feel his heart leap out of his shirt as he was chased through subways, cornered at train stations or bricked on coaches. Still, today's kids can't have everything, can they?

That Chelsea final left me with an unmistakable sense of unfinished business. Once again José Mourinho's side had got the rub of the green (Gerrard's own-goal equalizer came with 11 minutes to go), and something was telling me, maybe a scream from a lonely £20 note in a nearby bookies' drawer, that Rafa would have the last laffa.

So when Juventus were clinically removed by a Hyypia volley and a Garcia wonderstrike at Anfield and world-class defending in Turin, which meant Chelsea were the only obstacle on the road to an Istanbul final, I felt supremely confident.

Down at Stamford Bridge in the semi-final first leg, a back-four marshalled by Jamie Carragher stood immense and held out for a 0–0 draw. What a season he was having in the middle of defence. What a hero and role model he was turning out to be. Gerrard was grabbing the headlines, but Carragher was the heartbeat of this side, and quite possibly the most underrated player in the land. Against Juventus and Chelsea he was a colossus. The true driving force, composed and committed for 90 minutes, focused purely on giving his all for a cause that coursed through his blood.

Here was a man who couldn't bear to look in the eye one of his mates who'd just paid to watch him, without knowing he'd given everything. In an era where players began to see themselves as individual brands, their heads turned by sharks claiming 10 per cent of their disloyalty, Carragher struck a blow for the local heroes of yesteryear. Honest men who thought the way fans with one hundredth of their talent thought. Who go on record as saying, 'I want to stay here for life,' and mean it. Who don't simply spout clichés about performances 'not being acceptable for a club of this size' but actually do something about it, by showing a refusal to yield to defeat on the pitch, and an unswerving loyalty off it. Men whose desire is not to pine for a bigger stage, profile or pay packet but to pay back the fellow working-class men who have made them so fantastically rich.

Whenever I look at Carragher in the heat of battle I see Ian Callaghan, Tommy Smith, Phil Thompson, John Aldridge, Jimmy Case and Gerry Byrne. Scouse granite, bleeding red.

No night required this rock more than 3 May when Chelsea came to Anfield believing they only needed to pierce our defensive shield once to reach the Champions League final. I had never heard Anfield so loud as it was when I stood (nobody sat) in the Kemlyn Road that night. I'd never felt the will to succeed engulf the entire ground so powerfully. St Etienne was mind-blastingly magnificent, but the atmosphere against Chelsea surpassed it. St Etienne had been about the Kop but Chelsea was about every fan on every seat in every part of Anfield.

Against St Etienne we knew how good the Liverpool side were and how they were capable of doing it on their own. Against Chelsea, we knew how average Liverpool were, and by calling to mind the 33 Premiership points that separated us from Mourinho's men, how easy it would be for our dreams to fade and die. So for possibly the only time in Anfield's history, nobody sat back and wallowed in talk of being the Twelfth Man, they acted it out. They deliberately set out to make a frightening din of such loudness and intensity it would have a physical effect on proceedings. It was a form of black magic, and it worked.

When after just four minutes the Kop had sucked that Garcia shot over the goal-line (oh yes it was, José), and 40,000 hysterical voices press-ganged the officials into pointing to the centre-circle, the night was only ever going to yield one outcome. We hadn't waited this long, overcome all those false dawns, pulled off such miraculous results with a squad composed of such wafer-thin talent, to be denied by a shower of jumped-up mercenaries from the King's Road.

At last those six minutes of torture, otherwise known as added time, ended and I hugged Phil for what seemed like another six minutes. I was shaking, drained and close to collapse. My voice had gone. So had his. We just kept mouthing at each other, with clenched fists either side of our cheeks: 'We did it. We did it.' And then we were swept away by Gerry Marsden to another level of consciousness. I'd never heard The Hymn sung with such relief or pride.

That miniature shiny cup with red ribbons hanging from its big lugs loomed into my head. My gut instinct had been spot-on all along. It had been destiny. It had been fate. It was coming home to stay.

Pandemonium all around. Grown men tumbling over plastic seats, falling and not caring where or when they landed. A grandad next to me jigging like Michael Flatley. A mother in tears fitfully shaking, clutching a daughter in advanced stages of hyperventilation. Strangers squeezing the life out of each other. Screeches of Beatlemania proportions. Shirtless men sitting in aisles, heads between their knees, lifeless, disbelieving. Crashing music. Exploding fireworks. A blinding headache. Going under, being stood on, not caring, getting up and kissing someone I had never seen before and never will again.

Down on the faraway pitch men in all red, some on their haunches, alone in thought. Others dancing around in circles, vaulting advertising hoardings and diving into the fans. Players in white, collapsed on the turf, manually signalling at cameramen to train their lenses elsewhere. A stage being set up. One side of the ground emptying silently. Three sides bouncing maniacally. Songs starting up from different directions, then dying away as no one had the will or the patience to coordinate the choir in this twilight time between penalty shoot-out victory and trophy presentation.

A scoreboard. That huge blinding confirmation of the miracle at the far end high above the now-deserted Milan seats. A blazing neon sheet, blocking out stars in the clear, dark sky above a wasteland somewhere outside the old city of Constantinople, at the crossroads of Europe and Asia. A clock that was moving towards one o'clock in the morning.

I was incapable of Big Paternal Speeches. I'd never passed on the facts of life, or laid down the law about men having to do what they had to do. It had never felt right or necessary. But there and then, in that moment, in that place, I felt the most important piece of advice a father could ever pass on to his son speeding from my brain to my lips.

I grabbed Phil harder than I'd ever grabbed him and pulled him so close his face touched mine, in order for him to hear every single word I was about to yell above the ear-splitting bedlam.

'Look at that scoreboard. Look at that score: 3–3. Look at the words: Liverpool, Champions. And remember how it looked at half-time. And how you were dead inside. And whenever you feel life's beaten you, think of this scoreboard, and realize that anything, *anything* is possible. Will you do that for me?'

He nodded.

I gulped.

At 11 a.m. Turkish time, 9 a.m. Greenwich Mean Time, my mobile wakes me up from what seems like a few minutes' sleep. I feel rougher than a badger's arse after it's been through a paper shredder. Then I remember where, when and how, and I'm smoother than silk floating on top of a freshly poured pint of Dublin Guinness.

It's the *Daily Mirror* features editor (and fellow Red) Matt Kelly. He tells me everyone back home is going berserk about the Miracle of Istanbul. Even Radio Four are leading their news on it. So although I'm supposedly on holiday the editor wants 1,000 words in the next few hours. Click.

I'm sleep-deprived, dehydrated, starving, hoarse, confused, exhausted, still drunk and I don't even possess a pen and paper. I shower, go for a walk, see the front pages of all the Turkish papers dominated by the delirious face of a lad from Huyton's Bluebell Estate, eat my tenth kebab in three days, return to the hotel, pinch a pencil and some headed notepaper, sit in the lobby, where congas are still being performed by Liverpudlians whose heads have yet to touch pillows, and attempt to put down in words the greatest night of my life:

Being a football fan of 40 years standing, I am well used to rollercoaster rides.

But this was a rollercoaster that plummeted to the depths of hell before surfacing outside the gates of heaven.

As I write this in Istanbul, 10 hours later, hoarse from singing and bleary-eyed from too much lager and too little sleep, it still hasn't sunk in.

I keep having to walk past news stands to check if it really is the Liverpool team clutching that big shiny cup, below headlines in Turkish which talk of miracles.

Because you just don't come back from a 3–0 first-half annihilation by one of the best defensive teams in the world to lift the European Cup.

Especially with so few world-class players in your side.

That wasn't just any mountain Liverpool had to climb at half-time, it was Everest. Smeared in Swarfega. And us with only slippers on our feet.

Now I know why the only words Sir Alex Ferguson could muster after Manchester United came from behind to win this trophy six years ago were: 'Football. Bloody hell.'

Because this is a game that can cripple your central nervous system, leave you emotionally exhausted and unable to communicate in mere words.

A game that makes you do strange things. Why was I chatting to God at half-time, at the back of the stadium? Telling Him that I fully understood if He had better things to do than interfere in a football game but if He could just get around to knocking three goals into the Milan net, I'd believe in Him for ever.

Maybe it's because He's the only one with a track record of raising people from the dead. Maybe it's because I'd seen a mate earlier in the day, in the sea of red that was Istanbul's Taksim Square, wearing a wristband which said: 'God Loves Liverpool.'

Or maybe it was because I was a desperate man looking into a horrible pit of depression and only a miracle could drag me back from the brink.

The way the match was going, a humiliating rout looked a distinct possibility.

The four previous European Cups we'd won, and the huge reputation in world football that past heroes had forged so brilliantly, looked like being trampled into the dirt.

I could see the smug grins on Evertonian faces and hear the champagne corks popping in Manchester. And who could blame them?

I remonstrated with an angry fan who was leaving the ground in disgust. But it was only a half-hearted protest. To be honest, I could barely stomach any further humiliation either.

And then I walked back to my seat and heard You'll Never Walk Alone rising into the night air, looked around the two-thirds of the ground that Liverpool fans had filled, thought of all the money and emotion people had invested to get to the most far-flung capital in Europe and something told me things could not get any worse.

When everyone started singing 'We're gonna win 4–3' and my 15-year-old son joined in with hope in his heart, one per cent of me chose optimism. A mad, amazing, stunning 15 minutes later and that percentage was back up to 100.

Our name was back on the cup. The Force was with us. From being seconds away from getting in touch with the Turkish Samaritans, I was having one of the best nights of my life.

I'd been saying throughout that perfect day, as we drank with Milan fans in the warm sunshine, that this was what being a football fan was all about.

This is the reward for all those horrible Saturdays when a defeat won't allow you to watch Match Of The Day and the cat is left battered and bruised.

But at the end of this game as the biggest cup in the world headed back to Anfield for good, 'what it's all about' was an understatement.

Nothing outside of seeing your children born could touch the feeling.

After a 21-year wait, during which our team had seen their name changed to Once-Mighty Liverpool, this was as pure as euphoria gets. From the coaches which bounced back to the centre of Istanbul, we could see the locals lining the streets to applaud us.

My mind was dragged back to the time I was on a coach leaving the 1985 European Cup final after the Heysel disaster.

The few Belgians who hadn't locked themselves indoors couldn't bear to look into our eyes. How different it felt this time. Pride, not shame, oozed from my every pore.

At 4am, in a bar rocking with songs of past glories and tales of new ones, I caught the wonder of it all registering in my lad's eyes and I felt so proud of that wonderful, still-mighty football team of mine.

We've just heard that our flight home will be delayed for six hours. Who cares?

I've just been told Liverpool might not be able to defend their European Cup next year. Who cares?

I've just received a text from a friend that says: 'Now try to be mortal again.'

I'll find that hard to do, for all of this summer at least.

The price I paid Flight Options for the Istanbul package was £679. The amount I picked up from the bookies was £680.

Cynics and disbelievers, a pound for your thoughts.

27

OVER THE LINE AGAIN

1 MAY 2007 – ANFIELD

I stared at Rick Parry's sombre face on the telly, listened to his statement, shrugged, walked out the room and carried on washing the dishes.

'Steven feels he can do better elsewhere.' That's what he'd said. Steven. Frigging. Gerrard. Feels. He. Can. Do. Better. Elsewhere. It was a kick in the face followed by a bullet in the gullet. From the mouth of the club's chief executive came confirmation of our worst fears. The local hero we all hoped would become the biggest Kop legend of them all was turning out to be just another shallow, two-faced badge-kisser.

As I scoured the pans so hard I almost rubbed holes in them, I couldn't work out what my overpowering reaction was to the news that Gerrard had succumbed to the lure of the Rouble – six weeks after saying in Istanbul, 'How can I leave after a night like this.'

Sad, undoubtedly. Angry, unfathomably. Worried, beyond words. And not just about Liverpool's short-term prospects, but the future of football. It was Steven Gerrard we were talking about here. Huyton-born, Liverpool FC to his core, settled on Merseyside with a Scouse woman and a kid, surrounded by friends and family. He had just captained his boyhood club to victory in one of the greatest European Cup finals of all time. At twenty-five had won every trophy going with the Reds apart from the Premiership and the club were prepared to offer £100,000 a week to wear the red shirt, if he showed a little patience.

If *he* could walk out on the fans for a few more bob, and a London-based profile, to a circus of gold-diggers, what hope was there left? What was the point in carrying on and pretending that football had not become a grotesquely amoral, wealth-obsessed monster consuming everything that stood in the way of its march to global corporate domination? How could any of us who bought into it ever teach kids about the basic qualities of loyalty, decency, honesty and community? How far down the sewer pipes and out to sea had the legacy of Shankly drifted?

I went to bed on Tuesday, 5 July 2005, very angry and confused. When I awoke to news headlines claiming Gerrard had changed his mind, and he was staying, I was still angry and confused. He was now saying he thought he'd been 'taken for granted' but once the club had got their act together and met his agents' wage demands, he was staying for life. It was hardly time to crack open the Moët.

To be fair to Gerrard, it was another cock-up by a Liverpool management which seemed hell-bent on alienating its best players by damning them with indifference. Instead of sorting out a new deal for Gerrard days after Istanbul, to keep Chelsea at bay, they let it drift. In doing so they left their captain to stew over the rumours that they were happy to take £35 million off Roman Abramovich, thus giving Benitez a decent transfer budget.

Those close to Michael Owen say he went through the same agony the previous year. So was Istanbul a cruel mirage? Had winning that European Cup made no difference to us? Were we still a club of relatively little resources living off a big history and the passion of a big fan-base? That's how it felt, especially when Real Madrid transfer-listed Owen and he begged Benitez to take him back home, only to be told his priorities were buying a winger and a centre-half, to go with a new keeper (Pepe Reina) and a new striker (Peter Crouch).

As the transfer window shut with no world-class winger (a deal for Benfica's Simao was pulled at the last minute), no centre-half and no Michael Owen, the feeling among the fans was one of deflation. They believed the European Cup win and the fortune the club had made from it would see a poor squad overhauled and half a dozen class players brought in. But targets were lost because Liverpool either wouldn't meet the price, left it too late, dithered or insisted the player do all the running.

That summer we spent £18 million, recouped £12 million, and eighteen players left on transfers or loans, some big salaries included, chopping the wage bill considerably. It made fans wonder why the Champions League millions were not being splashed on signings, and dragged us back down to earth, which was where we stayed for most of the season. Apart, that is, from the FA Cup. Superb wins over Man United at Anfield in the fifth round and Chelsea in the semi-final set up Rafa's fifth Cup final in two seasons (we won the European Super Cup, but lost the Club World Championship despite having twenty clear chances.) We may have been off the pace in the League, but Rafa was ensuring the minimum obligation to his fans. A sunny day out, and a night on the lash, at the end of every season. This time against West Ham in Cardiff.

By now Phil was turning into an away-day veteran, going on coaches with his mates, picking up the knowledge of the best alehouses and open-air meeting points. So when we started our ritual crawl at 11 a.m. in Cardiff, he was pulling a face at all the pubs I was taking him to. Fabulous. As a trainee journalist I'd spent six months drinking in Cardiff, and now my sixteen-year-old son was telling me where to go. Literally and metaphorically.

I explained to him, as he led me to the pavement outside the City Arms, that this was the very same piece of concrete I'd slumped on to twenty-six years earlier, after a hulking Taff took umbrage at my rendition of 'Poor Scouser Tommy' and introduced his size nines to my mouth, knocking out two front teeth. But he wasn't listening. He was too busy handing out cans to his mates, keeping a plastic footie in the air and singing 'The Fields Of Anfield Road' to notice.

Another nail-biter, another Steven Gerrard corker saving our skin, another penalty shoot-out win. Another night of singing and carousing on the streets of a foreign capital, with a couple of sound Reds and excellent journalists Chris Bascombe and Tony Barrett. And a first. A treasured first. Phil buying me a Cup-winning celebration pint. I struggled to remember one that tasted sweeter.

Later on, back at the hotel, as I emptied the minibar and raised a glass to the reruns of Gerrard's last-minute beauty, I tried to remember exactly how many of these nights I'd had. Nights when hours-old memories of silver glinting above a red shirt keep a smile permanently pinned to your lips. I started to count, but soon lost my way. Far too many cups to remember. Far more than a supporter of any other English club could even begin to imagine. Far more than any man has a right to ask for. I tried the mental arithmetic season by season, but my pissed and aged brain got lost in the mid-seventies when UEFA Cups were being won. I was counting sheep branded with Liver Birds and cups on their backs when I fell into that long, dreamy sleep you go into on the night your team makes you happy.

As my head cleared on the drive home I tried to work it out again, this time more logically. Trophy by trophy. Five European Cups, three UEFA Cups, three European Super Cups, seven FA Cups, seven League Cups, that was the easy bit. League titles? Was it eleven or twelve. All those doubles and trebles in the eighties made it hazy. Charity Shields. Do I count them? Technically yes, because I'd had a good drink on the back of most of them, but morally no, because if I did would it make me sound like a Coventry fan, or even worse, Gérard Houllier.

When I got home I checked the records. It was twelve Leagues and nine outright Charity Shields (which would soon be ten) after beating Chelsea that August. Which meant that since I first set eyes on Alf Arrowsmith's quiff in 1965 I'd seen them win forty-seven trophies. In 42 years. During the same period Newcastle had won one.

Forty-seven times a Liverpool captain had put the spoils of

glory above his head, signalling a night of celebration. I was forty-eight. Had they picked up the Club World Championship that season, as they should have, they'd have won as many trophies as years I'd been on earth.

Who else, or what else, could give a person that much pleasure over so many years? This is what non-football people fail to grasp. We put up with all the heartache and frustration, the let-downs and the put-downs, because the highs, when they arrive, are pure and mind-blowing. No drug compares. The inevitable consequence of such vertiginous highs though are the ground-smacking come-downs. The pits of depression you can sink into during a bleak spell when you can't bear to pick up a paper. The diabetic reaction John Peel talked about that leaves you unable to talk about football for two days because you feel so ill and so angry.

I was suffering many of those two-day illnesses in the final months of 2006. Rafa, still in need of a budget that could order banquets at the Savoy, was still shouting orders through the McDonald's drive-in window, negotiating meal deals with medium fries. Scatter-gun, sub-£10 million buys like Craig Bellamy, Jermaine Pennant, Mark Gonzalez, Fabio Aurelio, Gabriel Paletta and Dirk Kuyt, aimed at shoring up glaring deficiencies in the squad, were bound to be hit and miss. They were also bound to take time to settle in. Yet nobody believed that their introduction to a side that finished only nine points off Premiership winners Chelsea would lead to such a calamitous start. By October we'd been beaten at Everton, Chelsea, Bolton and Man United. The expected assault on the title snuffed out before the clocks went back.

The team's confidence was shot to pieces. They'd lost their way, the Rafa critics were bursting out of the woodwork, citing Istanbul as a distant fluke, haranguing him for his obsession with rotating his players, and demanding his head. And Rafa, his patience exhausted at the club's failed attempts to attract investment that would allow him to compete with Chelsea and United in the transfer market, wasn't far off giving it to them on a platter.

The depression after those defeats was nausea-inducing, especially for someone whose job it is to read every newspaper from front to back every day. It becomes like a really bad hangover. Nothing you can do gets it out of your system quicker than it wants to. Only time can deaden the pain. Sometimes though, outside forces help.

On the Tuesday after the 2–0 defeat at Old Trafford which killed the title hopes, I was sitting at my desk pondering the point of life, when the phone went.

'Ariyt, son, Dennis Skinner here.'

I mentally trawled back through my columns to see what it was I'd written that the veteran left-wing MP was going to complain about. Nothing, and everything, were the two options that sprang to mind.

'What the bloody hell's happening to our football team? I can't fathom it.'

'*Our* team? I didn't know you were a Red.'

'Oh aye. Have been since Shankly made them a good socialist side.'

A conversation followed which lifted my jaw off the floor. Skinner was my second all-time hero after Shankly. A true socialist. A genuine Man Of The People, one of the very few left on God's earth.

I first shared his company in the House of Commons in the mid-nineties when I was interviewing him, and asked if he wanted a cup of tea. He said he'd never take a cup of tea off a journalist in case it was seen as a bribe. Just as he'd never own a passport on the grounds that having one would leave him open to the temptation of accepting foreign junkets. Priceless.

I loved the man, but never knew he was a Red. And there he was on the phone, reminiscing about Hunt, St John and Thompson; Keegan, Cormack and Toshack; Dalglish, Rush and Hansen, and wanting to know what was wrong with Gerrard, Carragher and Kuyt. It made me realize what a special club Liverpool is to so many people. What a unique place it has in so many hearts.

I was thinking that again strolling down Barcelona's Ramblas with Phil the following February, seeing every table taken over by Liverpool fans, and the main squares off it decorated with red flags and echoing to red songs. It was jumping-in-the-fountains time again.

There are certain away games you know you have to attend. Something in your guts tells you the day and night will go down in legend, and after the shame of missing Rome '77 I usually made sure I sucked it in first hand. Barcelona at the Nou Camp in the Champions League knock-out stages was one such game.

As in 2005 our domestic season lay in tatters but in Europe we were flying, despite being fancied about as much as a female sumo-wrestler with facial herpes. So it was another two-day sick note for Phil's teachers and another piece of real education for the lad.

We'd only been given 3,000 tickets but took three times as many fans, some of them familiar faces from past triumphs and tragedies, like Trevor Hicks, who I bumped into at Barcelona airport. We made a remarkable comeback from a goal down to beat the European champions 2–1. It was a fabulous tactical gameplan by Rafa, and one of our all-time great European victories against a team possessing Ronaldinho, Eto'o, Messi and widely regarded as the best attacking side in the world.

When the final whistle blew I thought of Trevor Hicks. And hoped he was giving a little nod to the sky, a knowing smile to his two beautiful girls Sarah and Victoria. Girls who by then would have been thirty-seven and thirty-four if they hadn't gone to watch Liverpool play in a semi-final. But, as Trevor had told me years previously, nothing on earth would have stopped them going that day to Hillsborough, so deep was their love for the club.

We were locked inside the Nou Camp for twenty minutes. I'd had worse lock-ins. As the huge coliseum emptied you could make out knots of Liverpool fans all around the stadium, dancing in the aisles, joining in with the few thousand of us up in the gods who were rattling through our entire repertoire for the tenth time that day. It was going to be a long night on the Ramblas.

'It doesn't get much better than this, does it?' asked Phil.

'Yeah, it does,' I replied. 'And it will this season.'

And I believed it. You have to. It's how it works. Every triumph this club has had has always been topped. There is always another emotional peak to be dragged over. And on the other side a valley full of vipers. You have to stay on the peak as long as you can. For the only certainty is you'll soon have a viper's tongue up your jaxey.

From six o'clock The Sandon was rocking. Rafa and the players had told the world that their Twelfth Man would once again be the crucial factor in pushing Liverpool past Chelsea into a Champions League final and nobody wanted to shirk their responsibility.

Inside Anfield the volume was turned up to maximum. It wasn't as manic as the semi-final two years before, mainly because three wins in the previous four games against Chelsea had made us believe they were far from invincible and the players might just be able to manage on their own. But it was still the loudest noise the Champions League had heard that season.

Anfield was a cauldron of emotion once again. Unstinting, fierce, frightening, incessant, hostile, overpowering, awesome. And unlike Stamford Bridge there were no shiny little plastic flags placed under the seats by stewards in an attempt to invent an atmosphere. Atmospheres, like fearsome reputations, are forged not invented.

Some things are invented though: mass terrace singing, mass scarf-waving, mass slogans on banners. Ask a veteran Kopite. Ask Inter Milan back in '65. Ask José Mourinho why he said in 2005 that Anfield was the only crowd he had ever seen win a game of football. Ask him why, on May Day 2007, he had to think about changing his quote to two games of football. And why, while he was thinking, we all had to think about ways of getting to Athens . . .

28

THE DEVIL WEARS PRADA

23 MAY 2007 – ATHENS

Loutraki is the Blackpool of Athens. A cheap and cheerful seaside resort for the working-class about an hour and a half from the city. We'd gone there on a three-day package with Roy Boulter, Kevin Sampson and Pete Hooton (Scouse writers once better known for some little group called The Farm who I'd become mates with due to our shared Red passion) and about eighty others, most of them part of Mono's Halewood mob.

The crack was of the highest order. Blackpoolopolis was colonized from late Tuesday morning, starting with an all-day bender in the sunshine which drifted into an all-night one in the town centre. Laughter, song, lager, ouzo and banter with the locals, punctuated with the age-old refrain about how shite it is following a club that never takes you anywhere. And, of course, occasional musings about the task that lay ahead at the Olympic Stadium tomorrow.

This time though, talk wasn't about how we'd get on against AC Milan but how people were getting into the ground. The question on everyone's lips concerned tickets. Who had one? Who had spares? Would there be any on sale at the ground? How much were the touts asking? And the most common one, accompanied by a scrunched-up piece of card being pulled from a pocket: What do you reckon to this forgery?

The word scandalous fails to do justice to the allocation of tickets for this final. A 71,000-seater stadium became a 63,000-seater before a ticket was printed, as 8,000 seats made way for the logos of UEFA's corporate sponsors. A further 9,000 tickets went on worldwide internet sale in the January, and 20,000 went to what they call the UEFA family. (In case you don't know, that's a family in some cases more amoral than the Borgias, more dysfunctional than the Simpsons and less accountable than the Windsors.)

Which meant Liverpool and AC Milan received a paltry 17,000 tickets each. A totally inadequate amount to satisfy Liverpool's 40,000-strong travelling army, made impossible by the club shamelessly handing 6,000 of those tickets to sponsors, corporate clients, shareholders and staff.

It meant the likes of me, Phil and every other season-ticket holder who had been to every home Champions League tie were thrown into a ballot with Fancard holders and given a one-in-five chance of winning the lottery. We failed.

To make matters worse, news of the long odds against getting a ticket was only relayed to fans a week after the Chelsea semi-final, by which time thousands who thought they had qualified (including us) had booked their trip – with prices averaging around £650.

Naturally no one was unpacking the Factor 12. Instead many snapped up one of the 5,000 decent forgeries that were doing the rounds in Liverpool pubs as a last-ditch insurance policy, heeded Rick Parry's last line of defence about 'Scousers always getting in by hook or by crook' and hoped.

I was so desperate I arranged for press-box accreditation through the *Mirror* but Phil wasn't so lucky. Despite putting out more feelers than a school of octopuses, no one was coming up with the goods. His uncle Terry, who'd been with us in Istanbul, was on a promise from a corporate contact which would sort Phil out, but as we left Speke on the Monday it hadn't come through.

I was in a state of mild panic. On the Friday Phil was sitting an AS Level in English Lit, and we were due back on Thursday night. I'd persuaded his mum to let him take three days off revision classes to undergo a further rite of passage, and now it looked like he'd be standing in front of a telly in a Greek boozer.

The panic deepened as we arrived at the Olympic Stadium on match-day, he was still ticketless, and I was told by the office that I would have to spend the afternoon writing. Meaning I had to head to the press box while he went into the centre of Athens in search of his elusive ticket. I got past a bored official on a gate by showing my press card. He barely looked at it. A forgery would have got a goat in. I walked around the stadium and saw no turnstiles. I looked at the pitch and realized I'd be watching the match across a long-jump pit. Surely this wasn't a ground fit to play the world's biggest game of club football in, between teams with huge, passionate followings and one set of those followers possessing the collective ability to bunk into the coffin at a state funeral.

What we had here was an athletics track with plenty of green space in the middle to put on a dazzling opening ceremony and excellent media facilities to beam images of it across the world. And that's it. But then it hadn't stopped UEFA playing the Istanbul final in an ill-equipped modern slum on a moonscape en route to the Syrian border, had it?

I spoke to fans outside the ground that afternoon, some in their sixties, who were milling around with long gobs on them, trying to sniff out tickets. When they realized there was none to be had they felt angry and betrayed.

The bad vibes were coming on over the hill and I could hear the vipers rustling.

As a 100-strong mob charged towards me it was a scene straight out of the Pamplona bull run: sprinting teenagers at the front of the crowd, electrified by the adrenalin rush. Those in their twenties and early thirties, manoeuvring with ease away from danger, and the middle-aged mass at the rear, struggling to keep up with the pace, bricking themselves at the realization that time had caught up with them and they could soon be hit or trampled underfoot.

The inevitable had happened. Three hours before kick-off a concerted surge from a mob had forced its way through a weak and complacent security cordon on the outer ring of the Olympic complex. The riot police waded in to shore up the defences and the hordes of genuine ticket-holders pouring out of the subway station were confronted with a line of baton-wielding, shield-holding Robocops. It became very ugly very quickly. Fights broke out, tear-gas was sprayed and heads whipped. Nobody involved, neither police nor fans, knew what the other was supposed to be doing. Or why they were having to do it.

After a twenty-minute stand-off during which the crowd behind the entry point was becoming increasingly large and boisterous, the police stood back and let everyone through. Now it was a free-for-all. The ticketless had only a single fence, a handful of stewards and no turnstiles between them and someone else's seat. I'd walked into the thick of it trying to find Phil to arrange where to meet after the game. He'd rung to say he'd got a ticket (his uncle's corporate mate had come good with the favour) and was on his way to the ground. But his phone had gone dead and we'd lost contact amid the anarchy.

Sadly that was the only word to describe what was happening outside the Liverpool end. Hordes were bearing down on the overwhelmed gatemen who panicked and let anyone past waving a piece of paper which looked remotely like a ticket.

Anyone with a forgery was through. As were fellas who told me they showed a cigarette packet, an aeroplane boarding card and, my favourite, a flyer for a Corfu lap-dance bar. There were fans arguing with each other, women who'd been gassed sobbing their eyes out, men venting their disgust at those trying to get in without tickets and those under verbal attack screaming back about having followed Liverpool for thirty years and being reduced to trying to bunk in like kids back in the seventies.

I took a phone call from one of the lads who'd been with

us in Loutraki saying the police were now stopping genuine ticket-holders as they poured off the underground, telling them the stadium was full and they should head back into the centre of Athens. I walked towards the police line he was talking about, could see the batons crashing down and hear the angry screams to be let through. It was deteriorating by the minute. If Phil was behind there I'd have to miss the match and get out of the place.

The phone rang. I didn't recognize the number but I did recognize Phil's voice. He was inside the ground, using a mate's phone. It had been a nightmare getting in, and he hadn't had to show his ticket, but he was safe.

With an hour to go to kick-off I made my way back to the press box, my head spinning at the sights I'd just seen and fearful about the ones I guessed I hadn't. I couldn't think about football. Which was just as well as I was passing through the long, sprawling section at the side of the ground which had been handed over to VIPs, corporate guests and their entourages.

The contrast with scenes outside the Liverpool end was both stark and pitiful. There were police lines here, but they were blocking out the riff-raff to allow limos to usher through the Armani army. The doors of those limos were being held open by staff as were the doors that led them off to their plush suites and the lobster and champagne receptions inside the stadium.

I just stood in amazement, looking at the high-heeled models strolling nonchalantly past the specially installed potted plants, making a dramatic late entrance, no doubt hoping to upstage their fellow freeloaders. I got so angry I wanted to drag them back from the stadium doors, hurl them into the black limos and drive them off Piraeus harbour straight into their yachts.

I knew there were thousands of genuine fans who had paid a fortune to be here tonight to see their team play on the biggest stage, who were being treated like criminals and told to go home. They may have had tickets but their presence was unwanted. These people were the lifeblood of football, yet in the eyes of the people who ran the game on their behalf they were an irrelevance. Worse than that, they were now a problem.

Unlike the VIPs who had paid nothing to be there, wouldn't have blinked an eye if they'd had their five-star trips cancelled, and couldn't care how little of the action they saw. (Witness the empty seats ten minutes into the second half caused by them not wanting to be dragged away from their half-time buffet.) They were considered the most important people in the stadium.

Here, in the space of a short walk, was an accurate snapshot of the world's most popular sport begun by men who wanted a healthy diversion from grafting ten-hour days in squalid pits and factories. This was how the Suits who ran the game thanked the British working-class for giving them this most precious of gifts. By telling them they didn't want their type around here any more before throwing them out of the tradesman's entrance. Here was the horrible reality of modern football laid bare: its soul had been stolen and crushed beneath Prada heels.

As for the final itself, I knew we were doomed when I left my 'Red Rafa-Lution' T-shirt in the hotel room and stuck on a slogan-less, short-sleeved formal number to stave off being thrown out of the press box. That red-and-white T-shirt, turned an anaemic grey through too many mixed washes, with Rafa's face super-imposed on Che Guevara's, had pulled us through all the big European nights since Olympiakos in 2004. (I opted for the Shankly and Paisley 'Invincibles' one for Benfica and look what happened.)

So I wasn't the least surprised when Inzhagi fluked that hand-ball at the death of the first-half. AC Milan were clearly into Name On The Cup territory, and we had little right to bollock God over such a biased arrangement after he'd put three past Dida and double-blocked Shevchenko in Istanbul.

Dirk Kuyt's goal aside, I didn't enjoy a second of the final. Not only was I sat in the press box, conscious of keeping my emotions pinned down to acceptable levels of taste and volume (and failing miserably on both counts), I kept eyeing up the densely packed mass behind the Liverpool goal, fearing we'd see injured fans being carried over walls and laid by the side of the pitch.

As we drowned our sorrows until dawn back at Loutraki, the mood was philosophical and sombre. There was debate over some of Rafa's selections and substitutions, derision over the shambolic organization at the stadium and anger at UEFA and Liverpool for forcing the fans into desperate measures. Everybody knew that on and off the pitch it had been a bad night for us, and hoped it would be quickly forgotten. The only chink of light came when someone remarked that Alex Ferguson might have over-exerted himself uncorking the bottle of vintage red he'd promised himself if Liverpool were beaten, and now had a variety of tubes sticking out of him in Wythenshawe Hospital.

THE MORE THINGS CHANGE
THE MORE THEY STAY THE SAME

2 MARCH 2008 – REEBOK STADIUM, BOLTON

It was a throwback to the days when the fire in workers' bellies had yet to be extinguished by apathy. A room as big and as cold as Alaska decked out in blood-red banners. Hundreds of solemn foot soldiers, hands pushed into pockets of dark coats, mooching around, nodding sagely at friends, weighing up strangers and reading leaflets left on chairs which outlined the struggle ahead. At the front of the room, on a raised platform, thirteen men sat at a long trestled table, some huddled, others pointing down the line, all wearing expressions laced with foreboding. A Scouse version of Da Vinci's *Last Supper*.

As in the golden days of Thatcher-baiting, angry men jumped to their feet and jabbed the air, gave passionate declarations to 'comrades' about corrupt capitalists stealing something precious from ourselves and our city. Something called a birthright.

When it came to 'Any more questions from the floor?', that same brother who couldn't finish a sentence without the words 'composite resolution' was there again, shouting 'chair' for the twentieth time, forcing you to tie a mental knot in a bladder that was dying to leak. Then the climactic speech, the unanimous show of hands, the defiant round of applause, and the decision to march through the streets to show the world, or at least everyone on the three number 26 buses backed up behind us, that we meant business.

The anger towards the new American owners had been building for months. By the middle of February, enough had become enough. More than 600 of us met in the Olympia Theatre in West Derby Road, three hours before the FA Cup fifth round tie with Barnsley to declare war on George Bush's buddy Tom Hicks, his Barney Rubble sidekick George Gillett, and any other rapacious piranha eyeing up Franchise Anfield.

It was my third anti-American march in as many months (the previous two being more like 100-yard shuffles from The Sandon pub to Anfield) to declare a love for Rafa and a loathing for our now absentee landlords. I'd been too young to join the anti-Vietnam marches and too busy chasing boob-tubed birds in Reading nightclubs to show unity with the dungaree-clad women down the road at Greenham Common. Yet here I was, aged fifty, dressed in an army jacket, wading through curry-soaked chip wrappers in Oakfield Road screaming 'Yanks Out' to anyone who'd listen. All I needed was a grey pony-tail and my transformation into a sad old hippy would have been complete.

In the Olympia, a Liverpool Supporters' Union had been formed called the Sons of Shankly (although when it was pointed out that the Messiah had only sired daughters it was changed to the Spirit of Shankly, neatly maintaining the SOS message).

And as events showed on that day when Barnsley belittled us, our soul was in dire need of saving. Back in August we'd believed that with dollar billionaires unveiling eye-popping plans for a 70,000-seater stadium and signing the record-breaking cheque for Fernando Torres, we would leap salmon-like into the title-chasing pack. Instead, the club became a dying trout rotting from the head downwards, its stench blowing all the way to Texas.

When Hicks and Gillett bought the club in February 2007 we trusted those who'd sold it, and gave our new 'custodians' the benefit of the doubt. They looked and talked like big hitters, promising to wipe out the debt, build a new Anfield, invest in new players, and pay for it out of their own deep pockets. All to make us the biggest club in the world again. And we believed them because we were desperate to.

The financial gap between Liverpool and the teams above had grown into a chasm. As the Glazers and Abramoviches colonized United and Chelsea, we prided ourselves on having a history money could never buy and an owner who, like us, was Scouse, Red and proud. But our history struggled to take us to within 20 points of the title. And it was becoming painfully clear that the most glaring thing David Moores had in common with us was the lack of a pot to piss in.

Fred and Barney on the other hand owned pots aplenty and a track record which suggested they could piss with the best of them. So we trusted them with our club. And they put their pots away and pissed all over us.

By November it was clear Liverpool had been sold under false pretences and Moores was admitting privately that he'd made a monumental mistake. The verbal promise about not saddling the club with debt wasn't worth a carrot. The loan that had bought the club would be restructured in such a way that up to £30 million a year would need to be found from annual profits to pay interest charges; the stadium plans were scaled down and the huge war chest they'd promised Rafa was an illusion.

Back in Dallas, Hicks was comparing his purchase of Liverpool to buying breakfast cereal: 'When I was in the leverage buy-out business we bought Weetabix and we leveraged it up to make our return. You could say that anyone who was eating Weetabix was paying for our purchase of Weetabix. It was just business. It is the same with Liverpool.'

In other words LFC was simply another underperforming consumer brand which could be bought with money loaned from a bank. Its customers could be fleeced to pay the interest on the loans, the share price enhanced, and the franchise eventually sold on at a huge profit.

We'd been taken for patsies. But maybe we should have expected it, because we'd known since the Premiership began and hard-nosed businessmen eyed up a hugely profitable industry that Liverpool FC was ripe for picking. The amateurish running of the club hadn't even begun to tap into its local, never mind global, earning potential. The Yanks came along, offered £500-a-share more than Dubai Investment Capital (DIC) was offering, and the men who ran the club went weak at the knees and handed them the keys to the Shankly Gates, seemingly with few questions asked. It was like taking candy from a baby.

Before this horrible reality dawned I bumped into the man who sold our club and was hit by a heavy dose of déjà vu.

It was early October, and I was talking with Phil and a journalist mate at the opening of Jamie Carragher's Cafe Sports England restaurant in Stanley Street, when Carragher's business partner Paul Flanagan called me over to meet someone. It was David Moores, who was about to turn into Graeme Souness on the day I was introduced to him in the Hilton Hotel – the only difference being I didn't fear the owner of this tan-and-tache combo was about to throw a headbutt. I was almost wrong.

'You were my predator,' he yelled in a tired and emotional voice, squeezing my hand so tight my eyes almost went as watery as his. 'You hunted me down. You were in with Steve Morgan trying to get me out.'

Before I could utter 'Pleased to meet you, Mr Honorary Life President', he called his wife over. 'Didn't this fella hurt me?' he implored. Marje smiled knowingly and tried to escort him away. But he wasn't going anywhere. So I joined in.

'I've never met Steve Morgan.'

'It didn't sound that way when you were hunting me.'

'How did I hunt you?'

'In the paper, you were always trying to bring me down.'

Over the years I had been critical of Moores. For not sacking Souness much earlier and for taking so long to sell the club when it was clear he lacked the funds to make us competitive. But I'd hardly pursued him on horseback with a pack of hounds. Besides, as a journalist I had every right to do so, and as I tried to explain to him, it was never personal.

'But it was, because you're a Liverpudlian. The fans knew you cared. That's why it hurt.'

'But I wasn't going to watch Liverpool go into freefall and say nothing.'

'Freefall? We won everything under me, except the League. And I tried my bloody hardest.'

I said nothing out of shame that my criticism had caused him so much pain.

'We're not that different me and you,' he said, grabbing my hand again. 'We've got the same heart.'

I could see Phil staring on, open-mouthed. Moores had clearly been in emotional limbo since selling the club, and on occasions like these it must have been hard for him. Before I could suggest we put the past behind us he released my hand and turned sour again.

'Well you got what you wanted, anyway. Me gone.'

And I couldn't resist it: 'You got what you wanted too, David. Eighty-eight million quid's-worth.'

His features hardened. 'It was never about money with me. You know that.'

Which was true. If Moores had been into money we may not have needed to sell the club to a pair of rednecks with no interest in football. We may even have closed the gap on the Mancs. His heart *was* in the right place, but sadly it takes more than a heart to run a football club. 'Are you sure you've sold to the right people?' asked a journalist mate. 'How can you look me in the face and ask that?' Moores spat back, disgusted that the question had even been asked. That response, as naive as it was honest, would come back to me many times over the next few months, summing up as it did the club's blinkered descent into civil war.

But back then, in early October, nobody could have forecast the horror of the trenches. They were happy days. I was back on the Kop now. After calls from a group called Reclaim the Kop

(Liverpool fans were now split into more people's fronts than Judaea in Monty Python times) the club set aside a section for traditional fans, or rather 'arl arses' who wanted to sing the songs of thirty years ago, and me and Phil now stood alongside Roy Boulter, Kev Sampson, Pete Hooton and Mono's Halewood mob. Stewards tried to make us sit down but we'd been given licence to go all retro and there was little the men in yellow could do about it.

Despite our inability to kill off some poor sides, I was enjoying going to Anfield more than I had done for twenty years. It's only when you've been away from the ground's spiritual heart for so long you appreciate there is no other place to worship.

Released from the straitjacket of the Kemlyn Road into this seething pit of passion was like swapping Sunday school at a Betwys-y-Coed Presbyterian chapel for Saturday night in a Dublin boozer. Diving over seats when they scored, swaying, singing as loud and as long as you wanted, was a joyous release. A throwback to an age of innocence. We even had a blond-haired golden boy, a cross between Alun Evans and Kenny Dalglish, called Fernando Torres, to drool over. And at one point, after a 6–0 demolition of Derby which took us to the top of the league, it genuinely felt as though, this time, it was no false dawn. The League was ours for the taking.

But there was a bomb ticking away underneath Anfield. All was not well with Fred and Barney. They had fallen out over the new stadium plans and were finding it hard to refinance their Royal Bank of Scotland loan. In fact since Rafa's Athens outburst, when he claimed they didn't understand how football worked, only one issue was uniting them. A desire to be rid of the troublesome Spaniard.

Performances and results had dipped and criticism was mounting about Rafa's rotation policy. When Torres was left on the bench for the visit of Birmingham, which ended in a dire draw, the unrest became vocal. The Americans were increasingly realizing there were like-minded anti-Benitez allies close to home.

In late November, Rafa's requests for approval of his January transfer targets was met with silence from across the Atlantic. His phone calls and emails were ignored until one flew back from Hicks telling him to focus on coaching the players he already had. Rafa was apoplectic, marched into a press conference and stonewalled every question with the phrase, 'As always I am focused on coaching and training my players.' He repeated it twenty-five times. The pretence of harmony was over.

For months the owners, board members, Rick Parry and Rafa had been briefing against each other, and now the poison was spilt. Liverpool FC was becoming unrecognizable, its dirty underwear hosed down in public, the schisms, alliances and bickering reaching untenable proportions. Even the fans, split over who was the biggest culprit in this shambles, began to turn on one another.

Like the majority of supporters I stayed loyal to Rafa, even though I could see the pressure was getting to him and he was making decisions that left me despairing (and I'm not just talking about growing that Max & Paddy goatee). Take the dreadful 3–1 defeat at Reading, when Peter Crouch and Andriy Voronin started as virtual wingers and Gerrard and Carragher were withdrawn in the final twenty minutes to save them for the trip to Marseilles. The white flag had been flown on another title challenge, and we were only a week into December.

By now the phone-ins and the letters pages were filled with anti-Benitez rants, and his critics within Anfield and throughout the media, sensing that the tension and uncertainty had got to him, cranked up the pressure. From what I could gather through speaking to Benitez and those close to him, he'd become convinced there was an agenda at the top of the club to replace him, and it was affecting his work. He felt isolated and besieged, frustrated at his inability to bring in his top transfer targets or plan ahead with confidence. He used a phrase about him driving an old BMW while the managers of other big clubs were in Ferraris. How he had to swerve and cheat to beat them. How he was capable of doing that but needed the money and the swift, professional backing to compete with the Ferrari drivers.

Much as I sympathized, he hadn't done himself any favours with outbursts like the press conference stonewalling, although when I found out what sparked his anger I laughed out loud. It was not so much Hicks telling him to concentrate on working with the players he already had that turned him into a raging bull, more the fact that he'd typed the command in capital letters. Benitez felt like he'd had his legs smacked and been stuck on the naughty step. This was too much for such a proud man to take. If only Hicks had realized how much damage he was causing by using the capital letter key on his laptop, he may have thought twice.

Or maybe not. Maybe Rafa was right. Maybe he was being deliberately pushed over the edge. How else do you explain Hicks confirming to *Echo* reporter Tony Barrett, without having to, that he and Gillett had offered Rafa's job to Jürgen Klinsmann? The second those words left his mouth Liverpool FC was officially at war. And the Yanks, the board and half of the players went missing in action. So too did the fans' restraint.

None of us escaped the pain. There were nights when I woke up for my three-o'clock pee and the previous day's abysmal result would sting me hard. They were followed by mornings when I couldn't face the daily work ritual of buying and reading all of the papers, knowing what torture lay in store.

That pungent whiff of failure was wafting around the nostrils again. Outsiders (and Joe Ainsworth my bitterest of Blue next-door neighbours) were relishing the club's crisis, celebrating Everton moving above us into fourth and arguing that Rafa's inevitable departure was the least of our worries. Because the way the owners were recklessly piling debt on to the club, and the way the performances on the pitch were going, Anfield would soon be twinned with Leeds.

*

I called Reg and Phil to the kitchen table, threw down tickets for the Bolton game, and told the youngest of the pair it was his eighteenth-birthday present. Phil's delight at the prospect of spending his most important birthday to date at an away ground surrounded by carousing Reds was broken only by the question: 'Is that all you're getting me?'

Reg just looked puzzled. 'I'm paying you back for taking me and Our Vic to Bolton for his eleventh-birthday treat. Remember?'

'Vaguely,' he replied, meaning 'no'. He was almost eighty now, his memory regularly plummeting to Arsène Wenger's level when asked to recall an Arsenal player's red-carded tackle.

'The FA Cup fifth round in 1965. My first game.' Still nothing. 'I sat on your shoulders and when Cally scraped that winner you slipped a disc. You had to crawl back to the car and were off work for a month.'

'Jesus, I remember. You're not getting on my shoulders this time.'

'They have seats now.'

'I bet the whole ground's changed.'

'Yeah, it's a shopping centre. They've moved to the Reebok.'

'The what?'

The Reebok Stadium. A plastic, soulless bowl constructed from B&Q flat-packs in a wind-blown wasteland four miles outside Bolton. When they sold off Burnden Park and gave naming rights to a firm that sells trainers they called their new stadium 'futuristic'. But it's merely a grim reminder of the future faced by fans whose clubs want to desert their historic city-centre homes for synthetic pastures new.

'Where's the nearest pub?' I asked the car park attendant at the entrance to a cemented field.

'There's two at top o' the hill but they're for home fans only. You're best going in the ground.'

Cue 10,000 Liverpool fans shivering in lengthy queues at three holes in walls, baying at a handful of harrassed kids to stop making hot-dogs and sell them overpriced Foster's in plastic cups.

Football, eh? Contrary to universal observations about the 'people's game', nothing has fundamentally changed. It may now cost a minimum of £30 to gain entry to these so-called futuristic leisure palaces but the fans who can't afford the corporate seats are still treated with the same contempt.

The 2008 visit to New Bolton could easily have been the 1965 trip to the old one. There was no Brylcreem, smog, or flat caps but the Tannoy's failed attempts to entertain still had me staring at the pigeons on the stand roof. Steve Gerrard scored a game-changing goal that was even jammier than Cally's causing the birthday boy next to me to go as berserk as his uncle had done. Liverpool triumphed again, and before the final whistle was blown the Lowry figures shuffled out mute and glum, back to their Lowry lives.

Something else which hadn't changed was the fans' decision to watch the game standing up despite there being plastic seats, meaning Reg's words as the match ended echoed those in '65: 'My bloody back's gone.' Once again he hobbled to the car like a war veteran with shrapnel for legs and grimaced in his seat with every twist and turn on the way home.

'It could have been worse,' I told him. 'You could have had me on your shoulders.'

'It feels like I did.'

'Well at least you don't have to worry about being off work for a month. You can stay in bed for the rest of your life if you want.'

'I think I'll bloody well have to. Still, for all the pain, I'm glad I went.'

So was Phil. He was heading back to his party but said seeing the Reds hand out a battering at their bogey ground would be what he most remembered about his eighteenth birthday.

As we sat for an eternity in a long metal queue in those concrete fields I felt a warm glow which had nothing to do with the harsh sun burning through the windscreen. When you win away with such class and authority, scoring three times when it could have been six, you view the future with a wild optimism. Those horrible defeats, 'Club in Crisis' headlines and dire forecasts about the end of the glory days, only serve to make the small victories even sweeter.

I thought back over the forty-three years since that first game at Bolton and realized that this lifetime obsession had not been sustained through winning all the glittering prizes. It was about days like this which mostly go forgotten.

It was about a cry of independence in a school playground. The theme tune to the most ecstatic of nights and gravest of afternoons. A proud defence against all the bile and lies thrown at a city which couldn't answer back. The most precious of photo albums, bearing images of long-gone idols, lost brothers, and a father figure with a Cagney smile. It was about an undying love for a bird on a shirt.

People who compare a fanatic's relationship with his team to a long marriage are wrong. It's a permanent adolescent infatuation. There are times you loathe yourself for allowing it to depress you so intensely, for having such a hold on your emotions, such control of your moods. But you cannot abandon it because it has you frozen in time, in that first flush of lust, the kicks to the floor serving only to make your besotted heart crave the highs even more.

As the car swung into that flat plain on the M62 outside Huyton, the sun was starting to set in all its splendour above the Liverpool skyline, the way it always did in May when you returned from Cup finals drunk on happiness. Optimism surged through me. The vipers were in retreat. This season wasn't over. There were still big nights of raucous bouncing on the Kop and long afternoons in sunny foreign squares, singing battle hymns with the rest of the Red Army, to be had. I could feel it in my bones. I turned to ask Phil in the passenger seat what his most enjoyable game was apart from Istanbul, but he was too busy sleeping off his first legal pint against the warm glass. In the back,

Reg's open-mouthed head was propped up against the baby seat, having managed to crawl through the pain barrier and reach the land of Nod.

So I told them mine, even though they couldn't hear and it hadn't happened. It was coming next week in Milan. I was going to stand shoulder-to-shoulder with other Sons of Shankly and watch the Reds claim revenge for the last time we visited the San Siro in '65 and some highly dubious refereeing in the land of the mafia broke the great man's heart and stopped us becoming the first British side to reach a European Cup final.

Forget all the Machiavellian scheming going on at Anfield and the Big Dick competition between foreign capitalists to win control of our destiny. Why waste another second seething with anger at the fools who sold our heritage so cheaply and so ill-advisedly? Feasting my eyes on a heart-jolting sunset over Liverpool on evenings like this made them all seem so utterly irrelevant.

All that mattered was we were going to Milan to right a wrong that had hung in the air for forty-three years. When we'd done it, we'd go on, Shankly willing, to conquer the bloody world.

And some day soon, maybe next May, maybe the one after or the one after that, a middle-aged man in a suit will wade through the sea of scarves in front of the Kop, pick one up and tie it around his neck like a docker, make a defiant fist with his left hand and hold the Holy Grail in the other, and stare at us the way the risen Christ looked at his disciples, eyes blazing with an intensity that says:

Tell me you never questioned me. Tell me you harboured no doubts. Tell me all the pain and emptiness was worthwhile.

Tell me I've just put flesh on your dearest dream.